MEMBER OF THE CLUB

MEMBER OF THE CLUB.

. . .

REFLECTIONS ON LIFE
IN A RACIALLY POLARIZED WORLD

LAWRENCE OTIS GRAHAM

HarperCollins*Publishers*

"Invisible Man" and "Harlem on My Mind" first appeared as cover stories in *New York* magazine. "The Black Lunch Table Is Still There" first appeared in the *New York Times,* "The Shame of the Black Middle Class" first appeared in *Essence* magazine, and portions of "Black Man with a Nose Job" first appeared in *New York Newsday.*

HarperCollins books may be purchased for educational, business, or sales promotional use. For information, please write: Special Markets Department, HarperCollins Publishers, Inc., 10 East 53rd Street, New York, NY 10022.

FIRST EDITION

Designed by Laura Lindgren

Library of Congress Cataloging-in-Publication Data

Graham, Lawrence.
    Member of the club : reflections on life in a racially polarized world / Lawrence Otis Graham. — 1st ed.
      p. cm.
     ISBN 0-06-018351-9
    1. Racism—United States. 2. Race discrimination—United States. 3. United States—Race relations. 4. Graham, Lawrence. I. Title.
    E185.615.G67   1995
    305.8'00973—dc20   95-7980

95 96 97 98 99 ❖/RRD 10 9 8 7 6 5 4 3 2 1

To Pamela—that brilliant black woman
I met in the halls of Harkness Commons.

■   ■   ■

CONTENTS

ACKNOWLEDGMENTS

B ECAUSE THIS BOOK was so long in the writing, and relied on so many resources, there are a great number of individuals who have won my deepest gratitude. Among them are friends, advisers, and confidants who have sent me articles, recommended books, shared ideas, and introduced me to people I needed to consult. They are Margaret Morton, Elisabeth Radow, James Grasfield, Brad Roth, Dauna Williams, Teresa Artis, Andrea and Keith Heyward, Kim Jenkins, Un Suk Ko, Teresa Clarke, Adam Cohen, Diane Faber, Alex Coleman, Brenda Boudreaux Coleman, Christopher Fearon, Nelson Smith, Joe McDaniel, Dolores Harris, Leora Thompson, Nancy Marx Better, Steven Price, Jamin Raskin, Carlton Long, David Jones, Steve and Marilyn Emanuel, Anne and Albert Gottlieb, Lawrence and Laura Gordon, David Goldhill, Naoko Fuji, Derrick Bell, Rosabeth Moss Kanter, Barry Stein, Alan Dershowitz, Claire Wachtel, Ted Lee, Randall Kennedy, Dominique Richard, Luke Yang, Gail Busby, Lou Schuster, Bruce Wilson, Marguerite Gritenas, and Jay Ward.

I want to thank Minerva Reed, Cecelia Drewry, Jim Merritt, John McPhee, Joyce Carol Oates, Cynthia Reynolds, Jody Seward, Pamela Hut, Roy Oppenheim, Stephen Pfleger, Pamela Henderson, Anita Jackson, Jordan Horvath, and Lawrence Hamdan, who befriended me during a very important period of my own racial soul-searching.

And although I have told them many times before, I can never sufficiently express my appreciation for Sarah Weddington and Ron Brown, who introduced me to two White House administrations and who demonstrated a sincere interest in the black professionals they hired, as well as the millions of citizens they served.

Others who have, directly and indirectly, offered advice and support on this work are Anne and Wyatt Tee Walker of Harlem's Canaan Baptist Church; William Howard of the New York Theological Seminary; Dr. Mirian and Donald Hinds, who introduced me to the movers and shakers in Harlem; Sen. Carol Moseley-Braun and Rep. William Gray, who were kind enough to discuss the issues of politics, race, and media during an intimate and unhurried breakfast; Percy Sutton; David Garth; Mark and Deni Green; Lucille Frand; Searcy O. Grahame; Leotha and Earlene Graham; Blanche and James Edwards; Earl and Phyllis Walker; Dorothy and Victoria Holloway; James and Robin Benerofe; John Jacob; Susan L. Taylor; Hazel Dukes; Edward Kosner; Tom Prince; Elliot Hoffman; Denzel Washington; Debra Chase; Michael Halpern; Courtenay Valenti; Jordan Schaps; Ted Hardin; Fawzia Mustafa; Irma Watkins-Owens; Edward Bristow; as well as my friends from the NAACP, Jack & Jill, the Drifters, the Westchester Clubmen, and the Links.

I want to thank the following libraries for providing me with reference texts, periodicals, and quiet spaces in which to gather data and construct these essays: Howard University's Moorland-Spingarn Research Center; the libraries of Princeton University, Harvard University, Fordham University, Pace University, and Columbia University; the Joint Center for Political and Economic Studies; as well as White Plains Public Library, Scarsdale Public Library, Greenburgh Public Library, Beverly Hills Public Library, Los Angeles Public Library, and the Schomburg Center for Research in Black Culture of the New York Public Library.

I am immensely grateful for the time and interest contributed to this project by my friends and advisers at ICM: Esther Newberg, Amanda Beesley, and Sloan Harris. They, along with the editorial guidance of Gladys Carr, Cynthia Barrett, Elissa Altman, and Deirdre O'Brien, helped me weave these essays into a manuscript that fully captures my view of race in America.

For fighting off the demons and for shaping my first impressions of what it meant to share in the rich heritage and culture of the black community, I thank my parents, Richard and Betty, for their patience and their courage. And for being my first best friend, I thank my brother, Richard.

And finally, I thank Pamela, who, along with her intellectual honesty, consultant's eye, three-books-per-week reading addiction, and deep spirituality, has helped me find my own moral compass and reach for places I'd never been and never knew existed.

Lawrence Otis Graham
New York, New York

INTRODUCTION

■ ■ ■

A FOOT IN EACH WORLD

A S A BLACK professional in America it is sometimes so difficult to find true acceptance in either the black or the white communities that I often feel like an outsider to both; alienation seems to be the price of living with a foot in each world.

When my black peers and I share the daily experiences that we face at work, in our neighborhoods, on vacation, in church, or even in local restaurants, we inevitably find ourselves commenting on the mounting feelings of frustration and alienation that accompany our roles as people who have become a threat to elements in both the black and the white communities.

Most of us were raised in integrated or totally white neighborhoods. We attended predominately white colleges and graduate schools, and we are employed by white-owned-and-run institutions where we work in positions that are almost exclusively held by whites. Our daily contact with other black people is sometimes so peripheral that our emotional and intellectual ties to the larger black community become weakened and we begin to be perceived as outsiders by our black brethren. The black community, which is primarily *not* professional and *not* middle or upper class, looks at us as sellouts who have abandoned the black agenda. When we do attempt to involve ourselves with the agenda of the larger black community we are accused of expressing views that are outside the parameters of authentic black concerns.

Similarly, we are alienated from the white community by daily reminders that while we can shop in the same stores, work in the same firms, and live in the same neighborhoods as our white peers, our acceptance will be challenged as we are shadowed by store clerks, passed up by cabdrivers, ignored by bosses who are looking for protégés, and rejected by clubs that offer networking opportunities.

The twelve essays in this book examine the black professional class and its ongoing dilemma as a group that has no real home— abandoned or ostracized by other blacks and resented or rejected by whites.

Relying on historical research, my experiences as a corporate attorney and a college professor, and the anecdotes of others, I examine the widening gap within the black community between professional blacks and others; the continuing, subtle racism of some white institutions; and the ambivalence that blacks living with a foot in each world feel when the two communities collide.

For example, "Who's Running This Race?: The Black Leaders We Like and the Ones We Don't" assesses how black leadership has failed black people by not recognizing that the black agenda needs to include more than just the challenges of the black poor. In this essay, I discuss the grave problems of the NAACP, the tendency of the black community to anoint ill-equipped or corrupt spokespeople, and how those more capable black leaders and civil rights groups should reorganize if they intend to remain effective. Black leaders and their organizations must implement what I call "Socioeconomically-Based Black Leadership," which would serve black people by dividing the black population's problems along economic lines. Socioeconomically-Based Black Leadership recognizes that the interests of a black corporate executive who earns $125,000 a year and lives in the suburbs cannot be met by the same black leader who is focused on solving the equally compelling problems of a black inner-city single parent earning $10,000 a year who lives in public housing. Up to this point, the black agenda has almost exclusively been dictated by the needs of the black poor and, while those needs are basic and compelling, they should not eclipse the cries heard from other blacks in need.

One of the issues that continues to plague blacks of all economic groups is the continuing subtle racism of some white institutions. The essays "Moving from 'Black Rage' to 'Bias Neutralizing': A New Paradigm for Affirmative Action"; "How White People Taught Me to Be a Good Black Neighbor: A Suburban Allegory"; "My Dinner with Mr. Charlie: A Black Man's Undercover Guide to Dining with Dignity at Ten Top New York Restaurants"; "'Head Nigger In Charge': Roles That Black Professionals Play in Corporate America"; and "Invisible Man: Why This Harvard-Trained Lawyer Went Undercover as a Busboy at an All-White Connecticut Country Club" each address the pain often faced by blacks who try to achieve success in institutions controlled by whites.

For example, the "Invisible Man" essay examines the climate at exclusionary country clubs. It was while researching my last book, *The Best Companies for Minorities*, that I interviewed minority professionals at more than six hundred American corporations who complained of feeling like outsiders in their own companies and professions. They said they were unable to build networks, find mentors, or even attract business opportunities because of their exclusion from private clubs that white peers were joining.

These remarks led me to camouflage my identity as a Manhattan corporate attorney and go to work undercover as a busboy at an all-white country club in Greenwich, Connecticut. The experience, which I wrote about in a cover story for *New York* magazine elicited responses that illustrate the breadth of the chasm between certain whites and blacks. Responding to my shock at learning that the Greenwich Country Club referred to its on-campus dormitory as "The Monkey House" because the building's inhabitants had traditionally been black club workers, a woman sent a letter attacking me for having given an unfair characterization of the club. After introducing herself as "the wife of a Greenwich

Country Club member," she argued, "Graham neglects to mention that the Monkey House offers suites with private baths for each unit . . . "

After several news organizations reported that the club had no minority or Jewish members, after a handful of junior club members told me that they disagreed with club policies, and after Warner Brothers announced that it would enlist Oscar-winning actor Denzel Washington to make a film based on my busboy experience, the club realized that questions about its membership policies weren't going to go away. So the following statement was issued: "The Board of Governors of the Greenwich Country Club regrets that Lawrence Otis Graham chose its club as the backdrop for his social commentary. . . . In its one hundred years, the Greenwich Country Club has had a tradition of being family-oriented . . . Today our members include a broad range of religious and ethnic groups. We have no policies or practices that would exclude anyone from membership because of race, creed or color. . . . Greenwich Country Club will continue to do its best to meet the high standards of its members and the community." To my knowledge, however, the club membership today remains as homogeneous as it was when the story was originally written.

There are individuals like General Motors CEO Jack Smith who are willing to take a public stand against discriminatory treatment. In 1994 Smith resigned from the Bloomfield Hills Country Club following that club's rejection of a high-ranking black executive. But in my experience too many members in the white community would rather ostracize those blacks who attempt to operate within their ranks.

The final group of essays in the book illustrates the painful situations where blacks trying to live in both worlds are criticized both by other blacks and by whites. In "The Underside of Paradise: Being Black at Princeton," I discuss my years as an undergraduate at Princeton and the difficulties I faced trying to have both black and white friends. In "I Never Dated a White Girl: Why Some Blacks Still Oppose Interracial Marriage," I examine the debate over interracial marriage and why it is that both blacks and whites are distressed by blacks who cross racial lines in their dating and marital choices.

Whether the issue is country clubs, segregated cafeteria lunch tables, affirmative action, interracial dating, or my own plastic surgery, the purpose of all of these essays is to offer another perspective of the black experience. My hope is that they will contribute to the creation of a society in which black professionals—and everyone else—need not be trapped between worlds that are either black or white. As more of us learn to openly discuss the ways in which we exclude members of our community and as we learn to candidly address our own biases, we can learn to live with both feet firmly planted in a world that is whole.

I

INVISIBLE MAN

WHY THIS HARVARD-TRAINED LAWYER
WENT UNDERCOVER AS A BUSBOY AT AN
ALL-WHITE CONNECTICUT COUNTRY CLUB

I DRIVE UP the winding lane past a long stone wall and beneath an archway of sixty-foot maples. At one bend of the drive, a freshly clipped lawn and a trail of yellow daffodils slope gently up to the four-pillared portico of a white Georgian colonial. The building's six huge chimneys, the two wings with slate gray shutters, and the white-brick facade loom over a luxuriant golf course. Before me stands the one-hundred-year-old Greenwich Country Club—*the* country club—in the affluent, patrician, and very white town of Greenwich, Connecticut, where there are eight clubs for fifty-nine thousand people.

I'm a thirty-year-old corporate lawyer at a Midtown Manhattan firm, and I make $105,000 a year. I'm a graduate of Princeton University (1983) and Harvard Law School (1988), and I've written ten nonfiction books. Although these might seem like impressive credentials, they're not the ones that brought me here. Quite frankly, I got into this country club the only way that a black man like me could—as a $7-an-hour busboy.

This piece appeared as a cover story for *New York* magazine, August 17, 1992.

After seeing dozens of news stories about Dan Quayle, Billy Graham, Ross Perot, and others who either belonged to or frequented white country clubs, I decided to find out what things were really like at a club where I heard there were no black members.

I remember stepping up to the pool at a country club when I was ten and setting off a chain reaction: Several irate parents dragged their children out of the water and fled. When the other kids ran out of the pool, so did I—foolishly thinking that there was something in the water that was going to harm all of us. Back then, in 1972, I saw these clubs only as places where families socialized. I grew up in an affluent white neighborhood in Westchester, and all my playmates and neighbors belonged to one or more of these private institutions. Across the street, my best friend introduced me to the Westchester Country Club before he left for Groton and Yale. My teenage tennis partner from Scarsdale introduced me to the Beach Point Club on weekends before he left for Harvard. The family next door belonged to the Scarsdale Golf Club. In my crowd, the question wasn't "Do you belong?" It was "Where?"

My grandparents owned a Memphis trucking firm, and as far back as I can remember, our family was well off and we had little trouble fitting in—even though I was the only black kid on the high school tennis team, the only one in the orchestra, the only one in my Roman Catholic confirmation class.

Today, I'm back where I started—on a street of five- and six-bedroom colonials with expensive cars and neighbors who all belong somewhere. Through my experiences as a young lawyer, I have come to realize that these clubs are where businesspeople network, where lawyers and investment bankers meet potential clients and arrange deals. How many clients and deals am I going to line up on the asphalt parking lot of my local public tennis courts?

I am not ashamed to admit that I one day want to be a partner and a part of this network. When I talk to my black lawyer or investment-banker friends or my wife, a brilliant black woman who has degrees from Harvard College, Harvard Law School, and Harvard Business School, I learn that our white counterparts are being accepted by dozens of these elite institutions. So why shouldn't we—especially when we have the same credentials, salaries, social graces, and ambitions?

My black Ivy League friends and I know of black company vice presidents who have to ask white subordinates to invite them out for golf or tennis. We talk about the club in Westchester that rejected black Scarsdale resident and millionaire magazine publisher Earl Graves, who sits on *Fortune* 500 boards, owns a Pepsi distribution franchise, raised three bright Ivy League children, and holds prestigious honorary degrees. We talk about all the clubs that face a scandal and then run out to sign up one quiet, deferential black man who will accept a special "limited-status" membership, remove the taint, and deflect further scrutiny.

I wanted some answers. I knew I could never be treated as an equal at this Greenwich oasis—a place so insular that the word *Negro* is still used in conversation. But I figured I could get close enough to understand what these people were thinking and why country clubs were so set on excluding people like me.

March 28 to April 7, 1992

I invented a completely new résumé for myself. I erased Harvard, Princeton, and my upper-middle-class suburban childhood from my life. So that I'd have to account for fewer years, I made myself seven years younger—an innocent twenty-three. I used my real name and made myself a graduate of the actual high school I attended. Since it would be difficult to pretend that I was from "the street," I decided to become a sophomore-year dropout from Tufts University, a midsize college in suburban Boston. My years at nearby Harvard and the fact that my brother had gone there had given me enough knowledge about the school to pull it off. I contacted some older friends who owned large companies and restaurants in the Boston and New York areas and asked them to serve as references. I was already on a short leave of absence from my law firm to work on a book.

I pieced together a wardrobe that consisted of a blue polyester blazer, white oxford shirt, ironed blue slacks, black loafers, and a horrendous pink, black, and silver tie, and I set up interviews at clubs. Over the telephone, five of the eight said that I sounded as if I would make a great waiter. During each of my phone conversations, I made sure that I spoke to the person who would make the hiring decision. I also confirmed exactly how many waiter positions were available, and I arranged a personal interview within forty minutes to an hour of the conversation, just to be sure that they could not tell me that no such job was available.

"We don't have any job openings—and if you don't leave the building, I will have to call security," the receptionist said at the first club I visited in Greenwich.

I was astounded by the speed with which she made this remark, particularly when I saw that she had just handed an application to a young-looking Hispanic man wearing jeans, sneakers, a T-shirt, and sunglasses. "I'm here to see Donna, your maître d'," I added defensively as I forced a smile at the pasty-looking woman who sat behind a window.

"There's no Donna here."

"But I just spoke to her thirty minutes ago and she said to come by to discuss the waiter job."

"Sorry, but there are no jobs and no one here named Donna."

After convincing the woman to give me an application, I completed it and then walked back into the dining room, which was visible from the foyer.

I came upon a white male waiter and asked him, "Is there a Donna here?"

"The maître d'?" he asked. "Yeah, she's in the kitchen."

When I found Donna and explained that I was the one she had talked to on the phone forty minutes earlier, she crossed her arms and shook her head. "You're the 'Larry' I talked to on the phone?"

"Yes," I answered.

"No way."

"I beg your pardon," I said.

"No. No way," she said while refusing to take the application I waved in front of her.

"We just talked on the phone less than an hour ago. You said I sounded perfect. And I've waited in three different restaurants— I've had two years of college— You said you had five waiter jobs open— I filled out the application— I can start right away—"

She still shook her head. And held her hands behind her back—unwilling to even touch my application. "No," she said. "Can't do it."

My talking did no good. It was 1992. This was the Northeast. If I hadn't been involved, I would never have believed it. I suddenly thought about all the times I quietly disbelieved certain poor blacks who said they had tried to get jobs but no one would hire them. I wanted to say then and there, "Not even as a waiter?"

Only an hour earlier, this woman had enthusiastically urged me to come right over for an interview. Now, as two white kitchen workers looked on, she would only hold her hands tightly behind her back and shake her head emphatically. So I left.

There were three other clubs to go to. When I met them, the club managers told me I "would probably make a much better busboy."

"Busboy? Over the phone, you said you needed a waiter," I argued.

"Yes, I know I said that, but you seem very alert, and I think you'd make an excellent busboy instead."

In his heavy Irish brogue, the club manager said he needed to give me a "perception test." He explained it this way: "This ten-question test will give us an idea of your perception, intellectual strength, and conscious ability to perform the duties assigned to you as a busboy."

I had no idea how much intellectual strength and conscious ability (whatever that meant) could be required of a busboy, but here are some of the questions he asked me:

1. If there are three apples and you take two away, how many do you have?

2. How many of each species of animal did Moses put on his new ark?
3. It's 1963 and you set your digital clock to ring at 9:00 A.M. when you go to bed at 8:00 P.M. How many hours will you sleep?
4. If a house gets southern exposure on all four sides, what color is the bear that walks by the house?

And the responses . . .

1. I answered "one apple" because I thought this was a simple math question, as in "three minus two equals one," but the correct answer was "two" because, as the manager said, "You've got to think, Larry—if you take away two apples and put them in your pocket, you've got two apples, not one."
2. Fortunately, I answered this question as it was presumably designed to smoke out any applicants who hadn't been raised in a Judeo-Christian culture. It was Noah, not Moses, who built an ark.
3. I scored major credibility points here by lying and saying, "Wow, I wasn't even born yet in 1963. . . ." The "right" answer was that there were no digital clocks in 1963. I took his word for it.
4. Although I believed that a house could get southern exposure on all four sides only at the South Pole—and thus the bear had to be a white polar bear—I was told that I was "trying to act too smart" and that all bears are, of course, brown.

APRIL 8 TO 11

After interviewing for advertised waiter jobs at five clubs, I had gotten only two offers—both for nonwaiter jobs. One offer was to split my time as a towel boy in the locker room and a busboy in the dining room. The second offer—which followed a callback interview—was to work as a busboy. When I told the club manager that I had only wanted a waiter job, he responded, "Well, we've discussed it here and everyone would feel more comfortable if you took a busboy job instead."

"But I've never worked as a busboy," I reminded him.

He nodded sympathetically. "People here have decided that it's busboy or nothing."

Given these choices, I made my final job selection in much the way I had decided on a college and a law school: I went for prestige. Not only was the Greenwich Country Club celebrating its hundredth anniversary but its roster boasted former president Gerald Ford, baseball star Tom Seaver, former Securities and Exchange Commission chairman and U.S. ambassador to the Netherlands John Shad, as well as former Timex spokesman John Cameron Swayze. Add to that a few dozen *Fortune* 500 executives, bankers, Wall Street lawyers, European entrepreneurs, a Presbyterian minister, and cartoonist Mort Walker, who does *Beetle Bailey*. (The Greenwich Country Club did not respond to any questions about the club and its members.)

For three days, I worked on my upper-arm muscles by walking around the house with a sterling-silver tray stacked high with heavy dictionaries. I allowed a mustache to grow in, then added a pair of arrestingly ugly Coke-bottle reading glasses.

April 12 (Sunday)

Today was my first day at work. My shift didn't start until 10:30 A.M., so I laid out my clothes at home: a white button-down shirt, freshly ironed cotton khaki pants, white socks, and white leather sneakers. I'd get my official club uniform in two days. Looking in my wallet, I removed my American Express Gold Card, my Harvard Club membership ID, and all of my business cards.

When I arrived at the club, I entered under the large portico, stepping through the heavy doors and onto the black-and-white checkerboard tiles of the entry hall.

A distracted receptionist pointed me toward Mr. Ryan's office. *(All names of club members and personnel have been changed.)* I walked past glistening silver trophies and a guest book on a pedestal to a windowless office with three desks. My new boss waved me in and abruptly hung up the phone.

"Good morning, Larry," he said with a sufficiently warm smile. The tight knot in his green tie made him look more fastidious than I had remembered from the interview.

"Hi, Mr. Ryan. How's it going?"

Glancing at his watch to check my punctuality, he shook my hand and handed me some papers. "Oh, and by the way, where'd you park?"

"In front, near the tennis courts."

Already shaking his head, he tossed his pencil onto the desk. "That's off-limits to you. You should always park in the back, enter in the back, and leave from the back. No exceptions."

"I'll do the forms right now," I said. "And then I'll be an official busboy."

Mr. Ryan threw me an ominous nod. "And Larry, let me stop you now. We don't like that term *busboy*. We find it demeaning. We prefer to call you busmen."

Leading me down the center stairwell to the basement, he added, "And in the future, you will always use the back stairway by the back entrance." He continued to talk as we trotted through a maze of hallways. "I think I'll have you trail with Carlos or Hector—no, Carlos. Unless you speak Spanish?"

"No." I ran to keep up with Mr. Ryan.

"That's the dishwasher room, where Juan works. And over here is where you'll be working." I looked at the brass sign. MEN'S GRILL.

It was a dark room with a mahogany finish, and it looked like a library in a large Victorian home. Dark walls, dark wood-beamed ceilings. Deep-green wool carpeting. Along one side of the room stood a long, highly polished mahogany bar with liquor bottles, wineglasses, and a two-and-a-half-foot-high silver trophy. Fifteen heavy round wooden tables, each encircled with four to six broad wooden armchairs padded with green leather on the backs and seats, broke up the room. A big-screen TV was set into the wall along with two shelves of books.

"This is the Men's Grill," Mr. Ryan said. "Ladies are not allowed except on Friday evenings."

Next was the brightly lit connecting kitchen. "Our kitchen serves hot and cold foods. You'll work six days a week here. The club is closed on Mondays. The kitchen serves the Men's Grill and an adjoining room called the Mixed Grill. That's where the ladies and kids can eat."

"And what about men? Can they eat in there, too?"

This elicited a laugh. "Of course they can. Time and place restrictions apply only to women and kids."

He showed me the Mixed Grill, a well-lit, pastel-blue room with glass French doors and white wood trim.

"Guys, say hello to Larry. He's a new busman at the club."

I waved.

"And this is Rick, Stephen, Drew, Buddy, and Lee." Five white waiters dressed in white polo shirts with blue "1892" club insignias nodded while busily slicing lemons.

"And this is Hector and Carlos, the other busmen." Hector, Carlos, and I were the only nonwhites on the serving staff. They greeted me in a mix of English and Spanish.

"Nice to meet all of you," I responded.

"Thank God," one of the taller waiters cried out. "Finally— somebody who can speak English."

Mr. Ryan took me and Carlos through a hall lined with old black-and-white portraits of former presidents of the club. "This is our one hundredth year, so you're joining the club at an important time," Mr. Ryan added before walking off. "Carlos, I'm going to leave Larry to trail with you—and no funny stuff."

Standing outside the ice room, Carlos and I talked about our pasts. He was twenty-five, originally from Colombia, and hadn't finished school. I said I had dropped out, too.

As I stood there talking, Carlos suddenly gestured for me to move out of the hallway. I looked behind me and noticed something staring down at us. "A video camera?"

"They're around," Carlos remarked quietly while scooping ice into large white tubs. "Now watch me scoop ice."

After we carried the heavy tubs back to the grill, I saw another video camera pointed down at us. I dropped my head.

"You gonna live in the Monkey House?" Carlos asked.

"What's that?"

We climbed the stairs to take our ten-minute lunch break before work began. "Monkey House is where workers live here," Carlos said.

I followed him through a rather filthy utility room and into a huge white kitchen. We got on line behind about twenty Hispanic men and women—all dressed in varying uniforms. At the head of the line were the white waiters I'd met earlier.

I was soon handed a hot plate with two red lumps of rice and some kind of sausage-shaped meat. There were two string beans, several pieces of zucchini, and a thin, broken slice of dried meat loaf that looked as if it had been cooked, burned, frozen, and then reheated. Lurking at the very edge of my dish was an ice-cream-scoop-sized helping of yellowish mashed potatoes.

I followed Carlos, plate in hand, out of the kitchen. To my surprise, we walked back into the dank and dingy utility room, which turned out to be the workers' dining area.

The white waiters huddled together at one end of the tables, while the Hispanic workers ate quietly at the other end. Before I could decide which end to integrate, Carlos directed me to sit with him on the Hispanic end.

I was soon back downstairs working in the grill. At my first few tables, I tried to avoid making eye contact with members as I removed dirty plates and wiped down tables and chairs. Having known so many people who belonged to these clubs, I was sure I'd be recognized by someone from childhood, college, or work.

At around 1:15, four men who looked to be in their mid- to

late fifties sat down at a six-chair table. They pulled off
ton windbreakers and golf sweaters.

"It's these damned newspeople that cause all the prob
said golfer number one, shoving his hand deep into a pop
bowl. "These Negroes wouldn't even be thinking about golf. Th
can't afford to join a club, anyway."

Golfer number two squirmed out of his navy blue sweater and
nodded in agreement. "My big problem with this Clinton fellow is
that he apologized." As I stood watching from the corner of the
bar, I realized the men were talking about then-governor Bill Clinton's recent apology for playing at an all-white golf club in Little
Rock, Arkansas.

"Holt, I couldn't agree with you more," added golfer number
three, a hefty man who was biting off the end of a cigar.

"You got any iced tea?" golfer number one asked as I put the
silverware and menus around the table. Popcorn flew out of his
mouth as he attempted to speak and chew at the same time.

"Yes, we certainly do."

Golfer number three removed a beat-up Rolex from his wrist.
"It just sets a bad precedent. Instead of apologizing, he should try
to discredit them—undercut them somehow. What's to apologize
for?" I cleared my throat and backed away from the table.

Suddenly, golfer number one waved me back to his side.
"Should we get four iced teas or just a pitcher and four glasses?"

"I'd be happy to bring whatever you'd like, sir."

Throughout the day, I carried "bus buckets" filled with dirty
dishes from the grill to the dishwasher room. And each time I
returned to the grill, I scanned the room for recognizable faces. Fortunately, I saw none. After almost four hours of running back and
forth, clearing dishes, wiping down tables, and thanking departing
members who left spilled coffee, dirty napkins, and unwanted business cards in their wake, I helped out in the coed Mixed Grill.

"Oh, busboy," a voice called out as I made the rounds with two
pots of coffee. "Here, busboy. Here, busboy," the woman called
out. "Busboy, my coffee is cold. Give me a refill."

"Certainly, I would be happy to." I reached over for her cup.

The fiftyish woman pushed her hand through her straw blond hair and turned to look me in the face. "Decaf, thank you."

"You are quite welcome."

Before I turned toward the kitchen, the woman leaned over to her companion. "My goodness. Did you hear that? That busboy has diction like an educated white person."

A curly-haired waiter walked up to me in the kitchen. "Larry, are you living in the Monkey House?"

"No, but why do they call it that?"

"Well, no offense against you, but it got that name since it's the house where the workers have lived at the club. And since the workers used to be Negroes—blacks—it was nicknamed the Monkey House. And the name just stuck—even though Negroes have been replaced by Hispanics."

APRIL 13 (MONDAY)

I woke up and felt a pain shooting up my calves. As I turned to the clock, I realized I'd slept for eleven hours. I was thankful the club was closed on Mondays.

APRIL 14 (TUESDAY)

Rosa, the club seamstress, measured me for a uniform in the basement laundry room while her barking gray poodle jumped up on my feet and pants. "Down, Margarita, down," Rosa cried with pins in her mouth and marking chalk in her hand. But Margarita ignored her and continued to bark and do tiny pirouettes until I left with all of my new country-club polo shirts and pants.

Today, I worked exclusively with the "veterans," including sixty-five-year-old Sam, the Polish bartender in the Men's Grill. Hazel, an older waitress at the club, is quick, charming, and smart—the kind of waitress who makes any restaurant a success. She has worked for the club nearly twenty years and has become quite territorial with certain older male members. Whenever I was on my way to hand out menus or clear dishes at a table, Hazel would either outrun me or grab me by the arm when she saw that the table contained important male members. Inevitably, Hazel would say, "Oh, Larry, let me take care of Dr. Collingsworth. You go fill this salt shaker," or "Larry, I'll take Judge Wilson's dirty dish. You go slice some lemons in the kitchen," or "Larry, I'll clean up Reverend Gundersen's cracker crumbs. You go find some peanut oil."

During a lull, Sam, who I swear reminded me of a Norman Lear creation circa 1972, asked me to run out and get some supplies from a Mr. Chang.

"Who is Mr. Chang?" I asked.

"You know, the Chinaman. Mr. Chang."

I had recalled seeing an elderly Asian man with a gray uniform in the halls, but we had not been introduced.

"And where would I find him?"

"He's down at the other end of the hall beyond the stairs." Sam handed me a list of items on a printed form. "He's the Chinaman and it's easy to remember 'cause he's right next to the laundry room."

Hector came along and warned me not to lose the signed form because I could be accused of stealing food and supplies if the signed list wasn't given to Mr. Chang.

Down a dark, shadowy hall, we found Mr. Chang, who, in Spanish, shouted phrases at me while swinging his arms in the air.

"Do you understand him?" I asked Hector.

"He said to follow him and bring a cart."

We followed the methodical Mr. Chang from storage room to storage room, where he pulled out various items like a magician. Lemons were stored with paper goods, cans of ketchup were stored with pretzels and simultaneously served as shelves for large sacks of onions. Bottles of soda were stored with old boxes that had "Monkey House" written on them. Combustible popcorn oil and boxes of matches were stored with Styrofoam cups in the furnace room. It was all in a disorder that seemed to make complete sense to Mr. Chang.

Back in the Mixed Grill, members were talking about hotel queen and Greenwich resident Leona Helmsley, who was on the clubhouse TV because of her upcoming prison term for tax evasion.

"I'd like to see them haul her off to jail," one irate woman said to the rest of her table. "She's nothing but a garish you-know-what."

"In every sense of the word," nodded her companion as she adjusted a pink headband in her blondish white hair. "She makes the whole town look bad. The TV keeps showing those aerial shots of Greenwich and that dreadful house of hers."

A third woman shrugged her shoulders and looked into her bowl of salad. "Well, it is a beautiful piece of property."

"Yes, it is, except for those dreadful lampposts all over the lawn," said the first woman. "But why here? She should be in those other places like Beverly Hills or Scarsdale or Long Island, with the rest of them. What's she doing here?"

Woman number three looked up. "Well, you know, *he's* not Jewish."

"Really?"

"So that explains it," said the first woman with an understanding expression on her tanned forehead. "Because, you know, the name didn't sound Jewish."

The second woman agreed: "I can usually tell."

APRIL 15 (WEDNESDAY)

Today, we introduced a new, extended menu in the two grill rooms. We added shrimp quesadillas ($6) to the appetizer list— and neither the members nor Hazel could pronounce the name of the dish or fathom what it was. One man pounded on the table and demanded to know which country the dish had come from. He told Hazel how much he hated "changes like this. I like to know that some things are going to stay the same."

Another addition was the "New Dog in Town" ($3.50). It was billed as knockwurst, but one woman of German descent sent the dish back: "This is not knockwurst—this is just a big hot dog."

As I wiped down the length of the men's bar, I noticed a tall stack of postcards with color photos of nude busty women waving hello from sunny faraway beaches. I saw they had been sent from vacationing members with fond regards to Sam or Hazel. Several had come from married couples. One glossy photo boasted a detailed frontal shot of a red-haired beauty who was naked except for a shoestring around her waist. On the back, the message said, *Dear Sam, Pull string in an emergency. Love always, The Atkinson Family.*

April 16 (Thursday)

This afternoon, I realized I was learning the routine. I was fairly comfortable with my few "serving" responsibilities and the rules that related to them:

- When a member is seated, bring out the silverware, cloth napkin, and a menu.
- Never take an order for food, but always bring water or iced tea if it is requested by a member or waiter.
- When a waiter takes a chili or salad order, bring out a basket of warm rolls and crackers along with a scoop of butter.
- When getting iced tea, fill a tall glass with ice and serve it with a long spoon, a napkin on the bottom, and a lemon on the rim.
- When a member wants his alcoholic drink refilled, politely respond, "Certainly, I will have your waiter come right over."
- Remember that the member is always right.
- Never make offensive eye contact with a member or his guest.
- When serving a member fresh popcorn, serve to the left.
- When a member is finished with a dish or glass, clear it from the right.
- Never tell a member that the kitchen is out of something.

But there were also some "informal" rules that I discovered (but did not follow) while watching the more experienced waiters and kitchen staff in action:

- If you drop a hot roll on the floor in front of a member, apologize and throw it out. If you drop a hot roll on the floor in the kitchen, pick it up and put it back in the bread warmer.
- If you have cleared a table and are 75 percent sure that the member did not use the fork, put it back in the bin with the other clean forks.
- If, after pouring one glass of Coke and one of diet Coke, you get distracted and can't remember which is which, stick your finger in one of them to taste it.
- If a member asks for decaffeinated coffee and you have no time to make it, use regular and add water to cut the flavor.
- When members complain that the chili is too hot and spicy, instead of making a new batch, take the sting out by adding some chocolate syrup.
- If you're making a tuna on toasted wheat and you accidentally burn one side of the bread, don't throw it out. Instead, put the tuna on the burned side and lather on some extra mayo.

April 17 (Friday)

Today, I heard the word "nigger" four times. And it came from someone on the staff.

In the grill, several members were discussing Arthur Ashe, who had recently announced that he had contracted AIDS through a blood transfusion.

"It's a shame that poor man has to be humiliated like this," one woman golfer remarked to a friend over pasta-and-vegetable salad. "He's been such a good example for his people."

"Well, quite frankly," added a woman in a white sun visor, "I always knew he was gay. There was something about him that just seemed too perfect."

"No, Anne, he's not gay. It came from a blood transfusion."

"Ohh," said the woman. "I suppose that's a good reason to stay out of all those big-city hospitals. All that bad blood moving around."

Later that afternoon, one of the waiters, who had worked in the Mixed Grill for two years, told me that Tom Seaver and Gerald Ford were members. Of his brush with greatness, he added, "You know, Tom's real first name is George."

"That's something."

"And I've seen O. J. Simpson here, too."

"O. J. belongs here, too?" I asked.

"Oh, no, there aren't any black members here. No way. I actually don't even think there are any Jews here, either."

"Really? Why is that?" I asked.

"I don't know. I guess it's just that the members probably want to have a place where they can go and not have to think about Jews, blacks, and other minorities. It's not really hurting anyone. It's really a WASP club. . . . But now that I think of it, there is a guy here who some people think is Jewish, but I can't really tell. Upstairs, there's a Jewish secretary too."

"And what about O. J.?"

"Oh, yeah, it was so funny to see him out there playing golf on the eighteenth hole." The waiter paused and pointed outside the window. "It never occurred to me before, but it seemed so odd to see a black man with a golf club here on this course."

APRIL 18 (SATURDAY)

When I arrived, Stephen, one of the waiters, was hanging a poster and sign-up sheet for a soccer league whose main purpose was to "bridge the ethnic and language gap" between white and Hispanic workers at the country clubs in the Greenwich area. I congratulated Stephen on his idea. He said he was tired of seeing the whites and Hispanics split up during meals, breaks, and evening activities. "We even go to separate bars and diners," he explained.

"I think a weekly soccer game might bring us all closer together."

Later, while I was wiping down a table, I heard a member snap his fingers in my direction. I turned to see a group of young men smoking cigars. They seemed to be my age or a couple of years younger. "Hey, do I know you?" the voice asked.

As I turned slowly toward the voice, I could hear my own heartbeat. I was sure it was someone I knew.

"No," I said, approaching the blond cigar smoker. He had on light green khaki pants and a light yellow V-neck cotton sweater adorned with a tiny green alligator. As I looked at the other men seated around the table, I noticed that all but one had alligators on their sweaters or shirts. Each one of them was a stranger to me.

"I didn't think so. You must be new—what's your name?"

"My name is Larry. I just started a few days ago."

The cigar-smoking host grabbed me by the wrist while looking at his guests. "Well, Larry, welcome to the club. I'm Mr. Billings. And this is Mr. Dennis, a friend and new member."

"Hello, Mr. Dennis," I heard myself saying to a freckle-faced young man who puffed uncomfortably on his fat roll of tobacco.

The first cigar smoker gestured for me to bend over as if he were about to share some important confidence. "Now, Larry, here's what I want you to do. Go get us some of those peanuts and then give my guests and me a fresh ashtray. Can you manage that?"

My workday ended at 4:20.

EVENING OF APRIL 18 (SATURDAY)

After changing back into my street clothes at around 8:00 P.M., I drove back to the club to get together with Stephen and Lillie, two of the friendlier waiters (and the only ones willing to socialize with a busboy), in Stephen's room on the grounds. We sat, ate Hostess donuts, drank wine, watched the Saturday-night NBC-TV lineup, and talked about what it would be like to be a rich member of the club.

Squeezed into the tiny room and sitting on the bed, which was pushed against the wall, we each promised to look out for and warn the others if anyone else tried to backstab us in the grill. Stephen was talking about his plans for the intercultural soccer league and what it could do for all eight clubs in the area.

"After spending a couple semesters in Japan," Stephen explained, "I realized how afraid Americans are of other cultures." Stephen told me that he was working at the club to pay for the rest of his college education. He was taking a two-year break between his sophomore and junior years at a midwestern university, where he was majoring in Japanese.

Lillie talked about the formal dinner that she had just worked at that evening. It was then that I learned she was half South American. Her father, who was from Colombia, was an outdoor groundskeeper at the club. "I'm taking college courses now," she explained. "And maybe I'm crazy to say this, but I think I'd like to go into broadcasting." Given her nearly flawless English and her very white skin, I wondered if the members were aware of her Hispanic background. She felt very strong about her South American heritage, and she often acted as interpreter for some of the club workers who spoke only Spanish.

They were both such nice people, I felt terrible for intruding under such fraudulent circumstances.

APRIL 19 (SUNDAY)

It was Easter Sunday, and the Easter-egg hunt began with dozens of small children scampering around the tulips and daffodils while well-dressed parents watched from the rear patio of the club. A giant Easter bunny gave out little baskets filled with jelly beans to parents and then hopped over to the bushes, where he hugged the children. As we peered out from the closed blinds in the grill, we saw women in mink, husbands in gray suits, children in Ralph Lauren and Laura Ashley. Hazel let out a sigh. "Aren't they beautiful?" she said. For just a moment, I found myself agreeing.

"So, Larry." Sam laughed as I poured fresh oil into the popcorn machine's heated pan. It was my second day at the machine in the

Men's Grill. "When you decide to move on from the club, you'll be able to get yourself a job at the popcorn counter in one of those big movie theaters."

I forced a smile.

"And you can tell them," he continued, "that you just about have a master's degree in popcorn popping. Tell 'em you learned everything you know from Sam at the country club."

I laughed. "Sure, Sam."

"Yeah, tell them I awarded you a master's degree."

I had already become an expert at yucking it up with Sam.

As I raced around taking out orders of coffee and baskets of hot rolls, I got a chance to see groups of families. The men seemed to be uniformly taller than six feet. Most of them were wearing blue blazers, white shirts, and incredibly out-of-style silk ties—the kind with little blue whales or little green ducks floating downward. They were bespectacled and conspicuously clean-shaven.

The "ladies," as the club prefers to call them, almost invariably had straight blond hair. Whether or not they had brown roots and whether they were twenty-five or forty-eight, they wore their hair blond, straight, and off the face. No dangling earrings, five-carat diamonds, or designer handbags. Black velvet or pastel headbands were de rigueur.

There were also groups of high-school kids who wore torn jeans, sneakers, or unlaced L.L. Bean shoes, and sweatshirts that said things like "Hotchkiss Lacrosse" or "Andover Crew." At one table, two boys sat talking to two girls.

"No way, J.C.," one of the girls cried in disbelief while playing with the straw in her diet Coke.

The strawberry blond girl next to her flashed her unpainted nails in the air. "Way. She said that if she didn't get her grades up by this spring, they were going to take her out altogether."

"And where would they send her?" one of the guys asked.

The strawberry blonde's grin disappeared as she leaned in close. "Public school."

The group, in hysterics, shook the table. The guys stomped their feet.

"Oh, my God, J.C., oh, J.C., J.C.," the diet-Coke girl cried.

Sitting in a tableless corner of the room beneath the TV set was a young, dark-skinned black woman dressed in a white uniform and a thick wool coat. On her lap was a baby with silky white blond hair. The woman sat patiently, shifting the baby in her lap while glancing over to where the baby's family ate, two tables away.

I ran to the kitchen, brought back a glass of tea, and offered it to her. The woman looked up at me, shook her head, and then turned back to the gurgling infant.

APRIL 21 (TUESDAY)

The TV in the Men's Grill was tuned to one of the all-day cable news channels and was reporting on the violent confrontations between pro-choice marchers and right-to-life protesters in Buffalo, New York.

"Look at all those women running around," a man in his late forties commented as he sat by himself at one of the larger tables in the Men's Grill.

At 11:10 A.M., the grill wasn't even officially opened yet.

As I walked around doing a final wipe of the tables, the man cried out into the empty room. "That's just a damned shame," he said while shaking his head and pulling at his yellow polo shirt in disbelief.

I nodded as he looked at me over his bowl of peanuts. "I agree with you."

He removed his sun visor and dropped it onto a table closer to the television. We both watched images of police dragging women who lay sprawled in the middle of a Buffalo city street.

"You know, it just scares me to see all these women running around like that," the middle-aged member continued as we both watched screaming crowds of placard-carrying activists and handcuffed protesters. "Someone's gotta keep these women reined in. A good, hard law that forces them to have those babies when they get pregnant will teach them to be responsible."

I looked at the man as he sat there hypnotized by the screen.

"All this equal rights bull," he finally added. "Running around getting pregnant and then running around doing what they want. Enough to make you sick."

Later, while Hector and I stood inside a deep walk-in freezer, we scooped balls of butter into separate butter dishes and talked about our life plans. "Will you go finish school sometime?" he asked as I dug deep into a vat of frozen butter.

"Maybe. In a couple years, when I save more money, but I'm not sure." I felt lousy about having to lie.

"Maybe? If I had money, I'd go now—and I'm twenty-three years old." He shook his head in disapproval. "In my country, I had education. But here I don't because I don't know much English. It's tough because we have no work in South America. And here, there's work, but you need English to get it and make money."

We agreed that since 75 percent of the club employees were Spanish-speaking South Americans, the club really needed a bilingual manager or someone on staff who understood their concerns.

"Well," I offered. "I'll help you with English if you teach me some Spanish."

He joked that my Spanish was a lot worse than his English. After all, I only knew the words *gracias, buenos días,* and *por favor.* So, during an illegal twelve-minute break, he ran through a quick vocabulary lesson while we walked to his minuscule room just across the sweaty congested halls of the noisy squash courts.

The room that he took me into overlooked the driving range and was the size of a walk-in closet. The single bed touched three walls of the room. The quarter-sized refrigerator served as a stand for a stereo. There were a small dresser and small desk plastered with many different pictures of a young Spanish-looking woman and a cute baby girl.

"My family" is all Hector would say in explanation while simultaneously pushing me out of the room and into the sweaty hall. "We go now—before we lose our job."

Just as we were all leaving for the day, Mr. Ryan came down to hand out the new policies for those who were going to live in the Monkey House. Amazingly, without a trace of discomfort, he and everyone else referred to the building as "the Monkey House." Many of the workers had been living temporarily in the squash building. Since it had recently been renovated, the club was requiring all new residents to sign the form. The policy included a rule that forbade employees to have overnight guests. Rule 14 stated that the club management had the right to enter an employee's locked bedroom at any time, without permission and without giving notice.

As I was making rounds with my coffeepots, I overheard a raspy-voiced woman talking to a mother and daughter who were thumbing through a catalog of infants' clothing.

"The problem with au pairs is that they're usually only in the country for a year."

The mother and daughter nodded in agreement.

"But getting one that is a citizen has its own problems. For example, if you ever have to choose between a Negro and one of these Spanish people, always go for the Negro."

One of the women frowned, confused. "Really?"

"Yes," the raspy-voiced woman responded with cold logic. "Even though you can't trust either one, at least the Negroes can speak English and follow your directions."

Before I could refill the final cup, the raspy-voiced woman looked up at me and smiled. "Oh, thanks for the refill, Larry."

APRIL 22 (WEDNESDAY)

"This is our country, and don't you forget it. They came here and have to live by our rules!" Hazel pounded her fist into the palm of her pale white hand.

I had made the mistake of telling her I had learned a few Spanish phrases to help me communicate better with some of my coworkers. She wasn't impressed.

"I'll be damned if I'm going to learn or speak one word of Spanish. And I'd suggest you do the same," she said. She took a long drag on her cigarette while I loaded the empty shelves with clean glasses.

Today, the TV was tuned to testimony and closing arguments from the Rodney King police-beating trial in California.

"I am so sick of seeing that awful videotape," one woman said to friends at her table. "It shouldn't be on TV."

At around two, Lois, the club's official secretary, asked me to help her send out a mailing to six hundred members after my shift. It seemed that none of the waiters wanted to stay late. And since the only other choice was the non-English-speaking bus staff and dishwashers, I was it.

She took me up to her office on the main floor and introduced me to the two women who sat with her.

"Larry, this is Marge, whom you'll talk with in three months, because she's in charge of employee benefits."

I smiled at the brunette.

"And Larry, this is Sandy, whom you'll talk with after you become a member at the club, because she's in charge of members' accounts."

Both Sandy and I looked up at Lois with shocked expressions.

Lois winked, and at the same moment, the three jovial women burst out laughing.

Lois sat me down at a table in the middle of the club's cavernous ballroom and had me stamp "Annual Member Guest" on the bottom of small postcards and stuff them into envelopes.

As I sat in the empty ballroom, I looked around at the mirrors and the silver-and-crystal chandeliers that dripped from the high ceiling. I thought about all the beautiful weddings and debutante balls that must have taken place in that room. I could imagine members asking themselves, "Why would anybody who is not like us want to join a club where they're not wanted?"

I stuffed my last envelope, forgot to clock out, and drove back to the Merritt Parkway and into New York.

APRIL 23 (THURSDAY)

"Wow, that's great," I said to Mr. Ryan as he posted a memo entitled "Employee Relations Policy Statement: Employee Golf Privileges."

After quickly reading the memo, I realized this "policy" was a crock. The memo opened optimistically: "The club provides golf privileges for staff. . . . Current employees will be allowed golf privileges as outlined below." Unfortunately, the only employees the memo listed "below" were department heads, golf-management personnel, teaching assistants, the general manager, and "key staff that appear on the club's organizational chart."

At the end of the day, Mr. Ryan handed me my first paycheck. Perhaps now the backbreaking work would seem worthwhile. When I opened the envelope and saw what I'd earned—$174.04 for five days—I laughed out loud.

Back in the security of a bathroom stall, where I had periodically been taking notes since my arrival, I studied the check and thought about how many hours—and how hard—I'd worked for so little money. It was less than one-tenth of what I'd make in the same time at my law firm. I went upstairs and asked Mr. Ryan about my paycheck.

"Well, we decided to give you $7 an hour," he said in a tone overflowing with generosity. I had never actually been told my hourly rate. "But if the check looks especially big, that's because you got some extra pay in there for all of your terrific work on Good Friday. And by the way, Larry, don't tell the others what you're getting, because we're giving you a special deal and it's really nobody else's business."

I nodded and thanked him for his largesse. I stuffed some more envelopes, emptied out my locker, and left.

The next morning, I was scheduled to work a double shift. Instead, I called and explained that I had a family emergency and would have to quit immediately. Mr. Ryan was very sympathetic and said I could return when things settled down. I told him, "No, thanks," but asked that he send my last paycheck to my home. I put my uniform and the key to my locker in a brown padded envelope, and I mailed it all to Mr. Ryan.

Somehow it took two months of phone calls for me to get my final paycheck ($123.74 after taxes and a $30 deduction for my uniform).

I'm back at my law firm now, dressed in one of my dark gray Paul Stuart suits, sitting in a handsome office thirty floors above Midtown. While it's a long way from the Monkey House, we still have a long way to go.

2

I NEVER DATED A WHITE GIRL

Why Some Blacks
Still Oppose Interracial Marriage

*"If any white person intermarry with a colored person, or any
colored person intermarry with a white person, he shall be guilty of
a felony and shall be punished by confinement in the penitentiary
for not less than one nor more than five years."*

—Section 20-59 of Virginia State Code,
struck down by the U.S. Supreme Court in 1967

I NEVER DATED a white girl.

At a recent black-tie thirtieth birthday party for a black
investment banker friend of mine on Central Park West in New
York City, I was reminded of how blacks of my generation discuss interracial relationships. As I made my way through a cluster
of guests, I overheard a black woman in a sparkling bugle-bead
dress initiating a conversation with a group of equally well
dressed listeners. "Now listen carefully," she said while lightly
tugging on a sleeve of glistening black and white beads. "What
do Clarence Thomas, Montel Williams, Diana Ross, Shelby
Steele, Marian Wright Edelman, and Shari Belafonte all have in
common?"

I struggled to catch a glimpse of the woman's expression as she addressed her audience of seven: five blacks who nodded knowingly and two whites who looked on with puzzled expressions. Without so much as a pause, one of the listeners—a black woman in a sequined gown—laughed and said, "And while we're at it, don't forget Berry Gordy, Barry Bonds, and our so-called godfather of soul, James Brown."

"And Gregory Hines, Iman, Congressman Major Owens, Henry Louis Gates, and the first black senator from Massachusetts, Ed Brooke," a tuxedoed black man added.

"And opera singer Marian Anderson," another black woman said, placing a hand on her hip with a knowing nod.

"And James Earl Jones," I added.

The only white man in the group smiled nervously and tugged at his black-and-silver-striped bow tie. Turning from me to the storyteller, he said, "I don't get it. They're all rich blacks that have done *what*?"

"And don't leave out Sidney Poitier, Richard Roundtree, Charles Barkley, and Quincy Jones," the sequined black woman added.

"Quincy Jones!" we shouted back in disbelief.

"Are you serious?" the bugle-bead asked. Even she had lost some of her composure.

The other blacks laughed doubtfully, but the sequined woman stood her ground. "Six mixed kids. Three blond women. Nastassja Kinski, Verna somebody, and Peggy Lipton—that girl from, you know—*Mod Squad*?"

"Ouch!" The bugle-beaded woman was visibly shaken. "Quincy Jones? How could I have missed that? I can't believe it." After a pause, she began again. "Are you serious?"

"Like a heart attack."

The rest of us made a mental note of Quincy—one of our biggest heroes—and some of the other names we'd heard for the first time, then shook our heads with silent, righteous indignation.

The white man turned to his date and said, "I don't think I like what I'm hearing."

Before any of us opened our mouths, his white girlfriend agreed. "I know. Criticizing famous black people who are married to whites."

The recurring litany—one that other blacks have been reciting, supplementing, and retelling in living rooms, beauty shops, and churches all across America—had once again drawn to a close. The blacks in the group took sips, almost in unison, from our respective Perriers and white wines; there was nothing more to say. But there was lingering angst in the group: Although each of us had collected a few new names for our repertoires, we'd done so at the expense of revealing the tension and anxiety that many of us feel over the issue of black-white relationships.

We all knew where the tension came from: the mixed messages that all black middle-class kids are given by their families. We were all raised in integrated or mostly white neighborhoods, told to befriend white neighbors, socialize and study with white classmates, live comfortably with white college roommates, join white social and professional organizations, and go to work for mostly white employers in order to assimilate ourselves into the white model of success. But after all this coaching on how to make ourselves happy with and comfortable with white people and their culture and values, we were handed a final footnote that read: "Oh, and by the way, don't ever forget that you are black, and that you should never get so close to whites that you happen to fall in love with them."

Acknowledging what could be described as black bigotry was hard enough that evening, but to have done it in the presence of white people we didn't even know was even harder. There was so much that they didn't understand, so much that they would misinterpret. What could we say to keep them from assuming that this was just black racism in its most naked form?

The white man standing there in the tuxedo and striped bow tie had already indicated that he missed our point. That didn't surprise me: Experience has taught me to anticipate a negative reaction from white people who have never considered the disappointment and humiliation we endure when our most talented role models use intermarriage as a means to disassociate themselves from the black race. Why would this man or any other white person sympathize with us when they fail to comprehend that our collective self-esteem is tied to the success of these black heroes and heroines?

Of course, not every black person feels this way. Two of the black men in our cluster had become visibly uncomfortable during the course of the conversation and appeared ready to bolt to opposite corners of the spacious room as the white man decided to press his point home, asking, "But what's your point?"

We'd all anticipated that question, but some of us resented his asking it in such an accusatory tone. The two black men just wanted a quick escape: They rocked back on their heels, with hands buried deep in their pockets. Meanwhile, the women rolled their eyes belligerently, then stepped in closer.

In a decidedly defiant gesture, the white man let go of his date's hand and crossed his arms at his chest. "I don't get your point," he said again—clearly determined to hold at least a few of us there to account for our remarks.

"I'll see you later, Shelly," one of the black men interrupted as he squeezed out of the circle and offered a sympathetic pat on the back. "I'll see you later. I think I see a partner over there from Morgan that I need to say hello to."

"I'll get with you later, Shelly," the other fast-exiting man said while making an obvious gesture at the late hour on his Rolex watch. "Call me about the Summit in Vail, 'cause, girl, I gotta *run*."

My brothers dispersed with urgency—leaving the white couple standing with Shelly and the other black women. The three sisters stood their ground and seemed poised to advance their arguments.

Just as they began to make their case, the white man articulated the question that the then absent black men had been hoping to avoid: *"What's wrong with a black being married to a white?"*

Like I said, I never dated a white girl.

Why? Well, it started with Emmett Till.

I was eight years old, away from New York on summer vacation visiting relatives, when I heard the story of Emmett Till. I was sitting propped up on two phone books and a large cushioned chair in a Memphis barber shop with my uncle just a few doors away from my grandparents' restaurant on Florida Street. It was the city's south side—the black part of town.

I was gazing out the front door into the August morning sunshine when a white woman in tight orange 1970s hot pants walked by on the arm of a dark-skinned black man. The man winked in what looked like my direction, then quickly turned away from my curious glance.

The black barber's scissors suddenly stopped clipping.

My uncle looked up from his newspaper.

One of the other black barbers stopped his electric clippers and darted to the door with the electric cord trailing like a serpent in flight. As our eyes stood frozen on the view outside, a small, metal oscillating fan recirculated hair and the hot Memphis heat throughout the room. The dark-skinned man and his lean female companion had disappeared from my vision as they crossed the street.

"He knows we watching him," Barber Leon announced in an accusatory tone. "That's why he cocks his head and then crosses the street all the time. Coming through here just to set us off. He just so sure we watching him."

Barber Joe spun me 180 degrees and resumed his clipping. "Sho 'nough. He better just watch *himself*—or he'll end up like that Emmett Till, and the rest of 'em."

"Yeah, Emmett Till." My uncle whispered the words in a barely audible voice, shook his head sullenly, then returned to the pages of his *Memphis Commercial Appeal.*

That evening, after some cajoling, I got my grandfather to tell me the short unhappy story of Emmett Till. In 1958, Till—a fourteen-year-old from Chicago who was visiting relatives in Sumner, Mississippi—flirted with a white woman in a store by addressing her as "baby" on a dare from his friends. Later that night, two white men dragged the boy from his house and into the woods, beat him, castrated him, shot him, then gouged out his eyes, tied a cotton gin to his neck, and dropped him into the Tallahatchie River.

The history of Emmett Till's death—and my grandfather's dispassionate recounting of it—was my introduction to interracial relationships in America.

I was too young to comprehend the fact that the deep South in 1958 was very different from anything I'd ever encounter in the North during the 1970s. Nonetheless, Till's death was still a poignant warning that black men and white women were best kept apart. I was obsessed with visions of young black corpses and Klansmen on horseback, so the rest of my summer became riddled with my imagined fears of violent racial confrontations. On trips to Goldsmith's department store or out to east Memphis, near Germantown, where the whites shopped for groceries, I avoided making eye contact with white girls and white mothers who pushed their shopping carts up the aisles. This thirteen-year-old story about Till altered the rest of my summer—and even though I had never formed an opinion about them before, my eight-year-old eyes were now filled with a fear and paranoia that suggested that white women might be a personal threat to my safety.

Before 1967, it was illegal for blacks to marry whites in at least sixteen states. These antimiscegenation statutes were first created during the seventeenth and eighteenth centuries and were designed to prohibit both interracial sex and marriage. Initially the statutes were drafted simply, with the primary purpose being to separate the slave and white populations. But as more white owners raped their black female slaves, the state officials drafted ever more complex laws to include mulatto offspring—whether slave or free—so that they, too, would be prohibited from marrying whites.

After 1865, many of these laws were further expanded to prohibit whites from marrying any person who had one-eighth (or in some cases, one thirty-second) or more black ancestry.

Whether simple or sophisticated, narrow or broad, all of these antimiscegenation statutes were eventually outlawed on June 12, 1967, when Richard and Mildred Loving, an interracial couple, successfully sued the state of Virginia in a nine-year battle that was finally decided by the Supreme Court.

Richard Loving, a twenty-four-year-old white bricklayer, and Mildred Jeter, a seventeen-year-old black woman, had been married in the District of Columbia in 1958 and immediately moved to a home in Central Point, Virginia. Shortly after, a county sheriff arrived at the Lovings' Virginia home to arrest them for violating a Virginia state law that prohibited marriages between whites and nonwhites. Specifically, Virginia State Codes 20-58 and 20-59 prohibited marriages between whites and nonwhites and provided for a punishment of one to five years in a state penitentiary for violators who had either married each other in the state or who had married elsewhere and then later resided in the state.

Once arrested, the Lovings were sentenced to a year in jail, only to learn that the judge would suspend the sentence for twenty-five years if the couple left Virginia and promised not to return for the next quarter century. After leaving town, the Lovings filed suit. Nine years later the Supreme Court ruled in their favor, concluding that states that used racial classifications to restrict the freedom to marry were in violation of the Constitution's equal protection clause.

More than twenty-five years after the Court's decision, social resistance to mixed-race marriages still exists, with the greatest social barriers erected against black-white unions. According to the Census Bureau, in 1993, only 2.2 percent of all U.S. marriages were interracial. An even smaller figure—just .4 percent of all marriages—were black-white unions. This means there are approximately 246,000 black-white married couples out of a total 1,200,000 interracial married couples and out of a total of 54,000,000 married couples in the United States. There are approximately one million children of mixed-race unions.

Even though the number of black-white interracial marriages has nearly quadrupled since 1970, when there were sixty-five thousand black-white interracial couples—and even though the weight of political correctness has rendered outright opposition to intermarriage unacceptable—a large segment of white America still remains strongly opposed to miscegenation. A 1992 Gallup survey, for instance, revealed that only 10 percent of whites would approve of a family member marrying outside the race. A larger group of whites—44 percent—said they had no objection to the "concept of intermarriage." "Concept," in this case, can reasonably be interpreted as "so long as it doesn't involve me." The only instances when a moderate percentage of whites (15 percent or more) said they would approve of an interracial union was when the survey participant was neither related to nor acquainted with the individuals being married.

Many of my white friends and colleagues say they are not surprised by these statistics. They rationalize white resistance to interracial marriage with elaborate explanations. So zealous are these friends that they claim white opposition to intermarriage may not be a manifestation of ongoing racism at all. It may simply be the residual effect of *past* racist practices and beliefs that were once, but are no longer, advanced, or just a desire to protect their families from the few remaining people who would make painful racist comments. Their myriad explanations for the current white opposition include white people's general lack of exposure to middle-class black people; historical practices that have reinforced the idea that blacks are inferior; a desire for whites to perpetuate their own white ethnic heritages; and a misapprehension that black-white gene mixtures could compromise the intellectual development of what would otherwise be an intelligent white child. These are the *"legitimate"* reasons that a supposedly open-minded white person might cite when arguing against interracial coupling.

Such perspectives can be found among leading thinkers in the white community as well as among average Joes. In a form of racial candor that has become far too rare, the writer Norman Podhoretz acknowledged, in 1963, his personal feelings about interracial marriage. In his *Commentary* essay "My Negro Problem—and Ours," Podhoretz discussed his desire for white people like himself to accept intermarriage—while simultaneously confessing that he wouldn't want his own daughter to marry a black man: "No, I wouldn't like it at all. I would rail and rave and rant and tear my hair."

Few whites—intellectuals included—offer the honesty that Podhoretz was excoriated for expressing three decades ago.

At the same time, however, my white friends who have a plethora of reasons that explain white opposition to intermarriage are completely bewildered by blacks who oppose interracial coupling. They ask with incredulity: "What could blacks *possibly* be objecting to?" Their tone of indignation belies their statements about an increase in interracial unions being positive and downright joyful evidence that racism is on the decline. It is my guess that many of these whites are shocked and insulted, for they feel that blacks should be grateful for the opportunity to form a union with a people that has historically been considered superior. The message they are sending is: "What do you mean, you're against black-white marriage? You should be honored that a white spouse has accepted you. You should be grateful to gain a white relative for your black family tree."

All this said, why *aren't* we blacks displaying greater appreciation for the freedom we have to marry whites? Of course, we are happy that the antimiscegenation statutes were struck down. But why aren't we applauding the ultimate manifestation of such *de jure* advances—such as the sight of that interracial couple that passes by kissing on the sidewalk? Why wasn't there an outcry from blacks around the country (and not just from a few members of the local NAACP and the Southern Christian Leadership Conference) when the white principal of Randolph County High School in Wedowee, Alabama, threatened to cancel an April 1994 prom if any students planned to take a date of a different race?

Where do our misgivings come from? We can't all be eight-year-olds dodging the ghost of Emmett Till.

Why Some Blacks Still Oppose Interracial Coupling: Six Objections

Within many segments of the black community, one hears numerous arguments against the mixing of the races. Some quite cynical, some not quite logical, these arguments are nevertheless taken seriously by blacks as we draw a line between members of our black community and the whites around us.

Objection 1: **When a black leader or advocate marries outside the race, his decision may be evidence that he will demonstrate less commitment to black people and our causes.**

The strongest objection voiced by the black community against interracial coupling seems to be rationalized as a means of keeping prominent black leaders loyal to their constituents. Within the black community, there is an expectation that any government official, minister, business leader, judge, or other policymaker who is black will necessarily make it a priority to combat discrimination and any other societal ills that specifically plague black people. Whether or not these leaders articulate this as their explicit objective, we nevertheless insist that they, as dark-skinned people, remain familiar with, sensitive to, and focused on the issues of concern to the larger black community.

Not surprisingly, black people believe that such commitment can only be demonstrated by an advocate's complete and uncompromised loyalty to black people and black causes. And as intrusive as it may be, "complete and uncompromised loyalty" happens to take into account those decisions that an advocate makes regarding his own home and personal life. So, when a black advocate decides to marry outside the race, his decision leads the community to draw a string of unfortunate conclusions: that the person does not value uncompromised race loyalty, that the person is willing to exclude blacks from his personal life, and that therefore the advocate must be capable of abandoning the policies that would benefit the black group as a whole.

Such concerns were expressed when the popular black U.S. congressman Adam Clayton Powell, Jr., from Harlem, married a nonblack woman in December 1960. The son of a well-known black preacher and himself a minister at the famous black congregation Abyssinian Baptist Church on Harlem's 138th Street, Powell had used his light complexion to "pass" as a white student during the early part of his college education at Colgate University in upstate New York. He had lied about his racial background when he dated a white minister's daughter in college, when he patronized whites-only clubs, and again, in his fifties, when he began courting his third wife, a well-connected white Puerto Rican who lived in San Juan.

Even if they were not privy to Powell's occasional penchant for playing racial misclassification games, certain black voters and onlookers interpreted this willingness to marry a nonblack woman as evidence that Powell might also have the capacity to abandon black people and betray their interests.

When a May 1992 *People* magazine cover photo showed the then recently confirmed Supreme Court justice Clarence Thomas posing with his wife, Virginia Lamp, few black people were surprised by the revelation that Thomas was a partner in an interracial marriage. It confirmed black people's greatest fears that he felt no connection to the black community. During the news coverage of the Anita Hill hearings, we learned of his high regard for the conservatism of Ronald Reagan and George Bush, his prior emasculation of the Equal Employment Opportunity Commission, and his willingness to humiliate his sister with the public revelation that she once received public assistance. These situations caused black people to question Thomas's loyalties, but there was still one final indicator that confirmed for black America where he stood in relation to the black agenda. Blacks felt that his choice of conservative or anti–affirmative action views might suggest antiblack political leanings. Those were, however, still only political or intellectual decisions. What really mattered was his decision to marry a white woman: The black community considered this decision—a personal and emotional one—to be something even more relevant than his political views. And this was more than many blacks could take.

In some cases, the black community considers a black leader's decision to marry a white as simply an aberration that invites the black population's greater scrutiny of someone previously thought to be "okay." In Thomas's case, with his political views already weighing against him, it became incontrovertible proof that this black leader was isolated from—and possibly permanently at odds with—the black community.

One of black history's best-kept secrets involves the marital relations of one of black America's greatest advocates, nineteenth-century black abolitionist Frederick Douglass. Although he distinguished himself with heroic abolitionist activities and political speeches on behalf of black people's rights, black people are quietly suspicious today, and were even more so then, when Douglass married his white secretary in 1884. This information has caused some to carefully scrutinize the activities of one of our greatest leaders.

When Walter White, the NAACP's most prominent black leader during its early years, decided to marry the popular white *Mademoiselle* editor and socialite Poppy Cannon in 1949, he simultaneously resigned his high-level executive position with the organization—causing speculation that his interest in white women was further proof that he had abandoned the NAACP and its pro-black agenda. History proved that, like Douglass, White remained deeply committed to black equality even after he married. Unfortunately, many of his constituents at the time couldn't help questioning the sincerity of his interest in black problems.

Because paranoia builds so easily atop our own damaging collective experiences as a group, we are always wary of black activists who might lose interest in our problems. Our response is to demand that our advocates be surrounded by and totally consumed by the black experience—at work, at home, and at play. Therefore, we burden them with demands for ongoing demonstrations of their compassion for the black struggle. And it is unlikely that even the most proven black leaders would be excused from this same standard.

If, for example, Rev. Jesse Jackson or Coretta Scott King or the president of the NAACP were to marry a white person, black followers would immediately wonder if their leader's interest was somehow diminished and would call our activist leader's identification with black people into question.

Because of their ability to influence policy and their standing as a proxy for a large percentage of the race, black political, intellectual, religious, and business leaders are held to a much higher standard than the myriad big-money athletes and entertainers who marry whites. While we feel that the black community fails to gain advantages when black sports figures and singers marry outside the race, it doesn't seem to upset as many blacks as when our past and present intellectual leaders—people like Wilbert Tatum, publisher of the *New York Amsterdam News,* the nation's premier black newspaper; Archie Epps, dean at Harvard; Franklin A. Thomas, president of The Ford Foundation; writers Alice Walker, Maya Angelou, and John Edgar Wideman; intellectuals Orlando Patterson and Martin Kilson; Children's Defense Fund head Marian Wright Edelman; Virginia governor Douglas Wilder; *Native Son* author Richard Wright; *Raisin in the Sun* author Lorraine Hansberry; black South African activist and *Kaffir Boy* author Mark Mathabane; ANC leader and South African Ambassador to the UN, Allan Boesak; the first black senator, Edward Brooke; and Harvard African American history scholar Henry Louis Gates—decide to marry or become romantically linked with whites.

Legal scholar and author Derrick Bell recalls the concern expressed by some of his black students at Harvard over the issue of black academics who were married to whites. "At the time I entered the academic world in 1969 at Harvard," he explains, "a clear majority of black male faculty members were married to white women. The absence of black-couple role models was so striking to the black female students on campus at Radcliffe that those black women made a special request to the school: If the school were to place additional faculty families in the faculty housing across the street from the college, the administration should make an effort to place at least one faculty family that included a black couple. My wife and I were immediately placed at the top of the housing list and we eventually became mentors to several of the Radcliffe students."

The intermarriage test may have little application to the average private citizen, but it continues to have great significance for those who seek to speak on behalf of our race.

Objection 2: **We fear that intermarrying blacks are making a statement to black and white America that black spouses are less desirable partners—and are, therefore, inferior.**

This could easily be called the "black woman's argument," since many black women believe it is no coincidence that 71 percent of all black-white couples in America involve a black man. Black women know that these statistics support their often cited theory that materially successful black men seek out white wives as the final accoutrement in their climb to the top. The white wife is perceived as the ultimate trophy in the black man's battle to match the gains and respect of the more successful and revered white man.

As powerful and accomplished black men marry less educated or less accomplished white women, the message being inferred by the black community—and by the *black female* community, in particular—is that no black woman, no matter how attractive or intelligent, would be satisfactory. This was an issue that became a focus of the black community's debate about O. J. Simpson's guilt or innocence in the 1994 murder of his white ex-wife. Black readers focused on the accounts that reported how the football star expressed romantic interests in white women exclusively.

Middle- and upper-class blacks' response to black-white couples can be particularly negative when a successful black marries a white spouse with characteristics and qualities that are deemed to be far less extraordinary than his own. When a white spouse is neither prominent, nor wealthy, nor accomplished, nor attractive, we find our anger further compounded and further justified.

On occasional Sunday afternoons, I get calls from black friends who've just finished perusing the *New York Times* wedding announcements. They've spotted an interracial couple's résumé that resonates with incongruities. We are all trying to maintain an open mind but still find ourselves saying, "Okay, maybe this obviously well-educated and prosperous black man had a hard time finding a large number of similarly placed black women, and therefore sought out a white woman with his same impressive qualifications. But what would cause him to marry a white woman who has none of these attributes?" More than a few blacks asked these questions about black TV talk-show host Montel Williams, who is married to a white blonde who once worked as an "exotic" dancer in Las Vegas. Because of his national talk-show forum and his record as one of the highest ranking black graduates in Annapolis history, he has become an outspoken advocate on behalf of black issues. Blacks were nonetheless disturbed when they discovered that this new advocate was married not only to a white woman but one who lacked academic and career prestige.

Reading about successful black businesspersons, charismatic TV personalities, college deans, actors, and politicians has become an experience familiar to most blacks. We flip through glowing profiles in *People, Ebony,* or *Business Week* quietly praising the latest black trailblazer and role model. Then we look for what we consider the final determinant of this person's black identity—that thing that will allow us to bestow our unqualified appreciation. We look for the litmus test of loyalty to the race: the photo of the person's spouse or significant other.

Not only have I done this to others; I have seen it done to me. In the August 17, 1992, issue of *New York* magazine, an out-of-focus photo of my wife's back appears in my article "Invisible Man." The print came out very light, causing some readers to conclude that my black wife was white. I received angry letters and calls, endured face-to-face remarks from black people who were proud of my modest accomplishments yet disappointed when they mistakenly believed I hadn't married one of my own. When I corrected them and explained that my wife was, in fact, 100 percent black, they said they were "relieved" to hear that. Notwithstanding my own history of race-checking the spouses of people I admired and read about, this experience brought home the ease with which absolute strangers will denigrate blacks whom they want to celebrate but who have "let them down" through their dating or marital choices.

Few blacks can imagine seeing a similarly accomplished white man marrying a similarly unaccomplished black woman. Therefore, they wonder: Why should the famous and talented Montel Williams reject all black women—accomplished or otherwise—for a white woman? Similar arguments were made when blacks heard that black Virginia governor Douglas Wilder was dating Patricia Kluge, a white woman who (while a liberal, generous, and wealthy divorcée) was a former belly dancer.

We blacks are surprised that whites don't understand our frustration at seeing our most accomplished members aggressively pursuing unaccomplished white spouses. After years of trying to offer my white friends a "white" analogy that would be as outrageous as certain famous rich black–poor white couplings, I came up with the following scenario:

Imagine if in 1965 Jackie Kennedy, then a recently widowed First Lady, had come to the conclusion that she would never find a white man to measure up to her understandably high standards and had decided to go ahead and marry a black store manager who worked at an A&P in suburban Boston.

Sounds mighty ludicrous when the colors are switched, doesn't it?

Unfortunately, there can be an even more insidious motive for this "marrying down" behavior between successful blacks and less successful whites: that some blacks simply do not find African Americans to be physically attractive. On more than one occasion this has been revealed about ex–football star O. J. Simpson. An August 29, 1994, *Newsweek* cover story asserted that his black friends criticized him for lusting after only white women. One black NBA player and friend of Simpson's said, "I never saw O. J. connect with a sister—it was white or nothing." In describing the physical features that attracted him, Simpson was quoted as saying, "California types . . . I'm in love with Farrah Fawcett-Majors's looks."

There were black guys in my own circle who also found black women unattractive. I spent my first college summer working as a research assistant in the White House. During that time, I became friends with a black student who was my age, lived in my dorm, and worked as an intern in a government agency near Capitol Hill. After seeing Kevin go out on dates with three different white women, I asked him one evening: "Why do you only seem to date white women when we're right here in Chocolate City—where we're literally outnumbered by smart, good-looking black women?"

Although I'd heard this from white guys before, the answer surprised me when it came from *his* lips.

"No offense to you and your girlfriend, Larry," Kevin said. "But I just don't find black women attractive."

I assumed that he was about to launch into that tired old argument about white women being more appealing because they come from traditional two-parent families where the husband is acknowledged as and treated like the "boss" of the household. I'd heard black guys offer innumerable stories of how black women challenge the black man's authority and become bossy because of their having been reared in families where black men were absent and where black women raised children on their own.

"No offense," he apologized again. "But I just don't feel black women are good-looking."

"No offense to *me?*" I asked incredulously. "How about no offense to your mother and to that black daughter you're gonna have someday—whether she's half-black or totally black?"

My challenge of his own self-hatred had absolutely no effect on Kevin. And unfortunately, I was to discover that there are hundreds of Kevins out there. I've never admitted this to the two white male friends of mine who guiltily confessed to me that they find black women unattractive, but there are many black Kevins whose definition of beauty is specifically linked to white skin, blond hair, and blue eyes.

I know I am not alone in resenting the Kevins and the message they send to black women and white America.

Take, for instance, the response when my friends and I heard that Roger and Karen, a popular black couple I had known from graduate school, announced that they were getting a divorce after only two years of marriage. When black friends and I heard rumors that Roger was verbally abusive to Karen and reckless with her money, none of us really agreed with Karen's decision to kick him out of their apartment. Even when we heard stories of Roger carrying on affairs with two other women, we challenged Karen to give him another chance. "He'll settle down—he just misses his bachelor days," we remarked, still not identifying with Karen's pain and frustration.

Then she dropped the bomb on us.

"And both of the women were *white*," Karen explained. "One is this blond secretary in his office."

"Dump him," we all instantly agreed. "He's hopeless." In the black community, there is no redemption for an "Uncle Tom." And while it sounds like an extreme characterization, one of the surest ways to be labeled an "Uncle Tom" is by undermining the advances or reputations of black people or by dating white women.

Cheating on Karen was an insult to her, as an individual, but cheating on her with a *white woman* was a political statement that offended us all. The act undermined the strength of our already weak black family structure by discrediting the black woman's physical and sexual desirability and by reinforcing white people's influence in our personal lives, our families, our stature, and our future. All of this caused us to rally around Karen and elevate her personal tragedy to a public and political statement about what was wrong with black men in America today.

"This is the problem with the black family," several of us lectured to no one in particular as the rumor spread from person to person in Karen and Roger's social circuit. "Black men who don't respect the black woman are also guilty of hating themselves and their people."

Objection 3: Interracial marriage undermines our ability to introduce our black children to black mentors and role models who accept their racial identity with confidence and pride.

Black parents already have a difficult job teaching their children not to be ashamed of their blackness. Millions of black children are challenged each day by news media and advertisements that suggest that to be black is to be poor, uneducated, unattractive, and threatening. The nation's devotion to long-haired blond models in print ads teaches our daughters that their dark, short, curly hair is unmanageable and unattractive. The gratuitous photos of both actual and falsely accused black male muggers and rapists on the evening news tell our sons that they will grow up to be criminals.

Because of all the negative black adult stereotypes in the media and society, we look for positive black role models and hold them up as proof to our children that black is beautiful, good, and intelligent and that they should be proud to be black. But when that role model turns out to be married to a white mate, our children say, "Well, if it's so good to be black, why do all my role models date and marry whites?" Children interpret the actions of these role models and conclude that their parents are misleading them. As a child growing up in the "black is beautiful" 1970s, I remember asking these questions when I learned that my favorite black role models—people like actors Sidney Poitier and Sammy Davis, Jr.; opera star Marian Anderson; Broadway actress Pearl Bailey; basketball legends Bill Russell and Wilt Chamberlain; TV and nightclub performers Leslie Uggams, Eartha Kitt, and Diahann Carroll; and Motown singer Diana Ross—were all married to or romantically linked with whites.

I'm reminded of a black mother whom I met on an Amtrak train from New York to Boston while I was in law school. It was 1988. The woman told me that her seven-year-old daughter wanted to grow up and become an Olympic skater just like the black skater Debi Thomas.

"My Cheryl has been the only black student in her figure-skating class for three years now," the woman said wearily. "And that's why I was so glad we had Debi to look to. Just hearing about Debi gave Cheryl a role model and it quieted the jokes that some of her white friends made about black people not knowing how to skate."

I looked over to Cheryl, who was sleeping quietly in the large reclined train chair. I thought of how Arthur Ashe had been my role model when I was just taking up tennis when I was six years old—standing on a court in Manhattan, surrounded by a group of white children who said blacks couldn't play tennis.

"Well," I said, "I heard Debi announced she's getting married."

The woman closed her eyes and shook her head in exasperation. She made a shushing sound, then whispered back, "To some white boy," she said. "I just read about it, but I'm not even telling Cheryl about it," the woman confessed. "You know, I can't stand it when our very best kids run out on us and just self-destruct. There she was, a premed student at Stanford, competing in the Olympics, on the covers of all those magazines. Cheryl wanted to be just like her—even had me do her hair like Debi."

"Wow," I remarked.

"And now I just read that she's dropped out of Stanford, moved to Colorado, and married this white boy, who's some kind of physical therapist or something."

The woman and I looked over to the dozing seven-year-old and shook our heads in silence. I tried to think of how bigoted all of this sounded—and how judgmental we were of black people who had, at one time or another, created some sensation and made us proud to be black. I recalled the stories about Debi's mother and how she had always been photographed in the stands and described as a stoic working-class single parent who had driven her daughter several hours each week to attend skating lessons as a child. We surely hoped that Debi and her new husband had a happy life together, but we were still left with the feeling that we had lost yet another role model for black children to emulate. We hoped that it wouldn't disappoint the little girl in the way it disappointed us.

Another way in which interracial marriages undermine our search for confident black role models comes from their treatment by both the media and the white public. For example, interracial pairings in the public eye often take on a comic or exploitative role. Consider the mixed couple Tom and Helen Willis of the 1970s Norman Lear TV series *The Jeffersons,* who were treated as one big joke for the entire history of the program. They were the "Zebra couple" that George Jefferson laughed at in every episode. There was nothing complex or interesting about them. They were comic relief *because* they were mixed. That was the joke. Instead of taking these pairings at face value, we see them as acts intended to provoke controversy or to entertain. Hence, they are never taken seriously.

Take, for instance, the well-reported relationship between black actress Whoopi Goldberg and white actor Ted Danson in 1993. It was in 1992, during advance publicity on their yet-to-be-released movie *Made in America,* that the public was first told about a possible love affair between the two stars. Initially, the media and the public—both black and white—laughed at this apparent public relations campaign. After all, what could be more comical than the pairing of this dark-skinned dreadlocked black woman who was known for a repertoire of jokes about "gullible white people" with this tall white man who'd become famous playing an Irish bartender in TV's most famous all-white Boston bar? All those black fans of Whoopi's from her famous role in *The Color Purple* chuckled to themselves, "Oh, that crazy Whoopi!" And all those white fans of Ted's from his role in *Cheers* laughed, "Oh, that crazy Ted!"

The movie *Made in America* came and went. But to many people's surprise, Whoopi and Ted were still here. Soon, the public realized that this interracial union was more than a wacky publicity stunt. It was real life. And that's what led to an event that made a complete mockery out of Whoopi, Ted, and the seriousness of interracial relationships.

For her initiation into the famous Friar's Club, Whoopi was "roasted" on a New York dais in October 1993. When it was time for Ted to give his comments and cracks about Whoopi, he appeared at the podium in blackface. Under the guise of poking fun at the racists who spoke derisively of their union, Ted launched into a crude litany of derogatory jokes that played into every possible antiblack stereotype (from monkeys to watermelon, and from anal sex to coons) imaginable. White America was embarrassed. Black America was insulted by Ted and furious with Whoopi, who they felt should be dating one of her own. Less than a year later, Whoopi was in the process of marrying another white man—this time, a little-known union organizer named Lyle Trachtenberg.

The racist shock-radio host Howard Stern is another who perpetuates the notion that interracial relationships are nothing more than bizarre and comical pairings. During a December 13, 1993, program, the increasingly popular host spent much of the show asking various white female listeners to admit if they'd ever "done it" with a black guy and to describe what it was like. After his producer's wife called in and acknowledged that she'd had sex with a black man, Stern insisted, "He must have been wearing a ski mask . . . or you must have been incredibly drunk." In the eyes of a Stern, and unfortunately many of his listeners, the only contexts in which interracial relations might take place are rape perpetrated by black men in masks or where a white woman was too drunk to know what she was doing. Such a pairing could be the result only of folly or criminal behavior.

Objection 4: **Because it diffuses our resources, interracial marriage makes it difficult to build a black America that has uncompromised wealth, prestige, and power, thus making it harder to empower other parts of black America and erase the stereotypes of a weak and impoverished black community.**

Following the example of white Americans who have built respected and influential family dynasties, such as the Vanderbilts, Roosevelts, Kennedys, and Basses, ambitious black Americans recognize the importance of hard work and strong family ties. The black community can gain much from powerful and affluent black families. Just as certain white families have shaped policies and contributed to causes that work on behalf of their larger group's interest, black dynasties could do the same for our interests. We fear that intermarriage diffuses both the support we already have and the strength of the dynasties we would otherwise build.

While Supreme Court justice Thurgood Marshall, Quincy Jones, Sidney Poitier, Lena Horne, and NAACP founder Walter White are all examples of black individuals who remained extremely committed to black causes in spite of their marriages to nonblack spouses, we still fear the cumulative financial and political losses that our organizations and communities might suffer if an overwhelming portion of our pool of wealthy, educated, and influential blacks were to marry outside the race.

These fears that we blacks harbor are derived from our recognition both that we are a disenfranchised people and that powerful families who share our ethnicity and who act as benefactors can bolster our position and our voice in society. Like other "shrinking" minorities (for example, Jews, who now intermarry at a rate of 52 percent, or Native Americans, who have intermarried at rates exceeding 50 percent since the 1950s), we are forced to think pragmatically. We are afraid to imagine what might have happened if some of the wealthiest blacks in recent American history, including *Ebony* magazine founder John Johnson, former Beatrice Foods and McCall's Patterns owner Reginald Lewis, actor Bill Cosby, insurance company founder Ernesta Procope, and TV show host Oprah Winfrey had joined with white lovers and white spouses.

Would Lewis have given $1 million to Howard University—a black college he hadn't even attended? Would Cosby have given a record $20 million to black Spelman College in Atlanta? Would Winfrey have given so many of her millions to black families, black schools, and housing projects on Chicago's south side?

Without the encouragement and enthusiasm of spouses and companions who understood and shared the minority experience from a personal perspective, it is possible that these people might have moved outside the black community physically, emotionally, and philanthropically.

***Objection 5:* We worry that confused biracial children will turn their backs on the black race once they discover that it's easier to live as a white person.**

There were 49,479 black-white biracial children born in 1990. Within the black community, there is a pervasive belief that biracial offspring will undoubtedly mature from insecure kids, who get teased by schoolmates of both races, into psychologically troubled adults who are scrutinized by neighbors and coworkers. In his column in *Interrace* magazine, Dr. Lawrence Tenzer frequently answers letters from black readers about the psychological problems faced by children who grow up part black and part white. In 1993, he appeared on *Sally Jesse Raphael* with a white mother who told of her Afro-Caucasian adolescent child who had committed suicide because of the ongoing rejection he had faced from others who objected to his biracial makeup.

Putting complete stock in the experiences of those fictional "tragic mulatto" characters from *Showboat, Pinky,* and numerous Dorothy Dandridge films (which parallel her own tragic life, which ended in suicide), some of us imagine that the only viable option for mixed-race children is living a life of "passing"—a game riddled with guilt for those who truly can pass and with rejection for those who discover they truly can't. These children are the stars in their own real-life versions of *Imitation of Life*.

Putting a more optimistic, modern-day spin on biracial children, other blacks think of biracial adults such as legal scholar Lani Guinier; film director Mario Van Peebles; movie actress Halle Berry; *Village Voice* columnist and daughter of poet Amiri Baraka, Lisa Jones; and New York City councilman Adam Clayton Powell IV, who openly acknowledge their blackness and demonstrate their lack of confusion about their multiracial heritage. But for every success story, there seems to be a story of a confused biracial child. Take, for instance, half-black *Flashdance* actress and Yale graduate Jennifer Beals. We all rallied behind her acting and academic career—that is, until we heard rumors about a news story claiming that she said she considered her biracial parentage to have made her "neither black nor white." The "colorless world" argument is one that disturbs black people because it sounds like the individual is actually claiming, "I'd rather be anything but black, so if it's necessary for me to call myself 'raceless' or 'colorless,' then that's what I will be." After hearing that remark, we felt we had lost Beals—and matters weren't helped by the mean-spirited cynics who viciously joked that she had, no doubt, considered herself black enough during the two seconds it took to check off the "African American" box on her Yale application. The cynics, of course, had no idea which box Beals had actually checked off, but they sure felt vindicated when they saw that she was getting married to a white man a few years later. Feelings of abandonment mix easily with paranoia, and almost no one gets let off the hook.

In 1994, the black-looking biracial actress Troy Beyer, of *Dynasty* soap opera fame, also confirmed black cynics' suspicions about her own racial allegiance when she announced that she was marrying white Hollywood producer Mark Burg.

Biracial offspring are often perceived by blacks as sellouts who take advantage of the confusion that their mixed identity creates.

Such a situation was created when black-sounding singer Mariah Carey became a national sensation in 1990. Both blacks and whites agreed that she was talented. But what they didn't agree on was her race. While a large segment of the black population thought the twenty-year-old singer was black, the white audience and mainstream media saw her photos and declared her to be a "white singer" with a "black sound."

After many months of mounting public confusion, Carey and her promoters were confronted by members of the press. Grudgingly, it was admitted that yes, she was half-black. Even though it was the fault of her promoters, this reluctant admission did not endear the singer to black audiences. Her eventual, well-publicized 1993 marriage to a powerful white record executive pushed her even further outside the black community's borders.

Many black people suspect that biracial offspring are eager to disguise their black identity through any means possible (such as explaining one's dark coloring by claiming to be part Brazilian, Cuban, Puerto Rican, Syrian, or any other dark-skinned ethnicity that remains distinguished from African ancestry). Like high-level "gene police" guarding a racially obsessed and racially pure people, these "guardian blacks" oppose new measures and racial practices that could blur a black child's racial identification and classification. Some blacks, including prominent officials at the National Urban League, have opposed proposals that the federal government classify black-white offspring as "biracial" as opposed to "black." Some of the guardian blacks argue that the recent campaigns launched by mixed-race families throughout the United States, as well as by the Association for Multiethnic Americans in San Francisco, to convince the Census Bureau to create a new racial classification of "biracial" or "multiracial" will have the effect of discouraging children of black-white unions from establishing connections and identifications with the black culture and community.

Publicly, many parents of black-white children, and the offspring themselves, claim that they are not evading the black world and black culture through a "nonblack" label or classification because, in the end, they are still both white and black. But there is evidence that many biracial black-white children who are light enough to "pass" as white will do so—and that many of the rest, like singer Mariah Carey, writer Shelby Steele, and actress Jennifer Beals, will ultimately divest themselves of all black culture by marrying whites. It appears paranoid to some, but black people fear that mixed-race offspring will choose to give greater emphasis to their white heritage, since society offers greater acceptance to and greater respect for those that are held out to be white individuals.

A child's appreciation of his own black culture has been of great concern to many well-respected black organizations that grapple with interracial issues. Opposition to transracial adoption is fueled by similar concerns. With its 1993 rejection of a resolution supporting adoptions of black babies by white parents, the NAACP joined the National Association of Black Social Workers in asserting that a black child's racial identity is injured when he is raised by nonblack parents. Several states have followed this logic and drafted legislation encouraging adoption agencies to place black babies with black families. For certain legislators and black organizations, the desire to perpetuate a uniquely black culture has taken precedence even over the urgent placement of black children into stable families.

I am reminded of a well-known, forty-something white-looking black businesswoman in Chicago who many blacks say has spent her entire career passing as white. I have met her on numerous occasions and have often noticed how she politely excuses herself to another corner of a party when I or other blacks appear in her presence. Why? Because standing next to a group of black people, she, indeed, looks like one of us. A relentless partygoer, this wealthy, accomplished woman surrounds herself with an almost impenetrable circle of powerful white people. Whether she's 100 percent black or 25 percent black, she's the kind of role model blacks would be eager to claim as our own. When asked, she describes her background as a patchwork quilt of ethnic groups. Articles profiling this woman never seem to include a patch called "black." For us, this woman represents the mature version of the traitorous biracial child.

Objection 6: **Today's interracial relationships are a painful reminder of a 250-year period in black American history when our sexuality was exploited beyond our control and to our detriment by white people.**

For many generations, stories about black sexuality have been used by white racists to polarize the black and white communities. The Ku Klux Klan and other antiblack groups dating back to the early eighteenth century circulated propaganda that demonstrated whites' obsession with the size of the black man's genitalia, the black male's capacity for sexual activity, and the black man's grand scheme to sexually conquer white women. Advanced with pseudoscientific research and propaganda publications, the KKK and others taught whites to perceive black men as sexually driven animals that couldn't be allowed near white women.

D. W. Griffith's 1915 movie *The Birth of a Nation* exploited this "black man as sexual animal" stereotype. Throughout the film, lustful black men offer lecherous glances and remarks to defenseless white women. Ultimately, the white heroine of the film throws herself off a cliff to avoid being raped by the black character, Gus.

Not only was the image of the black man as a sexual conqueror of white women utilized in propaganda films; it was also at the center of frequent, small-town black-white conflicts. One of the most well-known racial miscarriages of justice began with a lie involving black men and white women. The 1931 "Scottsboro Boys" incident began when nine young black men got into a fight with a group of white men on a train traveling from Tennessee to Scottsboro, Alabama. The whites, who were determined to get revenge after the fight, falsely accused the nine black men of raping two white women, and persuaded the police in Alabama to arrest them based on this charge. Without any evidence, a mob of whites attempted to lynch the nine innocent boys. Eventually an incensed all-white jury found the blacks guilty and sentenced them to death. The countless lynchings of innocent black men who were falsely accused of sexually assaulting or insulting white women attest to the white man's fixation on the imagined threat of the black man's sexuality.

The visceral response of white America to stories—even mere accusations—about a black man raping, attempting to rape, flirting with, or having consensual sex with a white woman has not changed significantly even now.

The 1991 "Central Park jogger attack" received more attention than any of the other hundreds of heinous rapes that took place in New York City that year—in large part because the brutal rape was perpetrated by poor black boys on a white woman. An equally repulsive 1990 gang-rape attack, also in New York City, of a black, middle-class St. John's University student by four white male students was reported in the newspapers, but it did not elicit the same outrage from the public.

In September 1993, the executive producer of a Dallas children's play, *Ramona Quimby,* was forced to remove a kiss between a black man and white woman after objections were raised by various white audience members who viewed the play. Many Texas papers reported that the kiss—which consisted of a peck on the woman's cheek—so incensed a Dallas investment banker that he threatened to picket the theater.

White response to these black-white interactions reveals the heightened anxiety that the white community continues to experience toward interracial sex—particularly when the participants are black men and white women. Reports—whether true or false—detailing violent acts perpetrated by black men against white women continue to be the ones that mobilize the greatest response from the white public. And this is no secret to white people, as has been evidenced by some of the greatest hoaxes involving crimes alleged to have been committed by black men against white women: In 1992, the city of Boston and sympathetic TV viewers around the world listened to the eerie audio recording of a white, wounded, and frantic Charles Stuart tell a 911 operator about how a black man had just shot and killed his pregnant wife. With great detail, Stuart eventually described the fictional black murderer. After the police had launched a citywide search in which black men in and around Boston were questioned and detained, it was discovered that it was Stuart, himself, who had killed his wife.

And as if we hadn't learned to question the use of that ubiquitous, yet mythical, tall, dark-skinned, woolen-cap-wearing black criminal, the general public once again rallied around another bizarre crime (with sketchy and unlikely facts) that he had supposedly committed against a helpless white woman. In November 1994, a great outpouring of sympathy was understandably offered when the white, twenty-three-year-old Susan Smith, of Union, South Carolina, appeared on national television and the front pages of national magazines to make a plea for the return of her two young sons, who had been kidnapped by a mysterious black carjacker in November 1994.

After innocent black men in the small southern town had become suspects in the criminal investigation and after the races had become visibly polarized in the community, Smith finally broke down and admitted that she had actually killed her sons herself by strapping them in her car and rolling it into a nearby lake where they would drown.

Only a month after this incident, twenty-year-old Josephine Lupis, a white student at the Long Island campus of the State University of New York at Old Westbury, claimed she was robbed, slashed, and then stabbed by a black man in the school parking lot. Like the mythical carjacker in South Carolina, Lupis's perpetrator was a six-foot-tall black man with a woolen cap. This time, however, he had also donned a scarf. Days later, Lupis admitted that she had actually slashed herself and made up the description of the black slasher. The *New York Times* and other New York media reported that Lupis explained her crime by noting that she had been depressed following a breakup with her boyfriend. I ask you, what better way to win his and others' sympathy than to have been victimized by a knife-wielding black man with a woolen cap in a dark parking lot?

The image of a sexual relationship between a black man and white woman stirs complex emotions in both races—and a marriage between the two can become a lightning rod for the resentment that such a relationship can engender. Even when the parties are willing, the disturbing image of white female victim and black male sexual aggressor keeps us from feeling good about the union.

The black community's response to this popular portrayal is complex. Within the community, one can see the black man's fear of, and anger about, being accused of having uncontrollable sexual appetites. One can see the suspicion that a white woman may be seeking sexual thrills at the expense of a sincere black man. And one can see the painful message underlying the notion that black men want white women at all: that *black* women are undesirable and that black men aren't attracted to their own kind.

So like many older black men, I, too, avert my eyes when an attractive white woman walks by. Our fathers and grandfathers averted their eyes to avoid a whipping by whites or a false accusation of rape by authorities. My friends and I avert our eyes for various reasons: in order to maintain favor with our white male employers; to deny white racists the opportunity to confirm their wild accusations; to deny white women the opportunity to believe they are more desirable than black women; and to restore pride and self-esteem in our own black women.

Discomfort with black female–white male sexual encounters has a related, but slightly different cast. The predatory nature of these relationships has become muted over time in public discourse, but many blacks still remember it painfully.

Sexual abuses were historically and routinely perpetrated upon black women as both slaves and servants by white owners and employers. Not only have many historians confirmed that even prominent white colonial leaders (like George Washington and Thomas Jefferson) fathered black children, but slave narratives abound with stories of white plantation owners who required black servants and slave women to silently endure their sexual advances. Black and mulatto women—well into the 1950s—were commonly portrayed in books and films as whores. Popular caricatures in film and television reminded black women and others that their role in society was limited to being the asexual "mammy"— or the forbidden sexual fruit.

Unwillingness to repeat these patterns—even consensually— may drive black women's overwhelming rejection of interracial marriage. An *Essence* magazine survey of black female readers found that only one-third of black women would consider having an intimate relationship with a white man. In a survey at the University of South Florida, 67 percent of black women polled responded that they would rather remain single if they couldn't find a husband who was black. In 1992, Census Bureau figures revealed that black women are half as likely to marry outside the race than black men.

I never dated a white girl.

I grew up in a predominately white setting, but always had a moderate number of blacks in my circle of male and female friends. By participating in adult and children's organizations that catered to middle- and upper-income blacks, my family was constantly introduced to other black children who were growing up in similar environments. Nationally organized black organizations such as Jack & Jill of America, the Links, the Deltas, the Alphas, and the Drifters sponsored the parties, conventions, and trips where I met other black families like my own. The Oak Bluffs section of Martha's Vineyard and Sag Harbor, Long Island, were the summer vacation places where this group of black families renewed friendships each June, July, and August. It was out of these groups and locales that I made my black friends and formed my dating relationships.

From as early as I can remember, my parents encouraged me and my older brother to participate in discussions of race-related incidents that were reported in the press, as well as those that took place in our own everyday lives at school and in our community. Notwithstanding the proximity of the white children who lived around us, Mom and Dad made sure to balance those interactions with positive influences and messages from the black world. It was through these almost daily overt and subliminal messages that I formed my black identity.

I imagine that my parents were well aware of the subliminal messages we were receiving as they introduced my brother and me early on to positive images of black women, along with all the other images of blacks.

In 1968, a few months after we had moved from an integrated suburban neighborhood into a completely white suburban neighborhood, my father and uncle drove me and my brother into the black, impoverished neighborhood of Bedford-Stuyvesant, Brooklyn, to meet and hang up posters for a black woman running for Congress. She was a former schoolteacher named Shirley Chisholm, and my uncle, a Brooklyn resident, said she wasn't going to succeed in Congress unless black people everywhere helped her. At the time, I asked my father why we were helping a schoolteacher run for "Brooklyn Congress" when we didn't even live there. I don't remember his answer, but I do remember being told that getting this black woman elected was going to be a historic event. (In the end, he was right because she went on to become an influential and effective congresswoman for fourteen years.) I also remember keeping a picture of Chisholm in her cat-style glasses pinned to my bedroom bulletin board for years until I went off to college.

In addition to the copies of *Ebony, Jet, Sepia, Black Enterprise,* and *Essence* that became a part of our required reading in our den, I was met each morning by photos and articles that my mother taped to the refrigerator door. They were of and about women whom she admired and whom my white friends sometimes referred to as fat, funny-looking, or ugly. These brazen eight-year-olds had no compunction, when visiting my house for lunch or a Ping-Pong game, about walking through our kitchen, looking at the refrigerator display, and remarking, "Boy, is she dark!" or "Wow, she sure is fat!" These photos, which I initially shrank from, introduced me to important people and historic moments: Fannie Lou Hamer talking to the press at a Democratic convention; Barbara Jordan being elected to Congress; Constance Baker Motley being honored for her civil rights cases in the Supreme Court; Betty Shabazz receiving an award in Washington; Pearl Bailey opening on Broadway; and Patricia Roberts Harris becoming an ambassador.

On the foyer table of my parents' home, there were then—and still are today—three delicate carved-wood busts of African women. Each woman has a large round forehead, a wide round nose, and full Negroid lips. And until I was twelve or thirteen years old, my discomfort and self-consciousness were obvious when white friends stood in our foyer studying these three women.

Through persistent exposure and gentle verbal reinforcement, my parents taught me that there was, indeed, such a thing as black beauty. As I look back on it now, I wonder how much of this was calculated by my parents to combat the all-white and antiblack atmosphere that bombarded us in the media and our white community, and how much of this art and image building was simply a reflection of my parents' taste.

When the TV show *Julia* aired during the fall season of 1968, my mother expressed an uncontrolled giddiness. Each week when we sat down to watch Diahann Carroll and her TV son, Cory, Mom seemed to introduce each scene and each commercial with, "Isn't she the most beautiful woman you ever saw in your *life?*!"

When I was six or seven years old, I remember asking my father who Lena Horne was. His response was, "She's the most beautiful actress in the world." He didn't say "the most beautiful *black* actress in the world." That was the way my parents talked to me. So it wasn't until months later that I discovered that Lena Horne was actually a black woman.

And, of course, if all this subtle reinforcement had not made an impact on my black consciousness, there were always more blatant messages being saved to shock me and my brother out of our white, media-driven standards of beauty.

"Where are the black women?" my parents would ask aloud to no one in particular when the Miss America pageant paraded its line of contestants across the stage each fall on the screen of our Zenith TV set.

"I can't stand it," one of them would say. "With all the beautiful black women in this country—look at your cousins, look at Cicely Tyson, the Supremes, Angela Davis, Beverly Johnson, Melba Moore—and they can never find a single black girl to put in that pageant?!"

With the exception of the year that Jayne Kennedy represented Ohio, and 1983 when Vanessa Williams won the contest, I think that we were instructed to switch the channel almost every year during the Miss America pageant. The point was clear: "There are plenty of smart, beautiful, and talented black women, and America is wrong to ignore them. So don't you!"

And outside the home, whether it was at the barber shop or a cookout at the homes of family friends, one heard the thinly veiled, disparaging remarks made by the older generation of black people—particularly those in their fifties and sixties—who were disturbed by prominent blacks who dated or married whites.

With all this reinforcement, there was no way I was going to betray my people. Unfortunately, raising black children with that sense of pride is difficult—and sometimes even the "best" families fail.

I recall my junior year in college when a white friend invited me to Yale for a football weekend. Mark and I spent the entire time partying with his rich white friends, most of whom belonged to and took us through some of the school's most famous secret society clubs.

When we later got back to his room, Mark pulled out a freshman face book, announcing that he was going to introduce me to a black woman whom I had read about numerous times in the black gossip columns and various newspapers.

"You know Carla Washington, and you waited this long to tell me?" I yelled as I tackled him on the steep granite staircase of his dormitory.

Carla Washington (not her real name) was a socially prominent and striking black woman who had been feted in the black press as a popular debutante and student body president while I was still a high school senior. She had come from an accomplished and prosperous Los Angeles family that many blacks, including my own family, had admired for their achievements in business, politics, and social circles. Rich, charismatic, and stylish, the Washingtons were considered one of the black "royal families."

Although my own family had spent summers in the same places and belonged to the same groups that many affluent black families joined, I was always surprised that I had never met Carla, nor met any black people who knew her well. Although I was as giddy as I would have been to meet the kids of Martin Luther King, Jesse Jackson, or another famous black person, I concealed my excitement from Mark, since I knew that, since he was a white person, the Washington family held little or no significance for him.

As we entered the locked courtyard of her dorm, Mark said that he had not called Carla in advance.

"Don't worry, we'll have plenty of mutual friends and acquaintances," I said, recklessly confident that while I'd never met another black person who knew her well, our first few words would, no doubt, open our respective black networks and quickly find common ground.

"Well there's something else you may want to know," Mark added as we walked down the dormitory hallway. "She doesn't know you're black— 'Cause I think she may only be into white guys."

Whoa!!

I don't think my shock was visible, but I do remember thinking that Mark should have known that this was an important piece of information. As clear as day, I was obviously not a white guy. And he knew that I had never dated a white woman, so he must have realized the significance of introducing me to a black woman who he thought did not like black men.

As frustrating and inopportune as it was, Mark's comment forced me to quickly reconsider whether I wanted to meet this woman at all. Not that I had any intentions of asking her out at that point; the attraction was primarily in the novelty of meeting a member of this prominent and accomplished black family. You could say I was somewhere between stargazing and social climbing. Nevertheless, I wondered if I could withstand the personal rejection that might result if this woman was not only uninterested in—but also repulsed by—black men.

There was still enough time for me to evade this unscheduled tête-à-tête and escape to the safe buzz of students who walked up and down New Haven's busy streets below. Though I was growing increasingly resentful of his remark, Mark's morose expression bespoke his seriousness. The "white guy" remark was not his idea of a joke.

As we paused near the door to her suite, it suddenly occurred to me why my parents and our black friends had never seen Carla's family in Martha's Vineyard or Sag Harbor, at Links parties, Jack & Jill conventions, the Urban League Beaux Arts Balls in New York, or any of the other gatherings where we saw our black network.

Now it all made sense. Carla's parents were never around because they had clearly chosen not to socialize with blacks. And evidently, she had followed their lead. It occurred to me that perhaps all those facts about the Washington family's prominence in society were nothing more than the historical legacy that helped them to climb out of the doldrums of black society and segue into a more desirable white social network.

I was now crestfallen. I wanted to turn on my heels. I was ready to call an end to this social expedition, but I realized that there was still another concern to address. Mark, my white friend, was still standing there, ready to witness the foibles and flaws of the black upper class laid bare. Here was a group that I had learned to revere and protect from white criticism and scrutiny, about to be exposed as self-hating hypocrites. Was I ready to embarrass myself and my people in front of this white guy who had obviously set me up for a major disappointment?

In the final seconds, I decided to knock. I at least wanted to prove to this skeptical white boy—and to myself—that, yes, there are black people in America who aren't as infatuated with white folks as he and so many other whites would like to believe. I wanted to show him that there were still black people who respected their own, first and foremost.

I wish I had been right. Carla's white roommate eventually opened the door and told us that Carla was *preparing* to take an afternoon nap. Upon being told who it was, Carla encouraged us to peek into her room as she raised her torso just above her pillow.

"Hi, Mark," Carla said. "Open the door some so I can see your friend."

As we opened the door, hoping to break the ice, I quickly rattled off the names of three or four black people whom I thought she would know at least vaguely. Over where she sat up in bed, where a stream of sun poured in, I could see a slight sign of recognition on her face.

I nodded at her from my dark, shadowy end of the room.

"How do you happen to know so many . . . " Her voice suddenly trailed off, then an odd expression of surprise combined with sudden revelation washed across her face. "Could you step in more so I can see you?"

As I stepped farther into the room, the light shone across my face, and I saw Carla's expression suddenly turn to one of simultaneous recognition and indifference. She leaned back on her bed and dropped her head to the pillow while I spoke of these mutual acquaintances.

"Mark," Carla interrupted as I was concluding my twenty-second introductory monologue. "I'm sorry that I can't say hello to you and your friend, but I really must take a nap." Without directing another word at me, she summoned her dutiful roommate to pull the door closed.

As we walked back across the campus for lunch at one of the all-white secret societies, I remained silent. As the leaves crunched underneath our feet, I shoved my hands deep into my coat pockets and thought of the indifference that had registered in Carla's voice and facial expression. When she heard the names of four black students, it quickly occurred to her that I might also be black. Her long black hair pushed from the front of her face, she got the opportunity to see that I was, indeed, a black man. Her expression communicated her total rejection.

For the next couple years, I queried blacks who had known Carla from Yale or from her childhood. "Well, you know, she hangs totally white." "She only dates white guys or Hispanic ones that look near white." "Carla doesn't really like blacks." The comments were consistent. I told these people of my experience, and no one seemed to be surprised. While their response should have made me feel good that at least her rejection of me had little or nothing to do with my own looks, personality, and stature, I felt numbed.

Up until two years after, whenever Mark recalled the incident, he tried to argue that our encounter was proof of Carla's lack of interest in black men. Angry that he would have intentionally embarrassed me and one of my own, I insisted that Carla was not into white guys at all. "We just caught her on a bad day," I claimed.

There I was, still trying to preserve the "face" of myself and my people.

Does black opposition to intermarriage differ from the arguments made by white racists who drafted antimiscegenation statutes a hundred years ago?

Well, for one thing, the goals are different. The goal of white racists was to humiliate and to permanently label one group as "inferior" and "subhuman." The primary goal of blacks supporting black-black marriages is not to develop ways to keep the races separate or to assign a status to one or another: It is to develop solutions for the loss of black mentors and role models at a time when the black community is overrun with crime, drug use, a high dropout rate, and a sense that any black who hopes to find education and career success must necessarily disassociate himself from his people with the assistance of a white spouse.

In the end, what is the black community calling for? An end to mixed marriages? Are we suggesting that people should not marry the individuals they love—just because the other person is of a different race? No, that is not what the community is calling for.

But what we *are* asking is that blacks who are inclined to date outside the race consider just two ideas that may never have been posed to them.

First, they should ask themselves if they are unconsciously avoiding lovers of their own race: Is there something about black men or black women that I just don't like—and therefore do not want to be linked to? Do I find black people physically unattractive? Am I avoiding members of my own race because I cannot face the burden of sharing in yet another black person's problems of discrimination because I have enough of my own?

Second, blacks should examine the *cumulative* effect of their *incremental* decisions to reject their own and marry outside of the race. After all, is it Diana Ross's marriage, or Shelby Steele's or Clarence Thomas's, or even John Doe's marriage that we actually care about? No. It's not the discrete decision of any one of these individuals that makes black America stand up and take notice. It is the cumulative effect of each of these personal decisions that bespeaks a frightening pattern for an increasingly impoverished and wayward black community. The cumulative effect is that the very blacks who are potential mentors and supporters of a financially and psychologically depressed black community are increasingly deserting the black community en masse, both physically and emotionally. They are moving into a different way of life and thought with their white spouses, who may lack sufficient understanding and empathy for the plight of black people.

My sense is that many blacks who intermarry would argue, "Yes, it's a shame that the cumulative effect of all these marriages may mean that less will be given back to the black community and that fewer respected black voices will be crying out for black causes. But it was not my goal to choose a spouse on the basis of what he or she could do to help me give back to the black community. It was not a part of my criteria when judging my potential mate. I just happened to fall in love with someone who is white."

I believe that most blacks—including mixed-couple blacks—really do care about the cumulative effect of black people marrying outside the community—and the civic decimation that it can, and has, caused. And it is because of this that we must revisit our personal criteria. If we really do care about the cumulative effect, we must examine the values underlying our incremental decisions. When searching for a mate, in addition to using criteria such as whether the person is intelligent, considerate, spiritual, attractive, and witty, I believe we must add the criterion of "someone who understands the problems that blacks face and who wants to help me give back to my black community." Whether that mate is black or white, one's criteria for selecting that individual should, along with feelings of love, trust, and compatibility, also include this standard. And if the mate is *not* black, herculean efforts should be expended to ensure that the children of the union honor the heritage of *both* parents.

Only then will the greater issue of strengthening the black community—its families, its image, and its children—be addressed. And only then will we feel secure enough with our identities and our futures to smile in the face of an interracial couple, and actually mean it.

3

"HEAD NIGGER IN CHARGE"

ROLES THAT BLACK PROFESSIONALS
PLAY IN CORPORATE AMERICA

Aᴌᴌ ᴛᴏᴏ ᴍᴀɴʏ have been more cautious than courageous and have remained silent . . . ," wrote Dr. Martin Luther King more than thirty years ago in his famous essay, "Letter from a Birmingham Jail."

Several months ago, I was asked by Harvard Business School to join a roundtable gathering of businesspeople and professors for a discussion on the black experience in corporate America. More than a few students in the audience raised questions about how a black professional can command respect from a bigoted white boss, while not being perceived as an assertive and threatening outsider. Some stepped beyond the typical B-school decorum and bluntly asked, "Do you play it safe and adopt a deferential persona in order to become more palatable to white employers, or do you speak up and possibly risk losing your job?" Meanwhile, many of the seasoned black professionals in the audience remained silent.

How much we have forgotten, I thought to myself.

Although Dr. King's words had been written to elicit support for a far more urgent issue than the one being discussed at this roundtable, the frustrated messages being conveyed by the students reminded me of the counsel that King was attempting to communicate in April 1963: We must resist our tendency to do what is personally expedient in the short term and instead attempt to do what is best for all.

King had clearly written his letter in order to demand that a moral stand be taken by reticent people—reticent white people, that is—who had remained silent in the face of ongoing discrimination in their communities. Three decades later, as we sat in front of a Cambridge, Massachusetts, audience, I felt that the same reticence was being exhibited by some middle- and upper-class blacks, with results almost as damaging. From what I see, the only people capable of introducing real change into corporate workplaces are the black people who sat before me that day: educated, bright, ambitious. But unfortunately very, very cautious when it came to this topic.

As hard as it is for some of my African American corporate colleagues to swallow, I believe that it is incumbent upon black professionals to prepare and reform their racially insensitive organizations for those black generations that will follow, despite the everyday pressures of work. Despite the risk.

Many of my black peers would find my suggestion to be outrageous and tantamount to committing career suicide. They can't imagine attempting to alter the racist views of coworkers—much less raise the issue of color or ethnicity—for fear of being labeled "a black who cares about such things."

And so it is not surprising that many black professionals have concluded that there is a more efficient way to succeed in their chosen careers. Rather than attempt to alter or challenge the bias in their workplaces, they instead try short-term manipulations of the system so that they can eke out next month's bonus and next year's promotion. Instead of asking what they can do to change a system that seems not to recruit, reward, or retain people of color, they are asking, "Now, how do I get what I want without seeming too black?"

The world of the black professional in America is complex and difficult. The tightrope metaphor has been appropriately used more than once to describe the emotional and physical restraint that must be used to bear the racial burdens placed on the shoulders of black professionals. I've had this discussion for hours at a time with my friend Rosabeth Moss Kanter, author of *Men and Women of the Corporation,* in the context of how the black experience contrasts with the experiences of the female professional. I think we both agree that—like women—blacks in the workforce must not only overcome their own self-doubts but also address and overcome the white-male biases and low expectations that often work against them. Even though large corporations may create difficult conditions for black professionals, they must create and take advantage of more opportunities to alter the uneven systems that operate to penalize minorities or women in the business setting. In essence, they must be more than hardworking but passive beneficiaries of slowly evolving attitudes in corporate America; they must be catalysts for change.

It is obvious that professional blacks have had to assume certain unenviable roles because they have determined that their alienating circumstances offer them no alternative. In organizations that are unwelcoming to nonwhites, some black professionals have concluded that to succeed they must adopt particularly unbecoming roles and behavior. Whether the organization's prior treatment of blacks indicates that those determined to succeed must become chameleons, or whether the new black employee makes this assumption on his own, there is today a generation of extremely cynical and self-serving black professionals who have concluded that to succeed in their organizations, they must relinquish their racial identities. Unlike their parents, who lacked the opportunity to work for or advance within the corporate setting, these young professionals have a choice. Unfortunately, too many believe that to succeed at their choice, they must keep their moral and racial views to themselves. And they may be right. But the price of success may be too high if it involves abandoning personal integrity.

During the two-year period that I spent interviewing executives at more than six hundred U.S. companies and professional service firms for my book *The Best Companies for Minorities,* and during the time I have spent teaching a college-level course entitled "Minorities and Women in Corporate America," I have collected sufficient data on black professionals working in predominantly white settings to have identified nine different negative personas among this group. They are all variations on a well-known negative stereotype discussed in the black community: the "Head Nigger in Charge (HNIC)." (As much as I would like to take credit for this terminology, I must admit that the term was created and popularly used by the black community many generations before I was born.)

I characterize the HNIC as the often cynical, sometimes self-serving, lone high-ranking black person in an organization. The HNIC, who may or may not be talented, is sometimes elevated to his high status by white bosses who feel a noblesse oblige toward the race; or who recognize a need to appease the media, black consumers, or activists; or who cynically conclude that a token black senior staff person might simultaneously attract government contracts and head off employment discrimination suits by individuals or government agencies.

During the late 1960s and early 1970s, HNICs proliferated in the community affairs and public relations departments of *Fortune* 500 companies. In these positions, blacks were considered harmless and fairly invisible in the company's internal agenda, yet visible to an outside community that wanted to see the company's commitment to diversity. Today, HNICs are found stuck in various staff positions where they operate with inflated titles that may be as lofty as senior vice president, yet have no staff beyond a secretary, no budget, and no decision-making power within the organization. In corporate America, the black senior vice president who lacks subordinates, a budget, and actual authority is really just a Head Nigger in Charge of nothing. He is an executive in name only.

The various types of HNICs that I have identified include: (1) The Informant; (2) The Rubber Stamp; (3) The Expedient African American; (4) The Affirmative Action Deal Closer; (5) The Two-Faced Henchman; (6) The Colorless Dreamer; (7) The Self-Flagellating Basket Case; (8) The Self-Made Bootstrapper; and (9) The "I'm Going to Save My Money and Plan a Backup Job in Case They Can't Put Up with My Demands for Respect" Black. These types will likely seem familiar to my colleagues in large corporations—and unfortunately some individuals are playing more than one of these roles at a time.

1: **THE INFORMANT**

Favorite statement: "Boss, I think you should know that I overheard some of my black coworkers calling the EEOC and talking to the NAACP about possible discrimination here. I'll keep you posted if I learn anything else."

The Informant is very much a product of ego and necessity. There is an eagerness on the part of some black professionals to prove their loyalty to their white bosses, and there is a willingness (at best) and a need (at worst) for insecure white bosses to test that loyalty when it's called into question. And what better way for that black man to prove his loyalty than to offer to spy on his own people (the fellow black employees) and report back to the white boss on his people's confidences and agenda?

In many large white organizations, a lone senior black often joins the "them" team in the organization's "us" versus "them" group dynamic. Where black groups find themselves segregated into particular departments or offices, and where the boss's senior professionals are all white except for that one useful black, it is not uncommon for the lone black professional to be transformed into a useful informant.

Whether he offers his services because of his own Machiavellian tendencies or because he is called upon by the boss, it is often logistically easy for the lone black professional to infiltrate the covert meetings and personal confidences of lower-echelon black employees. His role can easily switch over to that of interpreter in the *overt* dealings that the white boss has with the black masses inside or outside the organization. This Informant is the one who receives a frantic call from the boss after the company's black employee group or the local NAACP branch president has visited the white chairman's office and listed a set of grievances and demands.

The Informant gets shepherded into the boss's office and is asked questions like, "What did they mean when they told me they wanted the office to sponsor a Kwanzaa festival at company headquarters? What's Kwanzaa?" "When I respond to the NAACP, do I use the term 'blacks' or 'African Americans'?" "When that black business magazine comes to interview blacks here, can you sit in on all the interviews and let me know what the employees tell them and keep me apprised of what they're saying and doing?"

Cast in the role as informant and interpreter, this type of black professional serves a valuable but self-destroying function in the organization. Some companies have avoided putting blacks in this uncomfortable position because they have already established black or minority advisory groups or councils that serve to advise the chief executive on black employee agendas and concerns. Xerox Corporation in 1969, Philip Morris and Johnson & Johnson in 1976, McDonald's and Corning in 1980, Upjohn in 1989, and JCPenney in 1990 are just a few of the major corporations that have realized the value of creating minority-issue advisory groups.

Instead of turning black professionals into spies and haphazard interpreters, more white employers need to look for responsible black advisers who are openly identified as such and to create advisory councils, as many responsible companies have done. With this type of candor, black employees will feel more valued and white bosses will receive better guidance—and avoid creating the conditions that require an Informant's services.

2: THE RUBBER STAMP

Favorite statement: "Sure, Boss, I've got no problems with us holding the firm holiday party at a country club that doesn't admit black, Jewish, or female members. The point of this party is to have fun, not to make a political statement. And you can tell other people that I said it was okay."

This is the black professional who is called upon to give his seal of approval for corporate decisions that the employer feels would be characterized as racist and antiblack. The Rubber Stamp is there to assuage the boss's guilt and give the boss and the white coworkers permission to pursue decisions that they sense are offensive but that they nevertheless plan to carry out.

At best, The Rubber Stamp is used as the moral compass for a boss or organization that has lost its sense of right and wrong. At worst, and what is more often the case, this HNIC cynically goes along with his employer's offensive behavior and grants the corporation permission to say that he approved of the behavior before it took place. The implication is that The Rubber Stamp's approval (or any black approval) renders the behavior less racist. The Rubber Stamp gives the boss permission to offer his name and racial identity as evidence if anyone accuses the organization of acting insensitively. The employer knows his company has acted inappropriately but doesn't have to worry about the consequences, as he can always say, "Gee, I didn't know that the black community or the black employees would be offended by our inviting Pat Buchanan to speak at the company picnic. We ran it by Tom (the Head Nigger In Charge) and he said there was no problem. I wish I'd been told that people would be offended." In the end, even if there are subsequent complaints, the white boss has pursued the plan that he had first intended, yet he characterized himself as a well-intentioned, sensitive manager, since he went to the trouble of asking the advice of the black senior staffer. In the end, Mr. Boss is ultimately able to pass the blame and moral faux pas to someone else—the HNIC.

3: **THE EXPEDIENT AFRICAN AMERICAN**

Favorite statement: "It's true that I never talked to the rest of you black employees and it's true that I bad-mouthed you to white coworkers by saying you were all lazy freeloaders who only get ahead because of affirmative action. But I need your support now because I think I didn't get my promotion to senior vice president because of racism."

The names Clarence Thomas and Joseph Jett immediately come to mind.

These are blacks who have made reputations for themselves by criticizing other blacks, but who later appropriate the black identity label when it becomes expedient to do so. These HNICs have a warehouse of complaints about the blacks around them: criticizing them for being too lazy to pull themselves up by their bootstraps, criticizing them for relying on affirmative action, criticizing them for blaming discrimination or a "nonexistent racism" for their career failures or job and financial disappointments. These are the black professionals who are so critical of other blacks that they not only ignore them at the office but avoid them outside the office, cutting blacks out of their social life and avoiding every possible physical or emotional link with them.

The Expedient African American's hypocrisy is eventually revealed when he finds himself in a professional, ethical, or legal jam and decides that the only thing that can save him, his reputation, and his professional status is a quick and convenient association with black people and the rhetoric of racism.

Think of Supreme Court justice Clarence Thomas prior to his 1991 nomination to the Court by George Bush. He epitomized the HNIC who was willing to assume antiblack or problack positions, depending on how the circumstances would benefit his career. As a former head of the EEOC and undistinguished federal judge, he worked tirelessly to discredit civil rights organizations and black leaders and to undermine and deny black people's claims that they were victims of racism.

Surrounding himself with conservative white people (his white wife; white political supporters like Senator John Danforth; and Rush Limbaugh, who was later married to an aerobics instructor by Thomas in the Thomas home) who were overjoyed by his protestations about the nonexistence of racism, he was the convenient Head Nigger who stood willing and ready to oppose everything that black people espoused. But this attitude mysteriously disappeared once he saw his judicial nomination suddenly slipping away from him during the 1991 Senate confirmation hearings. Charges made by black law professor and former EEOC employee Anita Hill threatened the confirmation, and suddenly, Clarence Thomas was an angry black man. On October 11, 1991, he reached into his bag of tricks and pulled out the race card.

"This is a circus. . . . And from my standpoint, as a black American, it is a high-tech lynching for uppity blacks . . ." were the well-crafted and now famous words that elicited the sympathy of a Senate chamber and nation full of guilt-ridden white people. These were the words that Thomas used to complain of the very thing that he had criticized other blacks for complaining about during the prior two decades. For the moment, it would help him snatch his job from the jaws of mounting liberal and feminist anger that opposed his nomination. In the eyes of Thomas and all those whites advising him, it was indeed time for him to become conveniently African American and to appropriate the rhetoric of the people he had vilified for so long.

Thomas is not alone in this regard. Think of Joseph Jett, the thirty-six-year-old disgraced black trader who in 1994 earned a $9 million bonus at Kidder, Peabody & Co., then was fired and accused of fixing his numbers and misrepresenting his department's earnings. Portrayed in *New York* magazine, the *Wall Street Journal,* and the *New York Times* as a black conservative who—while a student at Harvard Business School—expressed disinterest in having black friends, Jett was frequently heard criticizing blacks as lazy and too dependent on affirmative action. Allegedly mocking blacks for blaming their failures on racism, Jett was a corporate version of the prenomination Clarence Thomas.

Jett took a 180-degree turn when, like Thomas, he was faced with a scandal that threatened to destroy his reputation and career. As the financial world's accusations and negative publicity mounted in the spring of 1994, Jett did the thing that had previously disgusted both him and Thomas: He cried "racism." As reported in a June 3, 1994, front-page story in the *Wall Street Journal,* Jett suggests that he was framed by Kidder because of his race, explaining, "This is a public lynching." Sound familiar?

4: THE AFFIRMATIVE ACTION DEAL CLOSER

Favorite statement: "Boss, with me on your team, I could front for you and the rest of the white guys here, and I could then get the mayor's office to award you that contract through some sort of minority city government set-aside deal."

A 1994 study conducted at New York University's School of Business found that approximately 50 percent of all "minority-owned brokerage firms" that took advantage of minority set-aside programs were actually white-owned-and-run businesses that misrepresented themselves with one or more well-placed minority figureheads "fronting" for them. When the Resolution Trust Company (RTC) was established in 1989 by the federal government to sell the defaulted properties owned by failed savings and loans, thousands of law firms, accounting firms, and investment firms competed for the new RTC business that was set aside for minority-owned firms. Not surprisingly, many of these majority-owned firms began hiring blacks to increase their chances of serving the RTC's needs.

Affirmative action, a concept that was implemented by President Lyndon Johnson in 1965, has been an important and beneficial program for minorities in corporate settings. In addition to making up for past discrimination, it has given many white bosses a clear reason to hire blacks when they might otherwise follow their own antiblack sentiments and establish all-white offices and departments in their companies. Unfortunately, the policy has an unfavorable dark side: Too many companies and vendors realize they need only one or two well-placed black executives in their offices to qualify for lucrative projects run by municipalities and major corporations that want to conduct business with firms or contractors with minorities. They reap the rewards without truly fostering black progress.

And sometimes it's not the boss at all who recognizes the value of hiring a black to elicit business contracts. Many times, it's the already hired but long-forgotten and little-valued black professional who steps forward, dusts himself off, and says, "Hey, Boss, I'm ready to be used. Stick me on your project team and I'll turn you into a minority contractor. Even if you don't want me working on the project, at least bring me to the meeting and I can make you seem more palatable when you go into that office to pitch your business to: (a) those government people, (b) your liberal client, or (c) that minority-run company."

In June 1994 it was reported that the city of New York had been duped by several dozen white-male-owned companies that had captured contracts reserved for minority businesses. How'd they do it? By hiring a very visible black or minority "front person" to make their business's personnel appear more diverse. An opportunity like this is an Affirmative Action Deal Closer's dream.

5: THE TWO-FACED HENCHMAN

Favorite statement: "Boss, I think I can go talk some street jive and get the brothers and sisters on board with your idea. They trust me. Just promise that you'll back me up on what I tell them. Once they're softened up, you can go in and break some heads."

The Henchman is the senior black staffer who is used when the boss wants to get the junior black employees to agree to some type of unfavorable settlement or wants to make a move that might have damaging public relations consequences if executed by a white person. At times of budget cuts, layoffs, or when racial spin control must calm a strike or similar disturbance, The Henchman is called in to perform the acts that a white person would like to do but can't because of possible justifiable or imagined racial implications.

Think of how black assistant secretary of education Michael Williams was utilized in 1991 when the Bush administration attempted to create a policy opposing college scholarship programs specifically designed to aid minorities. Had President Bush or one of his white cabinet members or white deputies made the announcement about canceling the minority scholarships, there would have been immediate accusations that George Bush was not only failing to live up to his "education president" status but that he was also revealing a blatantly antiminority agenda. Instead, the message was offered by a black man, which tempered the reaction of both the white and black press. Even though Michael Williams was attacked for the proposal, the effect of his making the announcement was to lead some to believe that the underlying motivation wasn't antiminority—particularly since a black man was the one to deliver it.

6: THE COLORLESS DREAMER

Favorite statement: "I've always believed that I'm the kind of person who can make others forget I'm black. When I walk into a room, people see a professional. It's much later that they even think about my race. Since I don't focus on color, neither do they."

This sixth type of HNIC is characterized by an acquaintance of mine whom I will call Roy. He is a black graduate of Yale Law School and was an editor on the *Yale Law Journal.* He drives a Saab with ski racks on the roof although he never skis. In addition to affecting a British accent, Roy often drops French phrases into the middle of conversations. He wears bow ties, horn-rimmed glasses, suspenders, and laced-up wingtip shoes purchased from Brooks Brothers.

Whenever Roy and his two fellow attorneys arrive at the office of a new client or opposing counsel, he is inevitably mistaken as the most junior attorney or the paralegal. He is not younger or less articulate than his fellow attorneys, but he is the only minority in the group. What Roy can't understand is why younger white attorneys are instantly accorded greater respect than himself. After all, he has selected his clothing, car, and accoutrements particularly because they run counter to the stereotypical styles of black people. He has intentionally picked his surroundings, his affected British accent, and the subject matter of his conversations to counteract his blackness.

When Roy senses that white clients or coworkers are still not respectful of his comments in conversations, he subtly reminds them that he is a graduate of Yarmouth Prep, Yale College, and Yale Law School ("I'm a member of the 3-Y Club"). Roy feels that he's done everything possible to make himself appear colorless in the eyes of white people around him, yet he senses that they often treat him with the same disregard with which they treat other blacks who have put forth no special efforts to assimilate. "Why are they lumping me together with the rest of the blacks?" Roy asks himself continually.

Perhaps it is cynical to criticize an optimistic black professional who believes that because he wants to ignore the color of his skin, so will others. If he is light enough to "pass" as white, then he's correct that whites will probably pay little mind to his skin color, but if he's clearly black, he may need to accept the fact that ours is still a race-conscious society that will focus on, and draw certain conclusions from, his black features. No matter how "supposedly nonblack" Roy supposes his suspenders, suit, bow tie, or Yale Law School education are, what will stand out in a room full of white fellow attorneys is Roy's black skin.

Whether Roy's organization is a Wall Street firm or a nonprofit California-based foundation, certain white workers—like everyone else—will bring their racial and ethnic biases into the office, regardless of the "perfect, colorless world" philosophy adopted by Roy or other black individuals. Even if all whites do not act on these biases, many of these coworkers will notice and focus on apparent racial differences. As Rosabeth Moss Kanter says in her book *The Tale of "O,"* which talks about the lone O in an office full of Xs, Xs never think about their X identity and their similarities with other Xs until an O walks into the room. The O (black person, in our example) not only stands out, but that O makes the X (white person, in our example) feel more like the other Xs in the room.

Of course, this is not to suggest that the black professional is wrong to judge others on a color-blind basis, but history suggests that we cannot persuade others to overlook our racial and ethnic identity merely by altering our fashion accessories or purchasing a brand of automobile that is uncommon in our racial or ethnic community.

7: THE SELF-FLAGELLATING BASKET CASE

Favorite statement: "Although I work harder, complete more projects, offer more experience, and have collected better credentials than my white coworkers, and although the clients like my work more than anyone else's, the boss says I'm not going to be promoted like my peers. I guess I'm just not smart enough to be in this business."

Perhaps the most pitiful of all black professionals, The Self-Flagellating Basket Case has learned to internalize all of the biases and hatred that have been directed at him. He has honestly begun to believe all the insults that biased white people have fired at him. He wonders if maybe he is, indeed, stupid, unattractive, lazy, and unable to perform the job.

Whereas yesterday's bigoted employer might have said, "You will never succeed here because we don't want blacks to become managers," today's bigoted boss artfully disguises this bigotry with unsubstantiated complaints about work product and "your inability to get others to like you." Herein lies the problem. Where yesterday's boss was candid, the black professional felt absolved from guilt as he concluded, "If I fail here, it's because they said they didn't like blacks."

But today's boss does no such favors for today's HNIC. No matter how strong the antiblack sentiment, today's legal and business environment has taught managers to apply discretion and avoid making such legally actionable statements. Instead, the boss looks to assign blame to the employee's work product and his attitude. And The Self-Flagellating Basket Case is ready to assume the blame because he refuses to acknowledge that bigoted bosses and racist organizations still exist. He is the poster child for white conservatives. Such a black employee is convinced that it is his fault that no one will eat lunch with him, stop by his office, or introduce him to others in the company.

The Self-Flagellating Basket Case worries about and eventually blames his imagined lack of intelligence, his lack of experience, his inappropriate clothes, his credentials—even his personality. Everything that goes wrong is necessarily *his* fault. Finding himself leaning somewhere between paranoia and the feeling that he just isn't good enough to be working in that job, the self-flagellating black psyches himself out before anyone else can. This phenomenon has been called "de-skilling" and is perhaps the most damaging experience a black professional can face. Believing he is incompetent, he actually *becomes* incompetent—less skilled than he was when he took the job.

8: THE SELF-MADE BOOTSTRAPPER

Favorite statement: "Why do the young black employees always come to me for advice? Nobody mentored me while I was pulling myself up by my bootstraps, and I made it."

This black professional does not believe that he has any responsibility to other blacks who are either outside the organization or who are looking to him for guidance within the organizational structure. He is proud of the fact that he was the first black to rise through the company, and he proudly wears the battle scars of past disappointments. Forced to suffer the pangs of loneliness as he climbed the ladder without assistance and watched white peers receive mentoring from white senior executives, the self-made HNIC wants to see every other black suffer in the same way he did. Truth be told, he has learned to take particular pleasure in his position as the only black near the top of the organization, and he is not eager to mentor other black professionals who might take his place or who might make his "first and only black" status less exalted.

While many white-run organizations hope and expect that their senior black professionals will attempt to recruit and mentor junior black staffers, a great number of organizations still pick the type of Self-Made Bootstrapping black who not only works hard to keep blacks out of the organization but who also refuses to guide and mentor those blacks who are already there.

9: THE "I'M GOING TO SAVE MY MONEY AND PLAN A BACKUP JOB IN CASE THEY CAN'T PUT UP WITH MY DEMANDS FOR RESPECT" BLACK

Favorite statement: "I could probably succeed here if I was willing to give up everything else in my life like social life, hobbies, and sleep. But what if I do give up everything else, and they still don't let me succeed? I need a backup."

I'd have to say that I'm a good example of the black professional who expects and plans for the worst. Having been raised in the liberal Northeast as the eternal optimist, always expecting white people—particularly educated ones—to do the right thing, I finally got burned once too many times. I trust white people as much as I do anyone else, but past disappointments caused me, sometime during my mid-twenties, to brace myself for certain types of all-white settings—settings in which white people could never imagine themselves being outnumbered.

After a childhood full of all-white birthday parties, bar mitzvahs, and confirmations that I didn't get invited to, or was completely ignored at; after an adolescence crammed with white Sadie Hawkins dances, high school poker games, and weekend tennis matches between white "friends" on my block who preferred that I respectfully decline to participate; and after an early adulthood in which I was told by white college classmates that I was "their kind of black" and advised by prospective employers that I might "never be able to gain the respect of white subordinates who did not like taking orders from blacks," I learned to buffer my ego, save my money, and brace myself for the worst. Even if blacks who have endured these experiences continue to work aggressively and place themselves in white settings as I do, they learn to at least protect their self-esteem and fragile egos from the reach of the potentially bigoted peer, boss, and organization.

The Save My Money black professional can be healthily insecure—not insecure about his intellect or talent but insecure about whom he can trust. The danger of this approach is that it can encourage an emotional distance and lack of commitment that ultimately inhibit success in a professional organization. Succeeding at the highest levels requires a bit of myopia for *anyone*—and a level of "over-the-top" commitment that this person is unlikely to make.

As long as white-owned-and-run organizations approach the hiring and promotion of blacks as a means to limit their hiring to one or two qualified blacks, and as long as black professionals perceive their future success as linked to playing the role of "Head Nigger" in a high-stakes game of tokenism, black professionals will continue to find themselves at risk for taking on the negative characteristics described here.

Some successful black professionals may defend their silence, lack of mentoring, and blind loyalty to their bosses as a legitimate means of doing business. They may use the hoary old chestnut, "It's not my job to educate white people about black people's problems." I ask these brothers and sisters to examine their motives: This is a sure path to HNIC-hood.

As white bosses become more willing to build their firms with groups of black professionals—as opposed to simply one or two representatives in an office or department—and when blacks are willing to take the risks of speaking out in the workplace on behalf of other members of their race, then black professionals can stop playing the roles of spy, informant, minority business "front man," and rubber stamp, and start focusing on their professional development and their contributions to the organizations that employ them and the black community to which they belong.

4

THE SHAME OF THE BLACK MIDDLE CLASS

I OVERTIP CABDRIVERS merely because they've stopped for me. I smile warmly just because a waitress hasn't seated me next to the kitchen door. I thank salespeople profusely when they don't throw my change on the counter.

My friends ask me why it takes so little to make me happy—why I am so quick to thank others for barely treating me with respect. They are misinterpreting my actions. I don't overtip because I want to. I do it because I *have* to. These acts of kindness are simply my attempt to minimize the shame that I feel as a black person living at a time when the public sees us as thieves, as shoplifters, and as a general threat to good business.

Put simply, I am a member of the black middle class trying to fight against a stereotype that is making me look bad and that I never created. I am that middle-class black who cringes each time a black person appears in the paper or on the evening news after being accused of or arrested for some heinous act.

As middle-class blacks, we react instinctively each time a crime occurs. We hear about the rape, then wait for the police description—clenching our teeth, hoping that the accused rapist is not a black man. We hear about the drug bust, then wait for the handcuffed chain of dealers to be led out of the row house—straining our eyes, praying that every face in that group is not a black one. We read about the unwed mother who neglects and abuses her three young children, then we turn the page to read the conclusion of the story—crossing our fingers tightly, hoping that there will not be a photo of a black unwed mother with curlers in her hair.

When the faces are black, we shake our heads in anger. We feel exhausted, betrayed, and embarrassed by our people. We hang our heads.

But when the faces aren't black, we shake our heads in detached pity. We feel anonymous, part of the masses. We have been given a reprieve. Our teeth no longer clench, our eyes no longer strain. We're very sorry that it happened. We're shocked by the dark side of human nature. We admit we just don't know what is going on with this world today. But most of all, we thank God that the face wasn't a black one.

Perhaps this is the *real* shame of the black middle class. While we delude ourselves into thinking that our shame is being associated with a body of black criminals, drug addicts, unwed mothers, and homeless people, perhaps our real shame is the detachment and relief we feel when we discover that those guilty, poor, or addicted faces were not black ones.

Like Jews or Italians, Republicans or easterners—like any faction—we middle-class blacks also look at ourselves as an identifiable group. We want to be respected, we want to be perceived as good. Like a family, we want our members to be good because they reflect upon us. They affect our reputation and image in other people's eyes.

Is there something wrong with this? Does it seem narrow-minded, parochial, egocentric? Cold logic tells me that it's wrong to look at my world and my people this way, but for some reason protecting my racial image has always been a natural reflex for me.

The black middle class is a small group, and I'm proud to belong to it. Just as I am proud of the achievements of others in the group, they are proud of mine. They're proud that I graduated from two Ivy League schools. They're proud that I'm a lawyer in a top law firm. The black middle class is proud to claim me. That's the pride of the black middle class.

But, as we see every day, we also have our shame. Since our group remains small and our hold on success remains both new and tenuous, we shudder when muggers, rapists, drug addicts, and unwed mothers of our own color chip away at our group's real or imagined position in society.

Yes, it's damning to admit this and it's shallow to look at my people in such a manner, but as long as I identify with other blacks, and as long as there is a black criminal—*any* black criminal—walking the streets, I will not be able to avoid feeling the guilt and the shame of the black middle class.

After this essay ran in the "BackTalk" section of the April 1991 issue of Essence *magazine, the publication received an unprecedented number of letters. There was such an outcry that the magazine asked a black law-school professor to write an essay rebutting my own. Most black letter-writers objected to my assertion that I somehow felt responsible or ashamed when I initially learned of a widely reported criminal act that had been perpetrated by a black person.*

Even though I made several televised public appearances to explain that I felt an equal collective pride when a black person received an honor or award, it seemed to make no difference to black readers who continued to write critical letters. It was not until I gave subsequent interviews and drew two specific analogies that black readers began to sympathize with my point. I commented on how many Italian Americans were embarrassed by the unsubstantiated accusations that the husband of then vice presidential candidate Geraldine Ferraro had mob ties. It reminded them of the Italian Mafia stereotype and made them feel a collective shame because Ferraro was a proud example of one of their own. Similarly, I pointed out that many of my Jewish friends cringed during the late 1980s when various insider-trading perpetrators were arrested and vilified in the press. Because some of those arrested had Jewish-sounding last names, many Jewish onlookers felt embarrassed and implicated by the acts of a few who also happened to be Jewish.

Two years later, on a December afternoon, I felt vindicated about my candor when I received a call from a New York Times reporter who wanted to ask a few questions. It had just been reported that Colin Ferguson, a thirty-six-year-old black man, had jumped aboard a Long Island Railroad commuter train and had walked down the aisle shooting and killing white passengers, one after the next, at point-blank range. "What I'm focusing on in my article," the reporter explained, "is the degree to which black people feel ashamed or embarrassed by what Colin Ferguson has done. Many blacks that I've interviewed tell me that they feel ashamed and somewhat accountable when another black commits a crime."

It was just another one of those awful, I-told-you-so opportunities that black people had been given to assess their honest feelings about their relationship between themselves and the black criminal.

5

MY DINNER WITH MR. CHARLIE

A BLACK MAN'S UNDERCOVER GUIDE
TO DINING WITH DIGNITY
AT TEN TOP NEW YORK RESTAURANTS

I WAS RECENTLY on an Amtrak train traveling north with a friend from New York City to Boston. Since we were unable to find adjoining seats, we looked for a place where we could talk without disturbing sleeping passengers. We found our way to the café car, which had just closed service after running out of food. Standing there, as I ate an apple I'd brought as a snack, my friend and I braced ourselves against the wall of the train and launched into a conversation about business and ethnic politics.

Ken, a Korean American, was a graduate student in Boston and had just returned from a job interview in the New York area. I was on my way to give a speech on business issues at his school. After about five minutes, two white men and a woman joined us in the café car and began their own conversation. The two men leaned against our wall while the woman braced herself by leaning on the food counter. Moments later, a white woman in her forties entered the car and walked directly over to me.

"I'd like two hot dogs," she said. "And give me two diet Cokes—no ice."

"I don't work here," I answered, barely turning away from my conversation.

Ken and I continued our conversation until another woman— also white—came into the café car. After staring at the menu mounted on the wall, she turned directly to me.

"Do you have cinnamon donuts?" she asked. "It doesn't say what kind."

"I don't work here," I answered again, still not turning away from my conversation.

After the fourth person entered the car—the last of whom walked directly to me and asked when I would be done with my break and "opening up the food service again"—Ken turned and changed our conversation.

"Larry," he said, "doesn't it bother you that he was like the fourth person to ask you to serve them food?"

I took another bite of my apple, then looked over at the three white people engaged in conversation. I then looked at Ken and then down at my pants and shoes. Having outfitted ourselves for the sleet and slushy weather conditions, the five of us were dressed in casual but heavy winter clothes. Ken and I were both wearing white oxford shirts underneath sweaters—his a V-neck and mine a crew neck. He wore blue jeans, and I was wearing black jeans. I was also holding a book in my hand. The three white people were equally casual. After considering Ken's question, I made a mental note to myself to never again conduct a conversation in an Amtrak café car unless there was a worker behind the counter.

While any one of these incidents could be dismissed as a result of innocent carelessness, their cumulative effect in a black person's daily existence is disturbing. The incessant questioning of our status, the never-ending attempts to put us in a subservient position—it is enough to keep us at home eating TV dinners. No other group is perceived as servants more than blacks. If we are spotted in a store, hotel, restaurant, or at a wedding by a distracted white person, our black skin—regardless of our attire or demeanor—suggests that we are there to serve them.

I stopped patronizing a Columbus Avenue restaurant that would inevitably seat me next to the swinging door of the kitchen regardless of my requests to sit elsewhere and regardless of the number of empty tables in other areas of the restaurant. There is a second-floor Italian restaurant in the East Sixties in New York City that I no longer patronize because its maître d' is never at the second-floor entry landing upon a guest's arrival, which has left me on three occasions to fend off incoming patrons who handed me their hats, jackets, and umbrellas for the coat check. And I almost always avoid restaurants with valet parking because of the times I've been handed keys by incoming white patrons who assume that I am there to park cars rather than waiting to have my own car delivered to the front door as I leave.

Whether it's because of the racial attitudes of the wait staff, the maître d', or the patrons, randomly selecting one of New York's better restaurants for a business meal, a first date, or a family celebration is a tremendous risk for even the most forgiving black person. So, what's the solution? Rarely do restaurant reviews address the issues that black people are compelled to deal with when we go out. As I found in even New York's best restaurants, food quality and ambience can take a backseat to common courtesy when it comes to being black and trying to dine with the same dignity that is accorded to white patrons.

I recently phoned and made reservations—under the name Charlie Wilson—at ten well-known restaurants in New York City. I was trying to get answers to the unasked questions of blacks all over the city: Can we bring a client (black or white) here and be treated with respect? Can we be confident that we won't always be seated opposite the bathroom or kitchen? If we celebrate our parents' thirty-fifth anniversary here, can we do it without having one of them mistaken for a bathroom attendant?

During my ten-restaurant odyssey around the city, I was handed five coats while waiting to be seated, given three coat checks while preparing to leave, berated for not setting a patron's table with the right kind of dishes, mistaken for the valet car parker, mistaken for a men's room attendant who had turned the hot water faucet too high, threatened by a fellow patron with the loss of my job when I did not get off the only pay phone when asked, and offered the table closest to the bathroom or kitchen seven out of ten times.

As a service to my brothers and sisters—and others who want to be "down" with the people at New York's best dining scenes—I've developed a set of "real" reviews we can count on. And when in doubt you can always get reservations at Sylvia's. *Bon appétit!*

KEY USED IN RATING RESTAURANT VISIT

Stare Factor:	Duration and intensity of stares that we attracted from patrons and staff.
Diversity Factor:	Visibly apparent racial mix of patrons and staff.
Seating Margin:	Proximity to bathroom, kitchen, or absolute back of restaurant.
Isolation Factor/ Avoidance Quotient:	Skill/willingness of staff to ignore us, fail to welcome us, bring menus, refill water glasses, ask about our meal, offer coffee, or ask us to return.
Buffer Zoning:	Distance at which we were placed from any white patron, or apparent moves to switch already seated white patrons or to place us alone or near other minority patrons.
Table Refusal Factor:	Consistency with which white patrons refused to sit at a table near mine.
Mistaken Identity Quotient:	Frequency with which we were mistaken for coat check, parking valet, bathroom attendant, or other restaurant worker.
Reservation Deletion:	Willingness of maître d' to suddenly lose all records or memory of a reservation that we had confirmed less than an hour before.

What the Scales of Justice ⚖️ Mean:

⚖️	Offensive treatment
⚖️ ⚖️	Treatment that is barely tolerable
⚖️ ⚖️ ⚖️	Slightly less than equal treatment
⚖️ ⚖️ ⚖️ ⚖️	Equal treatment (or as equal as it gets)
⚖️ ⚖️ ⚖️ ⚖️ ⚖️	Special treatment

MORTIMER'S
1057 Lexington Avenue
New York City (212)517-6400

HOURS: Lunch: noon–3:30 P.M. Monday through Saturday; Dinner:
6:00–midnight, seven days a week.
CUISINE: American and French.
ATTIRE: Jacket required.
STARE FACTOR: Extremely high for both patrons and workers.
DIVERSITY FACTOR: We saw no black waiters or busboys, no
black patrons, and no black hair.
SCALE OF JUSTICE RATING: ⚖️

Besides the dark wood and red-brick walls adorning the eating
area, one thing you'll immediately appreciate about Mortimer's is
its cozy, familiar feeling. These people are so familiar, in fact, the
maître d' and wait staff instantly knew we didn't belong here—in
spite of our eight o'clock dinner reservation.

"How can we help you?" greeted the apathetic maître d' as we
stepped through the front door of the dim but inviting foyer. It
was 8:00 P.M., and the restaurant was 25 percent full because of a
raging rainstorm outside.

I smiled. "We have reservations for a party of three."

"Are you sure, here—at Mortimer's?"

My two black companions—one a former Wall Street attorney
and the other a Hollywood screenwriter—looked at me as though
I'd just dragged them into a members-only locker room.

As we glanced around at the patrons and wait staff, the low

Diversity Factor was immediately evident. Not a single black in the place.

"Uhh—yes," I said. "If this is 1057 Lexington Avenue?"

Without returning to his reservation list, the maître d' shrugged and walked away into the dining area.

"Are we supposed to be following him?" one of my companions asked while urging me to follow.

"Well, we've got some open tables. You can take that one over there," the maître d' said while pointing across the almost vacant room to a front table. After leaving us with our wet overcoats and umbrellas, we noticed a slight two-table Buffer Zone created between us and the nearest patron in any direction. We quickly deposited our overcoats in an unattended coat-check room on the left side of the restaurant.

At Mortimer's, the segue from an early and intense Stare Factor into a high Avoidance Quotient is a smooth one. The patrons—all white and 90 percent blond or gray—went back to their conversations. The waiters, however, maintained their awkward glances for at least ten minutes—and it took almost that amount of time before one of them approached us.

"Can I take your order?"

"We don't have menus yet," said the screenwriter.

The young six-foot man looked embarrassed as he saw that we also had no drinks, napkins, or silverware. The table was bare.

What made Mortimer's unique was that the staff did not rush us or interrupt us during the meal. In fact, from the time that we ordered our meal (chicken with stuffed tomato) to the time that the check came, not a single person—waiter, maître d', or busboy—stopped by to check on how we were enjoying our food, offer us beverages, or refill our water glasses.

Midway through the meal, I happened to be spotted by an old friend who was sitting with a large group a few tables away. I had missed seeing him earlier because of the flock of waiters hovering around his table. Tad stood up and came over.

"Well, hello, Larry," he said, placing a hand on my shoulder.

Tall, blond, and well into his career as a fund manager, Tad and I had known each other for a dozen or so years.

"Are you folks enjoying your meal?" he asked.

"We're trying," answered the screenwriter with a devilish grin. "Are you a regular here?"

"I certainly am."

We chatted a few more moments before Tad waved good-bye.

"Let's see if that helps any," whispered the attorney.

I, too, hoped that the official sanction we'd just gotten from a "regular" would have made a difference. But Mortimer's deserves the highest marks for consistency—we were cheerfully ignored right through to our departure at 10:15.

The Bottom Line: Even though the Seating Margin was good, the Diversity Factor ran too low and the Avoidance Quotient too high for us. That, plus a thinly veiled attempt at Reservation Deletion, puts Mortimer's near the bottom of our list.

THE FOUR SEASONS
99 East Fifty-second Street
New York City (212)754-9494

HOURS: Closed Sunday. Lunch: Monday–Friday, 12:00 noon–2:00 P.M.; Dinner: Monday–Friday, 5:00 P.M.–9:00 P.M., Saturday till 10:30 P.M.
ATTIRE: Jacket and tie.
CUISINE: American.
STARE FACTOR: None.
DIVERSITY FACTOR: We saw one Indian maître d', one Hispanic bathroom attendant, three Asian patrons, and no black workers or guests.
MISTAKEN IDENTITY QUOTIENT: It doesn't get much higher. Guileless patrons can create identification gaffes downstairs, so avoid waiting in the lobby.
SCALE OF JUSTICE RATING: ⚖️ ⚖️ ⚖️

Our experience at The Four Seasons proved the theory that the greater the distance between a restaurant's tables and its bathrooms or front door, the more harassment you will face.

It was on a brisk March afternoon that I arrived at the stark, Philip Johnson–designed restaurant for a business lunch with a young black insurance manager I had recently met. With all of the well-known business and celebrity types who eat at The Four Seasons, I figured it would be a fun experience.

When I arrived a few minutes before 1:00 P.M. at the downstairs entrance, two other men and I stood waiting for our respective lunch companions.

"Here, thank you," a woman said as she pushed a small colorful F.A.O. Schwarz toy-store bag at me.

I stepped back as she unbuttoned her coat.

"Lady," I said while putting my hands in my pockets, "the coat check is over there. I'm a guest."

The disheveled woman, who appeared to be a tourist in her mid-fifties, took a camera from her coat pocket and put it in her purse as she stood with the F.A.O. Schwarz bag between her legs. "Oh, thank you so much," she said, without looking up again.

I moved deeper into the beige marble waiting area and stood by one of the hanging woven blankets with my arms crossed.

After the disheveled woman checked her coat and asked the worker how much it would cost her, she headed to the carpeted stairwell leading up to the restaurant. Suddenly she changed course and walked past both white men and over to me while digging in her purse.

I immediately stepped back and turned away. "Young man, can you tell me—" she began while pulling out a lipstick dispenser and displaying a big smile. "Where's your ladies' room?"

Arms crossed, I turned to the woman. "I—don't—work—here, lady. I told you already!"

With the message finally sinking in, she dropped her lipstick back in the bag. "I'm so sorry," she whispered while touching my arm and leaning in close. "But this is my first time here. I'm so sorry." Then she rushed up the stairs.

I quickly ducked into the men's room, where a gray-jacketed Hispanic attendant stood at attention near the sinks. Aramis cologne wafted throughout the room and its eerily lit stalls. In the mirror I looked up and saw Michael Korda, Simon & Schuster's famous editor in chief.

Although he wouldn't have known me, I felt like confiding, "Mike, man, you aren't going to believe what some old white woman just said to me."

After the attendant handed Korda and me white towels, we left our tips and walked out.

"Can you sign for this?" a voice asked as a brown hand held a small voucher and pen in front of me.

A young black delivery man held out a voucher and a large accordion folder bound in brown tape.

"That's not for me."

He looked down at the address on his voucher. "Isn't this 345 Park?"

Although I knew that the front of this building was where he should have been, I pointed to the coat-check window. "She's 345 Park."

A couple minutes before 1:00 P.M., gossip columnist Liz Smith ran in from the forty-degree breeze wearing a stylish beige suit and no overcoat. Obviously late for lunch, she dashed upstairs with two sheets of loose white paper in her hand.

Moments later, the attendant exited the men's room and walked out to the street. Through the glass doors, I could see him puffing furiously on a cigarette.

"Excuse me," a tall man in a blue blazer called over to me from the half-opened men's room door as I remained seated in the lobby. "Aren't you supposed to be manning this bathroom?"

Finally, in walks my friend. Before we greet, I grab his arm and dash upstairs without an explanation.

From the maître d's podium I can see Ralph Lauren seated with a group of men who look vaguely familiar.

"Charles Wilson," I said. "Two for one o'clock in the Grill

Room." Like many New Yorkers, I knew that of the restaurant's two dining rooms—the Grill Room and the brightly lit Pool Room—the Grill Room had the more prominent businesspeople. Tourists and nonbusiness types were stuck in the Pool Room down the hall.

Unable to find the reservation that I'd made less than twenty-four hours before and confirmed an hour ago, the maître d' said that he couldn't accommodate us at all, then offered us the Pool Room.

"I requested the Grill Room when the reservation was made."

The maître d' sighed, then led us through the Grill Room and up six steps to a table underneath an emergency exit sign. A foot away stood a busboy's station with two trays and a stack of soiled plates and glasses.

My friend looked at me with a crestfallen shrug.

I looked down at the table, which looked more like a part of the busboy's station than it did a place to seat guests. The table's two wooden chairs didn't match the stainless steel and black chairs that were used throughout the rest of the room.

Once we were seated, another maître d', an Indian man, came over and thanked us profusely. The service and food after that were great. Although I can't be sure, since we were separated from them by a high wooden wall, it sounded like all the other patrons were enjoying their lunch as well.

The Bottom Line: The Four Seasons offers some of the best food, staff, service, and people-watching in New York, but the low Diversity Factor and high Mistaken Identity Quotient created by visiting tourists downstairs make it a lonely place.

BICE
7 East Fifty-fourth Street
New York City (212)688-1999

HOURS: Lunch: Monday–Sunday, 12:00 noon–3:00 P.M.; Dinner: Monday–Sunday, 6:00 P.M.–12:00 midnight.
CUISINE: Italian.

ATTIRE: No dress code.

STARE FACTOR: None.

DIVERSITY FACTOR: No black patrons, waiters, or workers were apparent. And given our table's proximity to the swinging kitchen doors, we would've seen them if they'd been there.

AVOIDANCE QUOTIENT: Was it their New York rudeness, or was it us? No one welcomed us, asked about our meal, offered us coffee, or thanked us for visiting.

SCALE OF JUSTICE RATING: ⚖ ⚖

When it comes to food and ambience, Bice is among the best Italian restaurants I've ever visited. It is also the meanest. The space is noisy and vibrant, with a handsome decor that makes use of dark wood, colorful Picasso-style prints, and recessed golden lights. Long-legged women in black crowd the bar while their escorts smoke languidly at their sides.

I lunched with a female friend who works Midtown. Given the fashion-forward attire and European atmosphere on display, I expected a high Diversity Factor. However, a room-walking survey at three different times revealed no black patrons, waiters, busboys, or kitchen workers. I noted three Asians among the more than two hundred patrons. The waiters (approximately seven) were white, and the busboys (approximately ten) appeared to be Hispanic, with the exception of one Asian.

When we arrived, the restaurant was operating at about 90 percent capacity, so although we were the only blacks, we expected no Buffer Zoning. We noted no Stare Factor from workers or patrons, but we did have to wait through ten minutes of Reservation Shuffling while three white couples who arrived after us, and were listed after us on the reservation sheet, were seated before us at tables that we would have eagerly accepted.

I looked at the lined sheet and saw my name, "C. Wilson."

"Why are these parties of two going ahead of us?" my friend asked the tall, well-built dark-haired Italian maître d' who stood before us and who had yet to welcome us.

He smoothed the lapel of his dark business suit. "We have a table for you. Just a few more minutes."

A female maître d' walked up next to him. "Party of two?" She then waved two white women—one of them in blue jeans—past us to a table with four chairs near the front of the main room.

Six empty tables for two lined the left wall, the front, and the right middle sections of the restaurant.

"Wilson, two, this way."

We were escorted directly past five empty tables to a table in the far left corner, separated from the swinging doors of the kitchen by a step that led to the sunken kitchen.

One benefit to our Seating Margin location was that we had a clear shot at the spicy aromas wafting from the kitchen. Unfortunately, our location also offered two small black flies that beat a path back and forth from our table to the kitchen doors.

While our waiter fawned over two mature men in business suits to my left and two younger men in jeans and leather jackets across from us, he wasted no words on us.

"No appetizer," he suddenly announced after strolling over.

I beg your pardon.

"No appetizer," he repeated. This was not a question.

My friend ordered the linguine with lobster and mushrooms, then asked, "Would it be a problem to get it without mushrooms?"

"No."

We looked at each other. Did he mean it wouldn't be a problem or that he could only serve it with the mushrooms?

"No, what?" I asked, still wondering about this response.

"Mushrooms are part of the dish. That's what."

We were intimidated into taking ravioli with sausage, salami, and butter instead.

The Avoidance Quotient runs dangerously high in this place. Although our waiter walked by aimlessly several times, he never inquired about our meal or asked us about dessert or coffee. All around us, he presented a totally different demeanor. Twice, he offered the two older men Pellegrino refills, then smiled and swept crumbs from the table of the young men in jeans. Even the busboy who came out with ground pepper and cheese for my pasta acted imposed upon.

As our waiter brought over a black vinyl book with our check, I nodded at his averted eyes and, for some reason, I said, "Thank you."

Before the words were out of my mouth, he had thrown the book down onto the table so that it bounced up and knocked over one of our empty water glasses.

I immediately looked up, only to see his back turned in our direction, as he had already leaned to the older men to place their book on their table and refill their glasses from a Pellegrino bottle. "*Grazie, grazie.* Thank you so much, gentlemen," he said.

"Did he just *drop* that on the table?" I asked my friend.

She frowned. "No. I'd say it was more of a toss."

The Bottom Line: In the areas of speed, efficiency, and presentation, Bice is tops. But we got the clear impression that they don't like us *moulees.*

THE WATER CLUB
500 East Thirtieth Street (on the East River)
New York City (212)683-3333

HOURS: Lunch: Monday–Saturday, 12:00 noon–2:30 P.M.; Sunday, 11:30–2:30 P.M.; Dinner: Monday–Sunday, 5:30 P.M.–11:00 P.M.
CUISINE: American.
ATTIRE: Casual for Sunday brunch.
STARE FACTOR: None.
MISTAKEN IDENTITY QUOTIENT: During our ninety-minute stay, I was mistaken for a waiter, a coat check, and a parking valet.
BUFFER ZONING: None.
SEATING MARGIN: Poor.
SCALE OF JUSTICE RATING: ⚖ ⚖ ⚖

Although the only visibly employed blacks at The Water Club were the black man and woman who sit, respectively, in the men's and ladies' bathroom, a few patrons displayed enough open-mindedness to mistake me for a waiter, coat check, and parking valet.

But in all fairness, you will find a number of favorable aspects to this place. When I joined three friends for a Sunday brunch, we were awestruck by one of the best river views in all of New York. The front of the building is on land, but the dining room is actually on a boat that is firmly anchored to the pier.

When we entered the high, two-story skylit lobby, we found green walls and green metal battleship stairwells.

The guests in the dining room were uniformly white, but a high staff Diversity Factor was supported by two Asian waiters, one Asian bartender, two Indian waiters, and a half-dozen Hispanic busboys.

"Good afternoon," greeted the two maître d's at the front of the brightly lit dining room. Behind them was a crowded buffet that was right out of the wedding scene from *Goodbye, Columbus.* "Hi, Charlie Wilson party of four." Hoping he'd read my mind, I stared longingly at eight empty tables down at the water's edge.

"You're up here," he responded as he brought us not to the tables in the sunken dining area that sat against the East River but to a section of booths—up against a wall. Separated by yet another wall barrier, we lost our waterside view along with our remaining view of the room.

"I'd prefer one of the tables below," I said.

"Sorry, but you wanted no smoking, right?"

"I see five empty tables that can accommodate four people," I answered pleasantly. "Smoking or no smoking, I'd be happy with any of them."

"Sorry, but they were reserved by people out at the bar. And they'll be right in." He urged us to slide into the booth. "Your waiter will be over," he said while rushing back down to the main level.

One of my friends looked up at me. "The bar was empty."

I walked out to the empty bar and confirmed that fact.

For the next hour, four of the five riverside tables remained empty. When we left ninety minutes later at 2:15, two tables were still vacant.

On my way to the bathroom, I was stopped in the lobby by an older man who handed me his wife's large red puffy ski jacket.

"I don't work here," I answered while charging up the metal stairs.

"How long is the wait to bring our car around?" a voice asked when I got to the first landing.

I looked up at a young couple in their early twenties.

"I beg your pardon."

"We're with the Stillman wedding upstairs," answered a young man in a rented tuxedo. "You guys parked my car just a little while ago—but we're leaving earlier than we realized." He pushed a tiny square ticket underneath my nose.

Mistaken identities run dangerously high in this nautical café—especially since there are lots of separate rooms and open common areas that lead to bathrooms and stairwells. In the men's room, a balding black man was listening to a church service on a radio as he brushed a tiny lint broom across the back of a patron's jacket.

As I turned on the faucet and looked up for a soap dispenser, a middle-aged man stepped from a stall and pushed his hands under my running water.

"A little too hot, son."

"This is my water," I said while pushing my hands under the water—just above his.

"I said it's too hot," he snapped while pulling back and waiting for me to adjust the valves. "Too hot."

As I turned slightly from the sink, he looked me up and down and then turned to where the attendant was brushing a jacket.

"Oh, pardon me," he muttered while moving to an empty sink, "I thought you were the boy."

I dried my hands and left a dollar for the attendant, a sixty-year-old man who was deep into his Sunday radio sermon.

The Bottom Line: Enjoy the food, but don't leave your table and don't make eye contact with white people carrying small tickets with numbers on them.

21 CLUB
21 West Fifty-second Street
New York City (212)582-7200

HOURS: Lunch: Monday–Saturday, 12:00 noon–3:00 P.M.; Dinner: Monday–Saturday, 6:00 P.M.–midnight; closed Sunday.
CUISINE: American.
ATTIRE: Jacket and tie required.
STARE FACTOR: High in the foyer. None in the dining room.
DIVERSITY FACTOR: Almost none. All guests were white except for one black man. All workers appeared to be white except for two Hispanic busboys and a black bath attendant.
SEATING MARGIN: Poor.
SCALE OF JUSTICE RATING: ⚖ ⚖ ⚖

It is no accident that this place is called the 21 *Club;* there are few restaurants more intimidating in reputation and atmosphere. Because the restaurant is a popular dining spot for bankers and lawyers, the street out front is always blocked by long black limousines.

A friend and I met for a 12:30 lunch at this New Orleans–style, wrought-iron-covered, three-story town house on West Fifty-second Street. At the front entrance, you are confronted with a collection of old-fashioned miniature lawn jockeys lining the outside steps and balcony: twenty-one of them—none in blackface.

A uniformed doorman opened the double brass and glass doors for us and tipped his hat as we entered.

Inside is everything you'd imagine a turn-of-the-century men's club would be—right down to the haughty brown horse that stands at the front of the living-room area.

Because entering 21 is like entering someone's home, if you've never been here before, everyone can tell. There are no signs or hosts to meet you at the door. And here in the foyer, the Stare Factor is high, long, and blatant. Old white men stand around awkwardly surveying those who enter. The elegantly appointed beige living room on the right is filled with businessmen waiting for guests.

"What's with this damn Bloomberg financial news?" a man in his sixties asked another banker type who was following the stock numbers across the screen of one of the three living-room TV sets.

As I waited at the end of a hallway leading into a dark, basementlike room, a formally attired maître d' waved two male couples ahead of me.

"I believe I'm next," I interrupted.

"He knows what he's doing," said an older woman standing behind an ancient glass showcase.

No one could have told me that 21 would look as uninspired as this. The dining room is as dark and campy as a junior high basement Halloween party. Suspended from the low ceiling and covering every inch of headroom are plastic and metal model airplanes, model trucks, football helmets, and plastic construction hard hats.

"This way, please," the captain said as he led us through a dark room of casual brown wooden chairs and tables covered with red-and-white picnic-style checkered tablecloths.

"Cheap, cheap, cheap. Tacky, tacky" is all you can think.

Then I saw the famous financier from Lazard Freres, millionaire Felix Rohatyn, seated in the area closest to the doorway facing the kitchen. That's when I realized that the traditional restaurant seating rules were somehow reversed at 21. The most desirable seats were the ones closest to the door and kitchen. The dining room is divided into three sections. You first enter section one (where Felix was), where you pass lots of businesspeople who look vaguely familiar.

Walking steadily to your right, you pass through section two (my label, not theirs), where one finds fifteen or so tables of less recognizable men and women. Moving farther into the room, you hit section three, which offers a hodgepodge of white professionals in their forties and fifties: all nobodies. They sit side by side—Parisian style—on a long red-vinyl banquet couch. The walls are—for lack of a better word—decorated with pewter and porcelain beer mugs. We were placed in a hard-to-find corner next to three mid-fifties banker types (alas, no Buffer Zoning), who immediately picked up their plates of artichokes and slid an entire table's length down the bench (Patron-Initiated Buffer Zoning), leaving an empty table between us.

An attentive captain and waiter served shellfish chowder and the single most expensive hamburger I'd ever eaten—$21 before tax.

In the bathroom I saw what might be the sole black employee at 21: an elderly bathroom attendant. Handing out towels and adjusting the faucets at the three sinks for male patrons, the balding man smiled and bowed gracefully.

"So, Billy," asked a tall man who combed his silver hair in the mirror. "How are we holding down the fort today?"

"Just fine, Mr. Palmer, sir," the black man answered pleasantly with a Jim Crow smile and a light brush of Mr. Palmer's rear pants leg. "Doin' just fine, sir—just fine. Thank you for askin', sir. Just fine."

Mr. Palmer looked over the collection of cologne bottles, then sprayed the Calvin Klein Eternity. "Now, you stay out of trouble, Billy," he laughed after handing the old man a few singles.

"Sure will, Mr. Palmer, sir. Sure will."

I walked up feeling awkward and resentful. I had no right to judge the real feelings of these two men, but if Billy's radio had been tuned to a 1930s Harold Arlen song, and this had been a Shirley Temple movie set, we surely could have jumped up on that white marble sink and tap-danced our way through the wooden doors of the French-mural-painted toilet stalls.

Heading back to my seat, I was happily distracted by the sight of a female friend whom I'd met in graduate school. "Hey, Janet—"

Before I had finished my greeting, the tall woman had dropped her head and shrunk behind a phalanx of white male colleagues. As she quietly met my gaze, I noticed that the group all wore name tags from her Big Six accounting firm.

Like Billy and Mr. Palmer, everyone at 21 Club seems to know his or her place. I was just learning.

The Bottom Line: Good food, okay staff, very clubby. Bring your reflector glasses for the stares you'll get in the foyer.

THE RAINBOW ROOM
30 Rockefeller Plaza (GE Building)
New York City (212)632-5000

HOURS: Closed Monday. Dinner: Tuesday–Saturday, 5:30 P.M.–1:00 A.M., Sunday, 12:00 noon–10:30 P.M.
CUISINE: Continental.
ATTIRE: Formal.
STARE FACTOR: Low.
DIVERSITY FACTOR: Very low. We saw no black guests or black waiters during a four-hour visit.
MISTAKEN IDENTITY QUOTIENT: Since black tie is common at dinner, black men can be easily mistaken for uniformed employees.
SCALE OF JUSTICE RATING: ⚖️ ⚖️ ⚖️

Sixty-five floors above Manhattan is a historic restaurant offering Cole Porter, champagne, sequined dresses, and that famous skyline. When my wife and I arrived for our Saturday-evening black-tie dinner reservation, an art deco hallway carried us into a scene straight out of *The Wizard of Oz.*

"Welcome to the Rainbow Room!"

Swarming around with words of welcome were coat checks— five of them—outfitted in 1930s "cigarette-girl"-style maroon caps and jackets with bright gold buttons and stitching.

"Welcome to the Rainbow Room!"

The maître d' instructed an assistant to take us to our table. The large circular room overwhelms with its rainbow-colored dome ceiling, mirrored walls, art deco steel-and-glass railings, silver lamé tablecloths, revolving dance floor, and tables distributed on three different terraced levels.

The eight-piece Rainbow Room Orchestra struck up Gershwin's "Just in Time" as we walked across the dim room. And from the raised eyebrows that came our way from the waiters, bus attendants, and ultraserious waltzing and fox-trotting guests, it was immediately obvious that black people are an unusual sight here. We were the only black patrons in the huge restaurant, and other than a table where four Japanese men sat, the entire room was middle-aged and white.

"Good evening."

"Welcome to the Rainbow Room."

"How are you both this evening?"

Smiles and greetings came from every waiter we passed as we were led toward our seats—an endless obstacle course of people, chairs, and candlelit tables. Our odyssey moved us briskly—taking us farther and farther away from the front of the restaurant, the dance floor, the orchestra, and the sparkling view of the city. Looking up ahead of our guide, I saw two terraces with a line of eight empty tables: All were great seats.

We passed them. We were instead taken to a table against a wall. On the wall, at knee level, was a three-foot-wide, two-foot-high metal exhaust vent that was either heating or cooling the room.

"Here is your seat," the assistant said with a gracious smile.

I looked at my wife, then at the stream of vacant tables we had passed. Not only did the dance floor and orchestra feel out of reach, but our sixty-fifth-story view of Manhattan had also disappeared. After considering the fact that this meal was costing well over $200, I requested one of the eleven or twelve other vacant tables. After checking with the maître d', the assistant politely told us our only other choice was the table next to the kitchen. We took the exhaust vent instead.

That night we saw six black employees: an unpleasant coat-check girl, a soulful saxophonist, three bus attendants, and one bathroom worker who seemed to be performing the job of three. As I picked up the green tube of Estée Lauder Maximum Care Hand Lotion in the men's room, I saw him turning on faucets, handing out towels, and offering shoe shines.

"*Bon soir, mes amis,*" greeted our jovial young waiter. He quickly sold us on a Belvedere chardonnay and green salads ($8 each). For entrées, we had lamb chops on a tomato pastry tart and the restaurant's famous tournedos Rossini, a smooth filet mignon covered in a Madeira wine and black truffle sauce.

You'll appreciate the Rainbow Room's attempt at celebrating diversity. There was a wall montage near the Promenade Bar featuring pictures and stories of famous performers. One poster pays tribute to Benny Goodman, noting that he integrated his bands in the 1930s with black musicians who could not find employment with other white bands.

As I waited for my wife outside the ladies' room, I stood admiring the montage. I then turned to a man who had just finished reading the same storyboard.

"That's a great story, isn't it?" I commented.

The man, who looked to be in his early forties, nodded approvingly as he fished through his pockets. "Yes, it's hard to imagine people being unwilling to hire someone like Lionel Hampton. My wife just loves his music."

I laughed. "My wife loves it too."

The man then reached out toward me with something green and shiny in his hand. "She's actually in the ladies' room right now. Why don't you take this and run ahead to your station so we can have our coats when she's done. We're trying to catch a train."

I looked down at the green plastic coat check in his hand, then back at his face. He smiled approvingly, then pulled out two singles.

Before my wife returned from the ladies' room, I was stopped by two other patrons. One man asked for the hours of the bar, and a woman who had been humming to the tune of "I'll Be Seeing

You" gestured to a nearby glass counter that featured the Tiffany-made Rainbow Room place settings and politely asked me, "How come you guys didn't serve us with *these* plates? They're so much more elegant."

It wasn't worth fighting. "I'll tell the boss," I said with a smile.

The Bottom Line: Here's a place for a memorable double date with your parents. The staff is great, but men should wear a kente-cloth cummerbund and stick close to your dates just to keep guests from asking you to clear a table or hang their coat.

LE CIRQUE
58 East Sixty-fifth Street
New York City (212)794-9292

HOURS: Closed Sunday. Lunch: 11:45 A.M.–2:30 P.M.; Dinner: 5:45 P.M.–10:30 P.M.
CUISINE: French.
ATTIRE: Jacket required.
STARE FACTOR: Almost none. We did, however, stare at Jackie Collins, author of *Hollywood Wives* and *The Bitch*.
DIVERSITY FACTOR: We saw no black patrons and no black waiters, busboys, or staff. There were four Asian busboys.
BUFFER ZONING: High Buffer Zoning goes on here. A radius of three tables plus a glass partition kept us separate from the other patrons.
SCALE OF JUSTICE RATING: ⚖ ⚖ ⚖

We wondered if the French were any more progressive than the Americans when it came to equal opportunity dining, and decided to try one of the most elegant and expensive French restaurants in New York, Le Cirque, which is famous for its gossipy, high-society lunch crowd.

A black female friend of mine, a corporate attorney, met me for a one o'clock lunch. As we stepped under the small brown-

and-white awning and entered Le Cirque's tiny foyer, we immediately felt transported back to a Paris of the 1920s. The windows of the old-fashioned vestibule are covered in the same gauzy linen drapes that your grandmother had on her front door in New Orleans. It all seems homey and unpretentious—until you open the second gauze-covered door and step into the actual restaurant.

That's where you hit the maître d', whom we found on the phone, negotiating with customers who were unsuccessfully trying to get a table for the following night. To our right, seven faces stopped their conversations and turned to catch a glimpse of us. One woman picked up a pair of catlike glasses to note our arrival. The neutral gaze we got was not unfriendly. These were stares of curiosity—as in "Are you somebody we should know about?" That's what Le Cirque is like. Slightly bitchy.

"This place seems catty," my friend commented while taking in the green-and-white tulip light fixtures and the beige chairs. "It's also quite simian," I added. When you look around the room, you are immediately struck by the profusion of monkeys. Pastel green, yellow, beige, and orange wall murals feature monkeys in all types of roles: cooking in the kitchen, riding Revolutionary War horses, playing festive tambourines. The monkeys also appear in white ceramic forms throughout the restaurant, as well as on plates, saucers, and cups.

If these hairy mammals are meant to advance the circus (Le Cirque) theme, this is where the fun stops. This restaurant is serious business. And it starts with the seating plan.

After checking our coats, we were brought into the dining area, which seemed to be at 15 to 20 percent occupancy. The Diversity Factor was as low as it gets: all white.

"Smoking or nonsmoking?" a waiter asked as he marched us past these people. Facing the empty half of the room, we were clearly heading into a major Buffer Zone—or out some side door.

Before we were able to respond "nonsmoking," we had already passed the front half of the restaurant and were turning a corner into a narrow, almost hallway-type area of tables that connected the dining area with the bar. This out-of-the-way area, which contained six tables, was further blocked from the rest of the restaurant because of a glass partition and a busboy station that was stacked with two or three dirty plates. Depositing us beneath a mural of monkeys working in a late-nineteenth-century kitchen, a swarm of staff (two white waiters and two Asian busboys) encouraged us to sit next to each other Parisian-style on the light green velour bench seats.

Although they had just Buffer-Zoned us from the rest of the patrons, the staff was so jovial and so attentive I'd almost forgotten what happened. The only benefit to our seats was that we could get to Le Cirque's 1970s disco-style gold metallic bathrooms before anyone else. Quite simply, we were the farthest table from the main dining area. And until a single white male diner arrived sixty minutes later and was seated near us, we remained separated from the rest of the diners by at least a three-table radius. Every other occupied table in the room was contiguous to another occupied table.

In spite of the blatant Buffer Zoning, Le Cirque gets high marks for service and food. The captains (all appeared to be white), waiters (all white), and busboys (four Asians and two whites) constantly offer their assistance.

The Bottom Line: Although Diversity of patrons was at 0 percent, black people would not feel like a spectacle here. The exaggerated accents, shocking face-lifts, dramatic entrances, and the occasional celebrity make the place seem quite eclectic. When everyone is—or tries to be—a spectacle, the lone black couple just seems like a part of the mix. At least that's how it looked—from the sidelines—out in the six-table hallway area.

LA GRENOUILLE
3 East Fifty-second Street
New York City (212)752-1495

HOURS: Lunch: Tuesday–Saturday, 12:00 noon–2:30 P.M.; Dinner: Tuesday–Saturday, 6:00 P.M.–11:30 P.M.

CUISINE: French.
ATTIRE: Jacket and tie required.
STARE FACTOR: None.
DIVERSITY FACTOR: In a room of approximately a hundred patrons, we saw two blacks and two Asians. Except for two Hispanic busboys, the staff appeared to be uniformly white.
BUFFER ZONING: None.
TABLE REFUSAL FACTOR: For two hours, the restaurant tried unsuccessfully to fill the empty table next to us.
SCALE OF JUSTICE RATING: ⚖ ⚖ ⚖ ⚖ ⚖

If Le Cirque is the ultimate French lunchtime restaurant, La Grenouille is, by far, the ultimate French *dinner* restaurant. My mother and I arrived for an 8:15 P.M. Saturday reservation. And whether it was her mink coat, Chanel suit, or the alignment of the stars that put us over the top, the staff bent over backwards for us all night.

After checking our coats with a young man who stood with a French novel at his side, we stepped from a tiny vestibule into a room overflowing with flowers, desserts, and an army of waiters and attendants.

"Good evening."

"Bonsoir."

"Welcome to La Grenouille."

A sea of men with varying French and American accents smiled and nodded as we came into the crowded entrance, which had desserts at our right elbow, a bar in front of us, and a blinking telephone on our left.

"Welcome," said the tall, dark-haired maître d'. "You are—"

"Charlie Wilson—party of two," I said. "For eight-fifteen."

"Ahh, yes," he said. "Let us show you to your table."

Walking into La Grenouille is like walking down a Parisian model's fashion runway. The restaurant consists of one deep room that is lined on both sidewalls with a long, fire-engine red velvet wall banquet sofa. The patrons were seated side by side, Parisian-style, and facing into the center of the room. There was virtually no Stare Factor as we made "the walk" behind the maître d' to just beyond the room's midway point—a few feet from the two eight-foot-tall floral arrangements.

"How is this for you?" he offered as he directed us to a table in the dead center of the room, just in front of a table occupied by two couples in their early forties.

No Buffer Zoning. No Seating Margin. "Perfect," I responded.

I faced the front and my mother faced the rear—with a full view of a mirrored wall that reflected the entire golden-lit room. At every angle, we could enjoy small table bouquets of white and pink roses, oil paintings, and delicate ten-inch-high electric lamps that sat on every other white-linen-covered table. We shared a lamp with an adjoining vacant table. The floral red-and-green carpet continued the French garden motif.

There was an extremely low Diversity Factor among the all-male staff: no blacks, and among the approximately five captains, ten waiters, and three busboys, all were white except for two busboys who appeared to be Hispanic. The Diversity Factor among patrons was equally low: When we arrived, the room was entirely white except for two Asian women, each of whom was dining with a white man. Patrons varied in age from thirty to seventy, with most appearing to be American married couples in their late forties.

"Bonjour," announced our French-accented captain, a jovial man who handed us two large white menus. Two assistants came over to give us water and place a silver tray of small fancy breads on a table that was already heavy with silver utensils.

In spite of five years of French, the only thing I recognized on the menu was the term "$70.00," printed at the bottom.

We had lobster bisque and the mixed greens with foie gras for appetizers, and then the lamb and roast duck in a wine sauce.

By 8:40 P.M., the Diversity Factor rose slightly as a well-dressed dark-skinned black couple walked in and joined a white couple that had already been seated along the red banquet sofa.

"That's a sneaky trick," I said while giving them the Universal Friendly Black Nod.

"What?" my mother asked.

"Ask your white friends to arrive first, so you never get a bad seat. That's how I get a cab in Midtown."

Mom rolled her eyes at me, then looked over two inches from us at that still-vacant table. We shared its old-fashioned two-shaded electric lamp, which threw a nice glow on our plates. Although the place had been at 95 percent capacity for the last hour, the table remained vacant—one of three in the room.

By 9:00, as new patrons entered, it became obvious that the restaurant was finding it difficult to fill our empty table. The maître d' brought a young couple over. The man pulled out a chair to sit down, but his light-brown-haired date—an attractive woman in her thirties—gestured in another direction.

"Can we take that table in back, next to the kitchen?"

The startled maître d' led them toward the kitchen.

At 9:30, only two tables were left: ours and the one on the *left* side of the kitchen. The maître d' escorted a balding man in his sixties, along with a dowdy-looking wife with dark black hair. They stopped at the empty table.

Once again, the husband pulled out his chair. The wife grabbed at her husband's left sleeve.

"I can't sit here," the woman snapped. "Can't we take that table there?" She pointed to a table on the left side of the kitchen entrance.

The maître d' looked disappointed when I stared him squarely in the face. I felt sorry for having thrown off his seating plan.

At 9:45, as we selected our desserts, two waiters were sent over to separate the empty table from our own. They pulled out the chairs and slid the table about a foot and a half. With the table also went our lamp. The electric cord was now visibly stretched from our floor area to the vacant table's linen-covered top.

Moments later, the maître d' brought a third couple to the table. The woman in her late forties looked down at my mother and me as we refilled teacups from the elegant silver pitcher.

"Can you find us a place over there on the sofa instead?" the wife asked pointedly as her double-chinned husband clasped his hands in front of himself.

"There's really not enough room for two," the maître d' said.

The husband nodded. "We'll squeeze."

The couple walked back up to the front of the restaurant and waited with their arms folded as the maître d' gently asked a patron to slide closer to her party on the couch. Then a waiter and busboy fiddled with the electric lamp that flickered on the table of what was now being turned into the *second*-to-last seat in the house. Moments later, a waiter returned, smiled sheepishly at us, then pulled the nearby table away from us another two or three inches. It was now virtually standing in the path where waiters walked back and forth to the kitchen.

The double-chinned husband and wife took their seats only to discover a still malfunctioning lamp on their table.

"Excusez-moi, s'il vous plaît," whispered a waiter as he pulled their table from the red sofa and they stood up. He got down on his knees to reconnect the plug and outlet as the wife looked over to us and the vacant table.

I leaned over to my mother. "Doesn't this bother you?"

"Remember," she answered, "I grew up in Memphis."

At 10:00 P.M., our lemon tart and Floating Island arrived. Before I spooned into the scoops of meringue and long shiny needles of spun sugar, I took a walk to the front and then back to our table and the bathroom. Except for the elegant Hollywood-style mirrored bathroom, the only open seats at La Grenouille tonight were the ones next to us. They couldn't give them away.

Finally, as we finished our dessert at 10:05 P.M.—two hours after our arrival—and as the vacant table got moved over yet another inch or so, an elegantly attired couple in their late forties with heavy French accents were seated at the table.

As we left at 10:30, no fewer than six waiters and captains thanked us for coming. The maître d' rushed out to help my mother as the bottom of her coat just brushed the floor. He leaned out onto the cold sidewalk to open the door for us.

"Thank you for coming. We hope you had a nice evening."

I nodded. "It was great."

And it really had been. Our dinner at La Grenouille had been like dining in the Garden of Eden. The fresh flowers, the soft golden lighting, the swarms of unpretentious waiters bringing beautiful silver trays and handsome dishes and warm words made the experience flawless. The only sin committed—that of forcing space between us and the other guests—was through no fault of La Grenouille.

I grabbed hold of my mother's arm, and we turned west to Fifth Avenue.

The Bottom Line: James Baldwin and Josephine Baker may have been right about the French.

RUSSIAN TEA ROOM
150 West Fifty-seventh Street
New York City (212)265-0947

HOURS: Lunch: Monday–Sunday, 11:30 A.M.–4:30 P.M.; Dinner: Monday–Sunday, 4:30 P.M.–11:30 P.M.
CUISINE: Russian.
ATTIRE: Jacket required for dinner.
STARE FACTOR: None.
DIVERSITY FACTOR: High among the staff. Low among patrons: uniformly white except for two young Asian women.
BUFFER ZONING: None.
SCALE OF JUSTICE RATING: ⚖ ⚖ ⚖ ⚖

An Asian waiter in his mid-thirties stood at a table near the center of the room. He wore a bright red Russian caftan shirt with a cloth belt tied at the waist.

"Since you are clearly Russian," one of the dinner guests remarked with a laugh, "what would you recommend among the Russian specialties?"

"Hah, hah! Very funny," the man responded with a Chinese accent.

When I joined three friends for a Saturday-night dinner in this kitsch-filled red, green, and brassy gold dining room, I was immediately struck by the high Diversity Factor of the staff: an Asian manager, two red-shirted waiters (one black and one Asian), and what appeared to be uniformly Hispanic bus attendants, all in green shirts.

"So, who's a real Russian around here?" a woman at the next banquet table behind us asked her date. "Seems like a whole lot of minorities in here. That busboy's name tag says 'Jimmy,' but he looks pretty Spanish to me."

This is not a place that attracts soft-spoken people.

As the four of us relaxed on a red crescent-shaped banquet couch against the right wall of the dining room, I stared up at the brilliant Christmas ornaments. I noted that even with a roomful of camera-toting tourists, this place offers no Stare Factor.

The menu, of course, offers a wide selection of Russian specialties. Besides the à la carte menu, diners can choose from among three prix fixe menus, at prices of $28.50, $39.00, or $62.00 per person. We started with some salmon caviar, then moved on to hot borscht with pierogies, and finally côtelette à Kiev (chicken Kiev), which was buttered and spiced delicately. We ended with hot Russian tea sweetened with cherry preserves and cheesecake that was accompanied by apricot, currants, sweet cherries, and apples.

Although the waiters do not fuss over you here, there is no Buffer Zoning and no Avoidance Quotient. Our waiter enthusiastically explained the significance of each dish on the menu, as well as of the samovars, portraits, and mural along the wall. This place packs them in from 6:00 P.M. right on up to 11:00, when patrons walk in waiting for a late dinner.

The Bottom Line: Even though one hears an occasional offensive ethnic joke about Russians from the overwhelmingly white, middle-American people who pour into the place, it's a great pre– or post–Carnegie Hall treat.

PARK AVENUE CAFÉ
100 East Sixty-third Street
New York City (212)644-1900

HOURS: Lunch: Monday–Friday, 11:30 A.M.–2:30 P.M.; Brunch: Sunday, 11:00 A.M.–2:00 P.M.; Dinner: Monday–Saturday, 5:30 P.M.–10:45 P.M.; Sunday, 4:30 P.M.–9:30 P.M.
CUISINE: American.
ATTIRE: Jackets preferred.
STARE FACTOR: None.
DIVERSITY QUOTIENT: Among the guests, we saw two blacks and three Asians. On staff, we saw a black coat check, as well as an Indian and a Hispanic busboy. Great male-female ratio.
BUFFER ZONING: The Café has a front room and a less desirable back room. You may have to fight to stay out front.
SEATING MARGIN: Bad at first, then great.
SCALE OF JUSTICE RATING: ⚖ ⚖ ⚖ ⚖

If you're looking for Upper East Side dining but are averse to the treatment we got slapped with at Mortimer's, the Park Avenue Café is the place for you.

I met two friends for an eight o'clock Friday-night dinner at this eatery hidden away in an elegant residential building. When you step through the large dark green awning and grab hold of the sharp elk-head door handles, you'll quickly discover that the Park Avenue Café's seating arrangement lends itself to easy Buffer Zoning. With both a front and a back room, it's as if the architects had anticipated restaurateurs with elitist sensibilities.

Up front, there is a "see-and-be-seen" room of about sixty tables. Americana is everywhere: Elegant wood carvings and small sheaves of wheat are strategically placed on tables, in windows, and against ledges. Wooden Shaker-style chairs feature green-and-white seat cushions, and a wooden pig pushes a cart of fresh vegetables. The golden light and buoyant conversation make the room warm and inviting.

This room looks out on Park Avenue, and with the aid of a large glass window, two very fussy maître d's look out on the room. As soon as I saw these two characters, paranoia kicked in and I immediately got the sense that I wasn't going to get a good table. And in spite of twelve empty tables, I was right.

"Your name, please?" asked maître d' number one, a tall man in a green suit with a small red apple pinned to his lapel.

"Charlie Wilson—party of three," I answered.

Checking his list, he glanced past the window and pointed in a 180-degree direction that was opposite the dining area. "Yes, you'll be eating back in the *other* dining area." He turned away from us and went back to his book.

"Excuse me," I interrupted. "What *other* dining area?"

"Behind me, through the bar, up the stairs, past the bathrooms, and just beyond the coat check," he said, still without turning to face us.

Through the window of the room, I saw several vacant tables. My friends were also reluctant to walk to the back. "You must have some empty tables up front." I could see at least twelve.

"But you wanted—" He paused.

"Yes?" I asked.

"But you wanted—" He stepped back and fumbled for a seating list. "Uh, you wanted no smoking, right?"

"Well—"

He interrupted, "So if you want no smoking, it's upstairs in the back."

"So," one of my friends interrupted, "you mean, there are only *smoking* seats in this room?"

"That's all that's left."

I wasn't giving up. "Then we'll take *smoking*."

He looked on his sheet of paper, then turned to me. "Unfortunately, there are only *two* smoking tables in this room."

"Then we'll take one of them."

He forced a smile. "Unfortunately they're both spoken for."

I turned to my friends. "Then we'll take one of the empty ones that are *not* spoken for. I see almost a dozen tables."

He rolled his eyes. "Only two *smoking* tables left, Mr. Wilson."

"Look," I said, while making one final attempt to end this word game and head off his attempt at Buffer Zoning us. "What table do we have to accept—smoking or nonsmoking—just to make sure we sit in this front room?"

"Okay, I'm sorry," he said in a final retreat while looking down at his sheet of names. "I was thinking we only had *two* smoking tables in here. We actually *do* have a third one. Show them to table forty-two," he quickly said to his assistant while rolling his eyes and turning his back to us.

Pheww!!

From our table in the center of the room, I noticed a zero Stare Factor. A black couple in their forties was at a table with three whites. An Asian couple in their fifties was at another mid-room table. The rest of the room consisted of whites in their forties and fifties. It was just after eight o'clock.

The remaining "spoken-for" tables remained vacant for another ninety minutes, when the room got increasingly older.

As the fastidious maître d's roamed the room, chatting up each table, placing their fingertips on others' shoulders, they treated us to a high Avoidance Quotient. They remained silent until we passed them on our way out the door at 10:35. The friendly waiters and buspeople (women in our case) in green-and-white-striped uniforms more than made up for their bosses' behavior. When my friend commented on the number of female waiters, one of them noted that top restaurants rarely hire women.

"While I was job hunting," she said, "one restaurant manager told me he didn't hire female waiters but that Park Avenue Café did. I was insulted, but glad he gave me the scoop."

The panfried monkfish with shrimp and sausage on couscous and zucchini and the steak frites were magnificent. Dessert was even better. Head chef David Burke came out and leaned against the bar as we delved into the famous raspberry and lemon flatbed tart, which was an old-fashioned truck made of cookies, ladyfingers, and raspberries. We also tried Opera in the Park, a park bench and lamppost made of dark chocolate.

The Bottom Line: For a business lunch or relaxed dinner, this is a great East Side choice. But sharpen your nails and be prepared to fight for a seat in the front room, no matter what the vacancy rate is like.

6

HOW WHITE PEOPLE TAUGHT ME TO BE A GOOD BLACK NEIGHBOR

A SUBURBAN ALLEGORY

IRECENTLY RECEIVED the following letter:

Dear Mr. Graham,
My name is Anita Richardson and I am sending you this special delivery package because I have recently implemented a ground-breaking program that has succeeded at doing what others thought was impossible: erasing racism from our country's households. Before I go on to describe the contents of this package (you'll see several pamphlets, computer printouts, a map of several major cities, and two looseleaf notebooks), let me introduce myself.

I am a forty-five-year-old black real estate broker who has lived in the affluent, predominately white Chicago suburb of Winnetka for eleven years.

I have discovered that the only true way to bring about racial equality in the United States is to alter the views of influential whites who harbor negative opinions of African Americans. And there is no better way to alter these biases against the black race than by placing well-educated and well-mannered professional black families as neighbors on their blocks to both observe and dismantle the racial stereotypes that whites have been allowed to perpetuate.

By planting a well-trained, preapproved black family on a block of white homeowners, the white adults and their children can see the myths about blacks explode before their very eyes. This is when the black race will earn true respect and equality.

After a successful seventeen-year career of selling homes to both blacks and whites, I have decided to combat the time-honored practice of steering blacks into preintegrated towns and neighborhoods.

I have launched an initiative that is already changing the entire direction of civil rights. I have created something that may wipe out prejudice from the entire country. I have brought together a network of thirty-six open-minded white and black real estate brokers around the U.S., and I have established **The Foundation for Suburban Placement of Upper-income Blacks** (also known as "SPUB"). Our mission is to seek out affluent suburban towns and villages that have a less than five percent black population. We monitor the racial composition of each of the top-zoned streets and we place a professional black family (Suburban Placed Upper-income Black— SPUB) on streets that are currently 100 percent white. The SPUB must sign our **Quality of Behavior Statement**, undergo a sixteen-hour **"Be a Good Black Neighbor Training Course"** and then live his life as he would anywhere else, while keeping in mind that he is there to serve as a model for how good black people can be. By living a clean life and assimilating into the white community, the SPUB will change the negative images of all black people. Of course the SPUB is subject to spot checks every few months by representatives of our foundation.

Mr. Graham, like yourself, I am a black of superior breeding— and one who wants to give back. As a graduate of Smith and the wife of a surgeon, I have never considered myself an angry, downtrodden black activist, but I do think that the SPUB program is a groundbreaking step in American civil rights. It hits racism right where it lives!

Our client database includes the names of all blacks who both live within our fourteen targeted metropolitan areas and have graduated from the college, law school, business school, or medical school that is affiliated with an Ivy League university, a Seven Sister college, Amherst, Williams, Tufts, or Stanford. I give you my congratulations because you and your wife received a 98.5 out of a possible 100 percent on our SPUB Qualification Rating System. This makes you a highly desirable black neighbor. And we want to help you.

You'll note that I've enclosed a looseleaf notebook with the label: "W.A.T.C.H.—I.T.: White Areas That Can Help Integration Thrive" (WATCH IT). On the following page is a chart that lists some of the communities where our organization is in the process of finding homes for SPUBs. The objective is to turn WATCH IT communities into SPUB communities. You'll notice that the notebook begins with a unique description of certain "WATCH IT" communities that we deem ideal for our SPUBs.

IDENTIFIED COMMUNITIES

It is our policy to place SPUBs in towns or villages that are **less than** 5 percent black. And although we acknowledge that all of our listed communities have first-rate homes, we maximize our impact by placing SPUBs only on streets that are currently 100 percent white.

If you scan through the looseleaf WATCH IT notebook, you will see section dividers that name white suburbs throughout different parts of the country. The white communities are named in the alphabetical order of their home state, and then in the alphabetical order of the community's name. So, for example, you will see areas listed like: California—Bel Air, Brentwood, Pacific Palisades, Simi Valley; Connecticut—Darien, Greenwich, New Canaan; Florida—Boca Raton, Palm Beach; Illinois—Highland Park, Kenilworth, Wilmette; Massachusetts—Newton, Wellesley, Weston; Michigan—Bloomfield

Hills, Grosse Pointe; Minnesota—Edina, Wayzata; New York—Bedford, Locust Valley; etc.

You may want to look through the WATCH IT notebook now and allow my letter to guide you through a sample section.

To get a sense of how we characterize the neighborhoods, flip to the streets and homes listed in the suburban area of Bel Air, California, on page 77, for example. The streets, along with their respective homeowners' racial history and current racial, ethnic, and religious makeup, are listed alphabetically. For example: Airole Way, Ashdale Avenue, Bellagio Road, Bel Air Road, Bentley Circle, Beverly Glen Boulevard, and so forth.

On page 79, for example, you will see the following description of a white, 1939 five-bedroom colonial listed at $985,000 at 7 Heatherbloom Circle: "Populated by only 9 houses, this street has been 100 percent white, except for a five-year period when a well-assimilated Japanese couple lived at #6 (a 6-bedroom split-level) during the 1970s. Except for the three housekeepers and two live-in nannies, nary a black has walked this palm-lined street.

"The benefits are obvious: Lush trees, restrictions against sidewalks, no overnight parking, the Bel Air name, security and proximity to L.A., the exclusive Westlake School and Beverly Hills. Since neighbors have already had to put up with the Asian family that once lived on the street, they have already lowered their standards of homogeneity and have learned not to contact police at the sight of nonwhite children on the block.

"Drawbacks to this placement begin with the schools. Unlike nearby Beverly Hills, Bel Air is a part of the somewhat too-integrated L.A. Unified School District, which means that your kids will eventually attend schools with—and perhaps be mistaken for poor blacks from other parts of Los Angeles. Another drawback is that the only nonprofessional household on the block—an Irish American couple—is right next door at #9. They own a four-million-dollar plumbing supply company in Sherman Oaks, but both husband and wife lack college degrees—so expect some ignorance and a great degree of jealousy since you are better educated. Sources tell us they are quiet and spend their social time with friends in Van Nuys, the Valley community they left in 1969."

So, Mr. Graham, do you see how easy this is? Imagine how helpful this will be to the many quality black people who don't normally have access to this information—or more likely, those who lack the courage to venture into unchartered white communities. With SPUBs, they find out what they'd be facing.

Now, if you look at the yellow spiral folder labeled, "THE SPUB BEHAVIOR-MODIFICATION PROGRAM," you will see that we offer helpful instructions to our new black homeowners on how to fit in with their new white neighbors. Now, I know that you are of second- or third-generation black-quality, but some of our SPUBs are not, and it would be elitist for us to discriminate against them. So, we offer them some simple suggestions to keep in mind after they purchase and close on their new SPUB home. Some people have said that the advice seems a little extreme, but we must anticipate every possible situation. Remember, Mr. Graham, as you well know—*the behavior of each black resident is ultimately a reflection on the entire race!*

So, we tell them the following as they move into their new homes:

1: Contact the local police and introduce yourself and your children (particularly dark-skinned boys who might draw attention) so that they will know that a black family lives in your home. This will prevent needless harassment from police seeking constant verification of identity.

2: Rearrange your walking or jogging schedule so that you're off the street by 6:00 P.M. If you must walk at all, always cross to the far side of the street when spotting a white neighbor coming in your direction. Give a big wave or "hello" and somehow subtly remind them who you are and where you live. This relieves any anxiety they might be feeling. Never walk up behind a neighbor without announcing your presence from a distance of at least twenty-five yards.

3:    Maintain your home's outside appearance so that it is in keeping with the standards of the most affluent of neighbors on your block. Paint the outside white or a light pastel. If you keep a garden, avoid sunflowers, unusual vegetables, and other plants that suggest a southern agrarian background.

4: Since your neighbors have never lived near a black person, don't wait for them to introduce themselves. They may be afraid of you, so put them at ease. Stop by on a weekend afternoon with a large basket of unsliced, store-packaged, shrink-wrapped, sanitized fruit, or perhaps a brand-name European delicacy they would recognize. Don't insist on entering their home or sharing in the edible gift. It is likely to be thrown out if they suspect tampering.

5: Make sure your children and any relatives who visit understand that they mustn't yell, sing, turn on a radio, play basketball, or stand outside without shoes, jacket, tie (women should follow such formality). Remember that you may be the only black that your neighbors will ever meet. These first impressions will stick.

6: Within the first few days of moving in, contact every neighbor on the block and ask them to recommend a gardener, housekeeper, nanny, roofer, snow removal service, interior decorator, architect, chimney sweep, and limousine service. This call will establish that you are a consummate professional who will keep the house up to par without regard to expense.

7: Attend a neighborhood association meeting and formally introduce yourself to the entire gathering, announcing your name, professional credentials, and academic accomplishments. This will let your neighbors know who your family is and will prevent them from becoming alarmed when seeing you stroll through the neighborhood. It may also be helpful to pass around snapshots of each of your family members.

8: Never put one of your new neighbors in the awkward position of having to refuse an invitation to join you for tea or any other meal. They will not feel safe letting you into their home and will be very nervous about entering yours. A better alternative is to schedule an outdoor activity—like a cookout or a Frisbee toss—in a public park or open field.

Now that I've said all this, I'm sure you have lots of questions. I have tried to anticipate them on the next few pages of this letter and have, therefore, offered to discuss some specific families. (Should you call me after reading this letter, I'd be happy to put you in touch with some of our satisfied customers.) Let me first say that these blacks—or these SPUBs, rather—have become well-assimilated into their white communities. I should note that although the number of blacks in American suburbs has increased 35 percent since 1980, our SPUBs are so unique, so special, and so assimilated, they are often not included in these census statistics! To put it simply, our SPUBs have become a model minority in each of our cities.

As we have been expanding these last six years, most SPUBs have followed the rules and have conducted themselves just as our SPUB handbook advises. These are people who want superior services: getting trash picked up twice a week, seeing city trees pruned regularly, and having burned-out streetlights replaced quickly. They appreciate the best public libraries and the finest pools and, of course, phenomenal schools: top scores, top administrators, and the best teachers.

But of course, Mr. Graham, I must admit there have been a few minor problems. Even though SPUBs have assimilated into the white community and know more about white America than any of their white neighbors care to—or need to—know about black America, a few SPUBs have expressed an interest in teaching their children a small amount of history about the black race and its culture.

For example, one of our SPUBs was a woman we had placed just outside Kansas City, in Shawnee Rise. (I'm not sure of the current population, but it's a lovely town with a fabulous country club—they're thinking about admitting a black family soon!) The SPUB's name was Latasha Chambers, and we had placed her three years earlier. At the time, she was the mother of an eighth-grader and was concerned that her son's school, Whitehill Middle

School, did not teach anything about slavery, civil rights, or Dr. Martin Luther King in any of its history classes. Not a single course so much as made reference to black people, except for a seventh-grade mimeographed TV trivia quiz handout that mentioned the actor Eddie "Rochester" Anderson from the old *Jack Benny Show*.

As I understand it, Mrs. Chambers and her husband were aghast one evening when, at the dinner table, their fourteen-year-old son, Yusuf (Mr. Graham, where do they get these names?), refused to believe that blacks had once been slaves.

"We figured that a top-rated school system," Mrs. Chambers told me and my Kansas City counterpart, "would have taken care of everything and told our son all about black history. We assumed we didn't have to mention any of it to him ourselves. That's what good schools are for."

So, Mr. Graham, that's when we had to send out one of our staff at the SPUB Foundation to get involved. Along with our representative, Mr. and Mrs. Chambers visited the Whitehill principal and demanded that the school's seventh-, eighth-, and ninth-grade curriculum include one or two items in addition to the Eddie "Rochester" Anderson TV trivia quiz question in its discussion of blacks in American history.

Being an open-minded administrator who believed in gaining consensus before acting, the school principal—I think his name was Dick Fortright—told them he wanted to first survey the parents of their students to see how many also felt this was important.

Well, one week later, the results from the survey of four black families and 372 white families were: One family (the Chamberses, of course) favored, and 375 families opposed the black history issue.

Principal Fortright apologized, but said none of the white families agree with the Chamberses. He said that the whites said black history didn't matter to them. And evidently, the other black families in town felt that rehashing all that black slavery stuff was unnecessary. The blacks in the town felt it reinforced negative stereotypes about blacks being poor and subservient. They wanted to distance themselves and bring closure to some of these outdated images. So Principal Fortright agreed with the majority that times were good for black people and that they should just drop this black history thing.

It became apparent to the Chamberses that they lived in a town with no other black families who cared about this issue. Principal Fortright reminded them that their town had no local NAACP, no local Urban League, no black church, no black political leaders, no black press or population (not even a black hair salon) where this issue could be discussed. Our staffer talked to them about all they should still be grateful for—the beautiful neighborhood, the nice stores, the great city services, the potential of one day joining the country club. So they eventually agreed that they lived in a superior town that offered excellent services. In essence, they really had very little to complain about, so they dropped the dispute.

Mr. Graham, I guess I should also mention here that some of the SPUB families, over time, have lost some of their black identity because they had to hide any interest in African American culture in order to succeed. They all really managed to become the model minority by *not thinking* of themselves as a minority. They became color blind to their own race. And this, of course, allowed them to escape from the psychological burdens most other blacks must bear.

I can imagine that this is somewhat confusing, so I'll explain. If you are an educated black person (and indeed you are, or I wouldn't have written to you), you might read about a lynching of a black in a Mississippi jail, or about the discrimination that black South Africans face, or about the starvation that African babies continue to suffer. You pay particular attention to these reports because both you and these other victims are black. But when you stop thinking about your blackness, you stop identifying with these unfortunate people. And that's when you free yourself from the burden. If you pretend you are colorless like our SPUBs, you no longer feel the pain of your own people!

Fascinating, isn't it?

And I'm sure you're wondering how the white neighbors have been reacting as we transform WATCH IT (White Areas That Can

Help Integration Thrive) communities into SPUB neighborhoods. To tell you the truth, it's been even better than we ever expected. Of course initially, affluent whites hated the idea of this form of desegregation. Then after seeing it work for a couple years, the white homeowners began to accept SPUBs, but just so long as the SPUBs remained out of view when the homeowners' other white friends visited. A few of the white homeowners went so far as insisting that SPUBs warn them when the SPUBs were to be out in the yard for long periods—and if they were to do so, that they might wear business attire or a small SPUB sign on their backs so visitors would know they weren't ordinary blacks. Of course we rejected this outrageous suggestion.

A clear positive result of the SPUB project was that white children on SPUB blocks were found to be more open-minded. I'm thinking of a SPUB we placed in West Palm Beach, Florida—the Joneses—a truly remarkable black family. Special in every way. Always setting standards in school and in the community—what you would call a real credit to the race. After seeing the Jones family, the white kids in town began to challenge their parents with insightful questions like, "I thought you said all blacks were poor, dirty, dangerous and stupid?" The more socially aware and progressive white parents had to pause and explain, "Well, they *are*—it's just that the Jones family is different from other blacks."

So although the white kids learned to accept a negative general impression of black people, the Jones family gave SPUBs, at least, a good name as being a different and special breed of black person. SPUBs, like the Jones family, were a true exception to the black rule.

But there's one bad apple in every bunch. Unfortunately, all the whites did not see the Joneses as an exception. When one of the white teenagers on the Joneses' street—Julie Whitehead—made plans to go to the movies with the black Jones boy, Emmett, Julie's parents insisted that although the Jones family is different from other blacks, they are still black. Emmett wrote to me and the Foundation about this and said that when Julie pressed for a better explanation, her parents stated that although she and *they* knew the Jones boy was a SPUB, no *other* whites would realize it.

Emmett broke it down for us and said that the Whitehead parents had told their daughter, "Think about the policeman down on Main Street or the woman who sells the popcorn at the theater—put yourself in their shoes. How are they going to know Emmett is okay?"

"Or worse," added Julie's mom, "think about the people sitting in that darkened theater. They'll be distracted—looking at you throughout the entire movie, nervously wondering why you two are together and whether you are going to hold hands or share your soda."

"And another thing," her father added, "the fact that you're with the Jones boy means that other blacks will likely sit close to you because they all want to be near their own kind, and then you'll be just surrounded by other blacks—and *they* won't *be* SPUBs. So God only knows what will happen to you then."

Mr. Graham, of course these whites are raising some valid points, but it's enough to make one's head spin. We couldn't anticipate everything! As you can see from our modest stationery here, we are just a nonprofit organization run by a few middle-aged women! And after all, much more good than bad has come out of the SPUB concept. A wonderful result of the program has been that many of the very young SPUB children are growing accustomed to being accepted and treated almost equally by the white neighbors and the white policemen, mailmen, and residents that know they live on the block. These young kids have demonstrated greater confidence and vigor.

Of course the program has had a few minor problems with the youngest SPUBs—like the day little ten-year-old Tawana Williams pulled her eight-year-old brother, Rodney, around the corner on Tawana's shiny new red wagon. You might have heard about this when it was written about in *Ebony* and the other black news magazines. It's actually not such a terrible thing, but it seems that the Williams kids were spotted by a neighbor who had never seen black children on his block before, so he snapped a photo of the kids with his Polaroid and then faxed it down to police headquarters. The squad car arrived moments later, spotted Tawana and Rodney, and stopped them before they returned to their own street.

Now, here's where some of the TV news media seemed to have reported things incorrectly. From what I heard, one of the officers shouted, "Freeze, you kids."

Some of the media blew this up and said that he had tried to shoot the kids, when in fact, he had actually just fired a warning shot straight up into the air. Then he assumed the firing position down on one knee with his .38 pistol drawn on Tawana. He did not shoot at her. He just screamed over to her, "Where'd you steal that wagon?"

Rendered speechless with fear, little Tawana grabbed her brother's tiny hand and attempted to run back home—leaving her wagon at the curb.

Only minutes later, the red wagon was in Officer Lockwood's patrol car trunk and Tawana and Rodney were handcuffed together in the backseat on the way to the precinct downtown. What a disaster!

But thank goodness it all worked out in the end. The children were released into their parents' custody a few hours later and the neighbor sent the boy and girl a note and a McDonald's gift certificate apologizing for having jumped to conclusions. I flew out there with another Foundation board member and we met with Mr. and Mrs. Williams to convince them that even with occasional hassles like this, being a SPUB was changing the course of American civil rights. We urged them to stick it out, and we explained that it had all been just a big misunderstanding.

In a way, I guess Tawana and Rodney were lucky to learn their lesson at a young age, because to be honest, we have seen some problems with postadolescent SPUBs who have ventured into other communities or to colleges where people knew nothing about the SPUB identification. For the first time in their lives—even though some are eighteen years old—SPUB kids found themselves being followed around in fruit and vegetable shops, passed up by cabdrivers, ignored by professors in their college seminars, not invited to weddings and birthday parties, or stood up at the last hour before a prom.

At first, Mr. Graham, these innocent SPUBs thought it might have been something they had said, or perhaps their breath or deodorant. They noted a harsher tone in their friends' and classmates' voices. They began to hear these people call them by strange, almost unintelligible words that sounded like "nigger," "jigaboo," "spook," "black water buffalo," "shvarze," "moulee" or "spearchucker."

From what I can tell, throughout their SPUB childhoods, these adolescent SPUBs had never heard these words. And because they were SPUBs, their parents never saw the necessity of telling them about derogatory words, bigotry, racial violence, or America's history of civil rights or discrimination against the black race.

Almost all were National Merit semifinalists and advanced-placement history students, but many had never heard of Dr. Martin Luther King, Frederick Douglass or Sojourner Truth. They had never seen *Ebony* magazine, and many didn't know the difference between Thurgood Marshall and Cab Calloway. Their SPUB parents thought it wasn't necessary to teach them that stuff.

When the SPUB kids ventured into other areas where distinctions between SPUBs and regular blacks blurred in the eyes and minds of whites, many of these young SPUBs tried desperately to prolong their experience. They did this by wearing distinctive pink-and-green buttons that read, **"I'm Different! I'm a SPUB!"**

Now, of course there are a few SPUB children who are in therapy today—still grappling with feelings of despair and low self-worth. Their parents, who had long before experienced racism, made a better transition to the SPUB experience.

But, Mr. Graham, I've rambled enough. I hope you'll fill out the forms, review the notebooks, and register you and your family into the SPUB Program. You've got the credentials that make black people proud. Feel free to contact me at my home phone of (312)333-4444.

Sincerely yours,
Anita Richardson

7

WHO'S RUNNING THIS RACE?

THE BLACK LEADERS WE LIKE
AND THE ONES WE DON'T

I'M NOT A rap singer with a tenth-grade education.

I'm not a professional basketball player with my own line of sneakers.

I've never done time in prison.

I wasn't raised in a riot-torn ghetto or saved by a Southern Baptist preacher.

And I don't wear gold teeth and speak in rhyming metaphors.

Does this mean that I could never be a black leader in the 1990s?

As a member of a race that is desperate for direction, I have, at times, found myself supporting black entertainers, athletes, crisis-chasing street ministers, pseudo-intellectuals, and others—hoping against hope that if I remained loyal to the end, I could help anoint a new leader for the black race.

I recently attended the wedding of a close childhood friend, a bond trader, at a country club overlooking a very turbulent Atlantic Ocean in East Hampton, Long Island. One of the club's members had somehow found his way into one of the rooms swarming with wedding guests and helped himself to the champagne flutes that were being passed around. I watched him turn to one of the servers—presumably a club worker he recognized—and begin to tell a series of jokes that I'd never heard before. They went something like this: "What do you call a white man surrounded by ten blacks?" Answer: "The quarterback." "What do you call a white man surrounded by nine hundred blacks?" Answer: "The warden." "What do you call a white man surrounded by ninety thousand blacks?" Answer: "The mayor."

I know that my friend and his new wife would have been appalled to hear this in the midst of their reception, but it didn't stop the server and intruder from laughing aloud.

The subject of black leadership is a topic ripe for debate among virtually any segment of the population: earnest college students, cynical politicians, thoughtful clergymen, journalists, business owners operating in diverse communities, and even wise guys at the country club. Sometimes the debate seeks to determine why there are so *few* responsible black leaders. Sometimes it attempts to determine why so many black leaders seem to constantly contradict each other. Sometimes it just seeks to poke fun at the idea of a black person serving as a leader at all.

At the heart of these conversations, whether well-meaning or malicious, is a fundamental question:

"Who is responsible for running the black race?"

Notwithstanding the vigorous debates, the immodest jokes, and the thoughtful discussions, it is a fact that black leadership is in disarray. As black people, we have allowed too many unqualified, ill-equipped individuals to take the reins of authority from intelligent, thoughtful black spokespeople. And more and more, we have allowed whites to finance and control the civil rights agenda only to later accuse these people of asserting too much authority in an arena that had once been our own. We have indulged outdated black organizations to the point of letting them become irrelevant and out-of-touch fiefdoms that serve no other purpose than to exist for their own sake. We have failed to realize that a thoughtful and eloquent lesser known black leader with management skills, a Ph.D., or a law degree can be of greater assistance to our cause than a provocative rap star or recognizable basketball player who rises to the level of "spokesman of the moment" after a hit record, a sneaker endorsement, or a winning season.

Moreover, we have been slow to recognize or admit that black leadership has failed black people. A historical examination of the African American community reveals that many factors have contributed to the undermining of effective black leadership. I believe that if we can address these issues with honesty and candor, we can then develop solutions that will help rebuild an important force that once existed for black Americans.

Factor 1: **The oldest and most respected black leadership organizations have become disorganized and ineffective because they have been unwilling to reevaluate their agenda and their methods for solving problems since the 1960s.**

Many black civil rights organizations have done a poor job identifying their goals and a worse job at selecting the executives who counsel and manage them. There is a consensus among the media and the black public that black organizations have become increasingly ineffective since the 1960s. Numerous reports profiling the NAACP, the National Urban League, and other groups raise the question of whether such black organizations still serve a real purpose.

Founded in 1909 and 1910, respectively, the NAACP and the National Urban League are, without a doubt, the two most influential black civil rights organizations in America today. After nearly nine decades, they have become increasingly and alarmingly bureaucratic and paternalistic. Governed by large, unwieldy boards—both organizations have boards with more than sixty members—they are often unable to act quickly in a crisis, and almost never able to maintain uniformity in policy and programs between their main headquarters and branch offices in different cities.

The fact that the Urban League has never had a black to chair its board and that during the last seventy-five years neither organization has hired a woman to serve as its director are just hints of how these groups have lagged behind the advancement of the very issues they were designed to monitor in the outside world.

Like CORE (Congress of Racial Equality) and SCLC (Southern Christian Leadership Conference), these groups have exhibited a tendency to appoint and hold on to middle-aged, sixty-something staffers and directors. They aggressively favor out-of-touch bureaucrats and ministers who earned their "civil rights seniority" by merely outliving their colleagues rather than select younger, more innovative leaders. This is not only a symptom of but also a cause of these institutions' falling out of touch with younger constituents and new methods, attitudes, and management techniques.

For example, CORE, which was founded in 1942, has been headed by the same leader—the outspoken and oftentimes outrageous Roy Innis—for more than twenty-five years. And SCLC has seen one of its cofounders, the energetic and respected septuagenarian Rev. Joseph Lowery, hold tightly to his organization's reins since 1957. Even with a relatively younger leadership, up until 1993 the NAACP attracted members with an average age of fifty-two.

All four of these groups have contributed immensely to the lives and opportunities of blacks and others, but there are problems on the horizon. Of all these groups, the eighty-six-year-old NAACP is clearly the most troubled. In addition to its ongoing fiscal problems, the group relies increasingly on contributions from white individuals and corporations, and is attracting less and less individual support. Moreover, board members have alleged that donors such as The Ford Foundation, Mobil Oil, Philip Morris, and General Motors have expressed ongoing dissatisfaction over the NAACP's mismanagement. Worst of all, the once invincible

NAACP suffers from a widely accepted image among blacks and whites that the organization has allowed radicals and charlatans to take over and use the group as their own personal pulpit. The NAACP, in fact, may have recently seen the worst year in its history—finally culminating with the August 20, 1994, dismissal of its executive director, Benjamin Chavis, a combative, confrontational man who led the group for all of sixteen months.

The organization's reputation was so badly damaged during Chavis's tenure that by the fall of 1994, responsible black leaders were working diligently to either redirect the group or to disassociate themselves from the organization altogether. The prominent black U.S. Federal Appeals Court judge Damon Keith publicly urged NAACP board members to remove Chavis in order to preserve the group's credibility.

Going even further at the NAACP Legal Defense and Educational Fund annual dinner on November 3, 1994, in New York's Plaza Hotel, that group's executive director, Elaine Jones, focused a major portion of her opening speech on making sure that the interracial audience of corporate contributors understood that neither she nor her organization had any relationship with the NAACP. And to bring her point home, a special message had been spread across four inches of the evening program's cover. In large block letters was a disclaimer message that resonated throughout the evening:

THE NAACP LEGAL DEFENSE AND EDUCATIONAL FUND, INC. (LDF) IS NOT PART OF THE NAACP . . . LDF HAS HAD FOR 30 YEARS A SEPARATE BOARD, PROGRAM, STAFF, OFFICE AND BUDGET.

That the NAACP was spiraling out of control had been foreshadowed by individuals for at least three years before that night at the Plaza.

In a March 31, 1993, profile of the NAACP, the *New York Times* had reported: "The National Association for the Advancement of Colored People . . . is in transition. And no one is quite sure where it's going." The article went on to discuss the failures, the successes, and the surprisingly uneven and sometimes unrelated activities of the organization that had at one time focused on voting rights, desegregation, and equal opportunity in employment.

In a June 10, 1994, article, the *Wall Street Journal* reported that "the NAACP, the nation's oldest and largest civil rights organization, is engulfed in what longtime supporters say is the worst financial and philosophical crisis in its eighty-five-year history." Current and former NAACP officials have added their own criticisms as well.

In a May 23, 1994, op-ed in the *New York Times,* Jack Greenberg, a Columbia Law School professor and former director of the NAACP Legal Defense and Educational Fund, pointed out that the NAACP (he was referring to the NAACP, not the Fund, which was his old employer and which had, indeed, been a completely separate organization since 1955) is suffering from a lost identity but trying to "renew itself" by embracing minister Louis Farrakhan, embattled City College professor Leonard Jeffries, and rap artist Sister Souljah. As others had, Greenberg argued that the NAACP is desperate to find a meaningful role that will once again make it an organization that blacks will believe is focused and relevant.

Greenberg's theory is well supported by the NAACP's current broad and unfocused range of programs. Defying all logic, the organization's breadth of projects expands each year—in spite of the fact that its membership and funding have continued to stagnate or shrink over the last thirty years. As an example, with 18,872,000 blacks in the country in 1960, the NAACP had a membership of over one million. Today, with nearly 30,000,000 blacks in the United States (a 63 percent increase), there are barely six hundred thousand NAACP members (a 40 percent decrease). The group's record for demonstrating its relevance and attracting enthusiastic black supporters is made to seem all the more pitiful, since sources report that more than 10 percent of the membership today is made up of nonblacks and that only 75 percent of that six hundred thousand are actually dues-paying members.

While extremely successful at working with the media to maintain its public image, the NAACP has had uneven success with the management of its wide range of programs. The organization has spread itself too thin to be consistently successful with its growing number of programs. The NAACP has, in effect, become the ultimate "McCivil Rights Organization": It tries to offer too many things to too many people, with too little funding. While valiant, it has become a foolhardy exercise.

For example, in addition to studying and advancing voting rights and housing desegregation, the organization runs the following: a national high school academic competition (ACT-SO), a health education program, a national teacher-training program, a national educational advisory group and educational summit, a high school scholarship program, a minority teacher recruitment program, an economic development program that negotiates and implements fair-share agreements with corporations, community development programs, minority vendor relationships, educational programs with clergy through the NAACP religious affairs department, housing discrimination advocacy through the NAACP housing department, job and career fairs through the NAACP labor department, stay-in-school programs through its youth and college department, the monthly *Crisis* magazine, the prosecution of environmental discrimination cases and police misconduct cases through the NAACP legal department, SAT college admissions test preparation clinics, programs with correctional officers and prison inmates through the NAACP prison department, and activities aimed at gaining equal opportunity for blacks in the military through the NAACP department of armed services and veteran's affairs. In addition to all of these programs, the NAACP also maintains a research office and a special-projects department.

It seems unfathomable that any national institution—particularly one with the NAACP's bare-bones budget of $15 million and frequent annual deficits ($3 million in 1994)—should be attempting to address the myriad issues that this organization's annual report suggests it is addressing. When the National Association for the Advancement of Colored People's incorporation was filed in 1911—two years after its founding—it had been decided that the activities of the group would be legal aid, organizing mass meetings, sponsoring investigations, and attracting publicity for discrimination issues. Over time, the boundaries of the NAACP's goals have been stretched to take in virtually every problem that black people might confront.

Although the NAACP tackles the wide range of problems with the best of intentions, the effect of its actions has been self-destructive. Since I served on the board of my local NAACP chapter and have participated in many NAACP programs as a teenager and an adult, I recognize, firsthand, the demands and requests made on the organization—particularly at the local level, where it seems to be most effective—by black people in need. But the willingness of NAACP leaders to reinvent the organization for every outsider needing support has created a situation in which the group is unable to please *any* blacks. Since the organization does not appear to limit its scope, the black public is constantly demanding the NAACP's assistance, regardless of the issue.

When the group doesn't respond, people become frustrated and resentful. The group then suffers from the high, impossible-to-satisfy expectations of the public—much the same way that the organization Rebuild L.A. (a group I volunteered with in 1993) suffered after it failed to communicate its purpose to south-central residents and business owners following the 1992 Los Angeles riots.

As Jack Greenberg pointed out in his May 1994 *New York Times* op-ed piece, young blacks feel that the NAACP can't relate to them. Urban working-class blacks accuse the group of favoring bourgeois and elite blacks. Affluent blacks, on the other hand, feel the group is reckless and shortsighted with its grass-roots approach and sudden overtures to militants and radicals like Nation of Islam minister Louis Farrakhan. Many insiders have expressed frustration with the group's recent alliances. Elaine Jones was particularly critical of the NAACP's embracing of Farrakhan.

Longtime NAACP activist and former board member Hazel N. Dukes published a letter in the July 4, 1994, issue of the *New York Times* asking the public to judge the NAACP on the basis of its work on equal rights as opposed to the alliances forged between Executive Director Chavis, Chairman William Gibson, and Farrakhan. Without directly criticizing the group's relations with the Nation of Islam, Dukes reminds the public that the local NAACP offices she controls as president of the New York State Conference of NAACP Branches "continue to work with our brothers and sisters in the Italian, Irish, Jewish, Roman Catholic, Muslim, Protestant, Chinese, gay, Caribbean, and Hispanic communities for our common interest in a just society." In recent years, the NAACP has seen some of its most prominent and responsible board members—people like Dukes, Percy Sutton, and Julian Bond—vacate their NAACP board positions in frustration.

And it is in the absence of responsible advisers like them that the NAACP finds itself embroiled in costly and embarrassing confrontations such as the messy sexual harassment suit filed in July 1994 by former NAACP employee Mary E. Stansel against Chavis and the organization. Several board members claimed that they learned of the suit only when it was reported by the media.

What they found even more frustrating was the allegation that Chavis had quietly agreed to pay Ms. Stansel up to $332,400 for an out-of-court settlement following a breach-of-contract suit. Supposedly, he reported this $332,400 charge merely as an NAACP legal expense.

A willingness to allow other black leaders and organizations to take on some of the problems in the "black universe" and a reevaluation of NAACP goals are desperately needed. These changes will also have the effect of helping blacks who need the guidance of certain organizations. With clearly outlined goals and programs, these overburdened organizations can lower, or at least change, the expectations that blacks and others have about them. Clearly outlined goals and programs will also allow the increasingly affluent and influential black middle and professional classes to offer their help and funds when they understand the agendas and the funding needed to carry out long-term plans.

As a dues-paying member of both the NAACP and the Urban League, and as one who recognizes the groups' contributions to my own life and lives of other blacks, I still realize how much more relevant these two groups might be if, at every level, they were run and advised not just by those inside the old establishment but by those who place a higher value on efficiency and change. Even the most basic aspects of an organization can make the difference between success and failure. Here is an example:

In the spring of 1994, I contacted both the local offices and national headquarters of each organization to check on the status of my membership and any dues I still owed. I was told by both organizations that the membership rolls were not computerized. As early as the 1992 annual report of the NAACP, outgoing executive director Benjamin Hooks stated in his letter to members that the national office was "computerized." Following my repeated calls, it took six weeks to learn of my membership status at the NAACP. After two calls to the national office of the Urban League, I was told that it had no central record of memberships—I was to check with my local branch. After making several calls to my local branch office over a two-month period in which I left messages and spoke to secretaries, I was told by a receptionist that I had paid $25 in the prior year but that she had no idea what I owed in the current year. She was also unable to explain why I had never received a single mailing from the Urban League.

It was similarly difficult to receive an application form to attend the two organizations' national conferences, which were to take place in July. I ordered both information packets in April. When I still hadn't received any information by the end of May, both national offices informed me that the conference was not until July and they were behind on the mailings. I received the Urban League brochure in early June, and I never received the NAACP material despite repeated calls to the national office in Baltimore. Finally, after contacting an executive in the NAACP labor department in late June, I was transferred to the conference department, where an administrator promised to fax a copy of the registration form. By this time, the application deadline had passed by nineteen days. With this type of mismanagement, I was saddened but not surprised when, on November 1, 1994, the organization ran out of cash and announced that it would have to temporarily stop paying its professional staff.

The NAACP is just one of the large black civil rights groups that could benefit from a reevaluation of its post-1960s agenda. The NAACP, the National Urban League, the Southern Christian Leadership Conference, and the Congress of Racial Equality are all credited with fueling the civil rights advances of the 1950s and 1960s through hundreds of boycotts, voter registration drives, marches, and peaceful sit-in demonstrations. There is no reason why they cannot continue to have a great impact on civil rights issues.

The Urban League was created, and remained for many years as, a social-service agency that avoided the boycotts, protests, legal controversies, and publicity that made the NAACP so influential. The Urban League instead focused on giving guidance to blacks who had migrated from southern rural areas to southern and northern urban areas. It aided them in job training, and it confronted company and government officials with demands for equal opportunity and integration among the corporate and governmental workforces.

Having always maintained a closer relationship with white industry leaders than other black organizations had, the Urban League distanced itself from many of the black protests that took place before the 1960s.

But the different evolution of these two organizations does not explain the confusion that has plagued them.

Because while evolution and change of direction are understandable as unanticipated problems and queries from the black community develop, black organizations start to become inefficient when they fail to communicate their change in focus to their executives, active members, contributors, clients, the media, and the general public they serve. Clients of the NAACP and Urban League no longer know what to expect from these organizations because the organizations have failed to redefine their mission. And this has left clients feeling frustrated and abandoned. Organization members who want to work or volunteer their time on certain programs are confused as they learn that certain programs have been replaced with others that have no relationship to prior ones. The Urban League has addressed this problem through the recent hiring of new executive director Hugh Price, a well-respected attorney with strong ties to the corporate and foundation worlds. The NAACP is still plagued by these issues.

The problems are magnified at the NAACP and Urban League because they are organizations that attempt to work from a combination of national offices and local chapters. Mixed messages, opposing agendas, and conflicting methods for tackling the same problems are a particular challenge when national black groups see their local chapters take on issues or set policies that fall outside the overall group's agenda.

Because each of the local affiliates in different cities are semi-autonomous, this has been a major problem for the National Urban League headquarters office. But no local-national office conflict was as troubling as the 1990 NAACP public relations crisis that followed President George Bush's nomination of the black conservative Clarence Thomas to the U.S. Supreme Court. NAACP executive director Benjamin Hooks announced that he was inclined to challenge the nomination but that the organization would hold its opinion until it had performed the necessary research into Thomas's past work and writings. No sooner had the national NAACP office said this than a local NAACP branch in Compton, California, announced to the press that it was giving its unqualified support to the conservative judicial nominee.

Alliances with racist radicals, infighting between local chapters and the national leadership, reliance on outmoded and inefficient internal office systems, and the acceptance of outdated or poorly designed agendas are issues that the NAACP and Urban League—as the two largest black organizations—need to address if they want to remain innovative and attract the next generation of blacks as members and contributors.

Factor 2: **Ever afraid of being labeled "elitist," the black power structure is reluctant to develop and implement what I call "socioeconomically based black leadership," which would more efficiently and effectively serve black people by dividing the black population's problems along economic lines.**

Can the interests of a black corporate executive who earns $125,000 a year and lives in the suburbs be met by the same black leader who is focused on solving the problems of a black $10,000-a-year inner-city single parent who receives public assistance and lives in public housing that is under siege from gangs and drug dealers?

The intuitive answer is no. If we were discussing any other ethnic group, it would be such an obvious answer that the question would appear silly and naive. However, both blacks and whites continue to believe that *one* person should be able to speak for increasingly divergent black interests. Up to this point, the agenda for black America has been defined almost exclusively by the needs of poor blacks.

Historically, and for good reason, the problems of impoverished blacks have drawn greater empathy from the media, governmental groups, and white benefactors. Because their problems have seemed more compelling, because many black organizations were designed to focus on the problems of poor blacks, and because of the lower-income blacks' lack of reticence in dramatizing their plight and calling out for assistance, the needs of middle- and upper-income blacks have long been eclipsed when it came to dictating the black civil rights agenda. No group in America speaks at a greater volume, marches with more determination, and attracts more news coverage than poor blacks who are proclaimed—both by the media and by themselves—to hold the mantle on who is authentically black in American society. The most visible civil rights activism leaves onlookers with the impression that the only blacks in the U.S. population and, therefore, worthy of attention are poor, urban, and uneducated. Statistics, though, reveal that blacks represent a wide range of incomes and lifestyles.

According to the U.S. Bureau of the Census, there are 29,986,000 African Americans living in the United States. Thirty-seven percent of that population consists of families earning less than $15,000 annually. Fifteen percent of all black families have incomes between $35,000 and $50,000. And another 15 percent of black families have incomes in excess of $50,000. Approximately 5 percent of all black family incomes exceed $75,000. Although 57 percent of all blacks live in urban areas, 27 percent live in suburban communities and 16 percent reside in rural areas. Nearly 53 percent live in the South, while 9 percent live in the West and another 38 percent are evenly divided between the urban areas of the Midwest and Northeast. According to the Bureau of Labor Statistics, almost 23 percent of all employed blacks are laborers, while 50 percent are in service, technical, or administrative support jobs, and another 16 percent hold managerial or professional jobs. Approximately 11 percent of all blacks are unemployed.

It is because of these differences in income, employment status, and lifestyle that we need black leaders from a range of distinct backgrounds. Our race needs black leaders who are as diverse as its population: as affluent and well-versed on the professional black class and corporate world as Hugh Price, the recently appointed National Urban League head who graduated from Amherst and Yale Law School before moving on to positions in public television and Rockefeller Foundation. And as street-smart and passionate as Rev. Al Sharpton, who was born into a middle-class family only to see his father abandon it, forcing Sharpton and his mother to move into cramped quarters in the working-class neighborhood of Flatbush, Brooklyn. His mother began working as a maid in order to support the family's new lifestyle. Sharpton's sensitivity to the working class was heightened by his teenage experiences as a director with Reverend King's Operation Breadbasket and other grass-roots groups.

Although Price and Sharpton have dramatically different experiences, and although each is evolving because of his own goals and his constituencies' concerns, both are necessary to the success of black America. Their value lies in the fact that they focus on different methods and different issues that impact on the black community. Without ever consciously choosing to favor one black group over another, Price and his organization have distinguished themselves as being particularly skilled at creating partnerships with white corporate America, as well as bringing prominent black business executives into black schools to build a black professional class.

Sharpton, on the other hand, has proven his talent at organizing public protests on behalf of inner-city disenfranchised black victims or of blacks unfairly accused of criminal activity. Although sometimes disruptive, and oftentimes dramatized for the benefit of the media, the marches and protests organized by Sharpton are effective at drawing attention to the problems of people who deserve to be helped. With the possible exception of his involvement in 1986 with the representation of alleged kidnapping victim Tawana Brawley in upstate New York, Sharpton has directed most of his energy to helping working-class urban individuals and families who have been ignored or mistreated by society, government, or the private sector. His coalitions in the inner city (like those of Rep. Maxine Waters in south-central Los Angeles or Ministers Wyatt Tee Walker and Calvin Butts in New York's Harlem) are just as important and as necessary as the corporate ties forged by Price and the Urban League.

For several decades following the emancipation of black slaves in the South, black leaders such as Frederick Douglass, Mary McLeod Bethune, and Ida B. Wells focused on the basic concerns that blacks of all backgrounds during that period faced—the right not to be lynched or harassed because of their color, the freedom to exercise their right to vote, and freedom from *de jure* discrimination in housing and education.

The struggle for equal treatment in these basic areas continues in some pockets of the country. But in most cases, these rights are no longer so blatantly flouted without legal challenge and prosecution. Today, the challenge has more often been to address a wide range of concerns that tend to fall along socioeconomic lines and deal with quality-of-life issues.

Today, it is virtually impossible for any one segment of black America to agree on which black problems deserve the greatest attention and resources. What one group sees as compelling may very well be irrelevant to another group.

The black professional class, for example, is debating issues such as the glass ceiling in corporations and its inability to move into important business networks like private golf and country clubs. The middle class, on the other hand, is concerned about housing discrimination, school busing in the suburbs, affirmative action, and white flight from public schools. Simultaneously, working-class and poverty-stricken blacks argue that gang violence, police brutality, teen pregnancy, AIDS awareness, and unemployment are the most crucial issues to address. It is likely that each of these three different groups has a different opinion about the magnitude of the problems of the other group. For instance, it would not be surprising to learn that a working-class black activist would have difficulty empathizing with a black accountant whose membership is rejected at a country club where he would meet potential clients. Even worse, that working-class activist might actually perceive this ambitious black accountant as espousing self-absorbed, elitist views that create the basis for harming all other black people.

The only logical solution to this dilemma of addressing divided interests and concerns is to implement what I call "socioeconomically based black leadership"—dividing black problems and concerns along socioeconomic lines and assigning certain problems to certain leaders.

What black America needs is a division of labor among black leaders. For example, leaders of poor, less powerful blacks might design a platform that focuses on such issues as the quality of public housing, AIDS awareness, teen pregnancy prevention and care, getting guns off the streets and out of schools, voter registration, job-training programs, truancy among students, the death penalty, and treatment of the incarcerated. Those spokespeople who focus on the middle-class black population might target such issues as multiculturalism in the suburban public schools, affirmative action in education and employment, discrimination in bank loan offices, redlining of suburban house buyers, and other forms of housing discrimination. And finally, those advocates who address the concerns of the professional black class might establish a platform that focuses on such problems as the glass ceiling in corporate America, the support of black colleges and arts institutions, minority representation on corporate boards, corporate set-asides and vendor programs, and the dwindling number of black Ph.D.'s in research and teaching.

Such a realignment of responsibilities would be far superior to the current situation in which many organizations and leaders are addressing the same problems, causing what I call "leadership overlap." I use this term to suggest that as opposed to being divisive or at conflict, there are well-meaning black leaders who have the same goals and utilize the same methods but are repeating programs and campaigns that overlap with the programs and campaigns of other leaders who are already successful at reaching the exact same people. Leadership overlap unnecessarily exhausts resources and invites a great amount of inefficiency.

An even more dangerous aspect of leadership's overlap is leaders who try to solve problems that deviate from those which their professional training and expertise have prepared them.

At first blush, to most blacks, this type of compartmentalizing might seem elitist and divisive. But socioeconomically based black leadership would not only improve both the efficiency and the effectiveness of civil rights organizations and leaders, it would also allow for a more equal distribution of efforts—giving attention where it is needed as opposed to where the constituents have the most clout. If only the most competent of leaders were assigned to address certain issues, we would be more likely to find solutions in a short time period. After all, our primary concern is that the problem be solved, not to debate who should get credit for having solved it.

For instance, imagine what could be accomplished on a long-term basis for blacks if Rev. Jesse Jackson were permitted to focus his attention for a four- or five-year period on addressing only those issues that specifically affected the black working class—one of the areas where his talents have been virtually unparalleled. He has had tremendous success on dozens of problem issues, but that success has been diffused because it has never been concentrated in one area or focused on one group of constituents. Jackson has done things for the black poor, the black rich, the black middle class, blacks in the military, as well as blacks and minorities in third-world countries.

It is hard not to praise Jackson when he has tackled such a wide range of problems facing the black community. It is a tribute to his intellect, energy, and charisma that he can serve so many different groups, but he is nonetheless less effective in his work when local black groups and communities demand that he make himself available for every local conflict or dispute.

Jackson has proven himself in a wide range of circumstances, including organizing voter-registration drives; working with gang leaders; organizing crime summits; getting country clubs to offer better benefits to workers; negotiating the release of hostages in foreign countries; staging boycotts of baseball teams that don't hire black management; spearheading foreign diplomacy projects dealing with Africa, Haiti, and the Arab world; convincing auto companies and fast-food companies to open their dealerships and franchises to affluent black business investors; raising interest and money for black political leaders; and running a host of other projects.

The list of Jackson's accomplishments is mind-boggling, yet the demands that are made on Jackson by the black community are ongoing. And it is hard to criticize the end result of his individual projects, because as long as he is still managing them, they remain effective. But guess what happens when we suddenly throw another crisis at him and demand that he negotiate a solution to a problem three thousand miles away from the last one? What happens to the once troubled community that has now been calmed by Jackson's intervention? As Jackson moves to the next high-profile issue that is demanding his help, who picks up where he left off? No one, and that's part of the problem. We appreciate that Jackson has solved our problem, but we have set up no organizational structure to take over this problem in the future.

Black America needs a civil rights program and approach that is not only more organized but also promises greater continuity and stability. As conscientious as he is, Jackson has become the moving target that can't be hit, criticized, or held responsible. Because he's given help to every group of blacks, and because there is always another group waiting for his arrival, no one group can hold his attention on a permanent basis. He is accountable to no group, and as long as he moves from issue to issue, attracting attention to a cause, solving some problems, merely touching upon others, he evades criticism and fails to give any single group of blacks true stability and continuous direction.

In executing socioeconomically based black leadership, one need not upset the philosophies of civil rights leaders or the organizational structure of any civil rights group. The goal is just to make these leaders and organizations more efficient at, and more tied to, what they've accomplished in the past. With stable leaders who will remain their advocates on an ongoing basis, black people will move beyond their problems.

The first step in implementing this leadership approach would be to identify a bipartisan group that could serve as a type of "clearinghouse," as well as serve a "legislative" function. This group could review problems and then assign individual leaders and organizations to address those problems. An ideal candidate would be a civil rights organization that is already recognized and accepted as an umbrella group for other black organizations. The Leadership Conference on Civil Rights, founded in 1950, which already acts as an umbrella group for nearly two hundred organizations, would be a good candidate for this clearinghouse function. Such an umbrella organization would ask major black civil rights groups and leaders to join a consortium where "member" organizations and member leaders agree to work together for certain specified goals.

The umbrella group would ask member groups and member leaders to agree to allow a moderate percentage of their projects (perhaps 20 to 25 percent) to be placed under the codirection of this umbrella group. It would ask the leaders to submit a summary of their prior ten years of programs, which would detail their target constituents, funds raised, contributors solicited, and projects sponsored during that period.

In conjunction with this information, each member leader and member organization would submit a five-year plan explaining which black-related problems and which black clients would be targeted in the future. Using this proposal and other data, the umbrella organization would then determine which specific projects and which black constituents would best be served by the particular leader. The umbrella group would consider the geographical strengths, available funds, and staff experiences of each member organization but focus most of its attention on the socioeconomic group best served by the skills of the particular leader or organization. After the umbrella group has made a determination, each leader and organization would then be charged with concentrating at least 20 to 25 percent of its efforts and funds on issues affecting the targeted socioeconomic group. The umbrella group might even require that its member organizations and leaders pool the funds into a common fund to be overseen by the umbrella group.

The practice of designating or creating an entity that distributes pooled funds for charitable causes is already followed by the well-respected United Way organization. But my framework would go even farther and allow for the collaboration of expertise and learned experience. While it may be a challenge for the egos of well-known and respected leaders to relinquish some of the breadth of their power, such a practice would contribute to the common good.

The concept of "legislating" specific responsibilities or actions to certain "member" groups is not very different from the manner in which admissions offices at Ivy League universities are accustomed to working now. Clearly in the position of competing for many of the same students, the seven colleges belonging to the Ivy League have, over the years, developed a very close working arrangement, where they have agreed to coordinate their application format and deadlines, admission notification dates, and offers for financial aid. Even more analogous is the agreement negotiated between the NAACP and Urban League fifty years ago when the two groups first agreed not to duplicate each other's projects in the civil rights battle.

The idea of getting organizations to agree to focus a modest percentage of their work in a particular area where they have already demonstrated competence and success should allow member leaders and member organizations to feel sufficiently unrestrained to still invest in new areas that were not assigned to them.

Through coalitions and ongoing communications between black leaders and black organizations, talented black leaders and well-meaning black organizations will become better organized and more successful at solving problems in our communities. As it stands now, we have many organizations investing hundreds of thousands of dollars into areas where they have little experience or where more experienced leaders and organizations are already investing resources. Encouraged to divide responsibilities and resources along socioeconomic lines, these groups can get a better grasp on the specific community they are trying to serve, or a new grasp on areas that have not yet been addressed.

Factor 3: **The black public has not yet learned how to utilize black leaders who represent a multirace constituency.**

When Carl Stokes became the first black mayor of a major American city—Cleveland—in 1967, his election created a dilemma for black people. David Dinkins's election created the same dilemma when he became the first black mayor of New York City. And so did Douglas Wilder when he was elected governor of Virginia, Tom Bradley when chosen mayor of Los Angeles, Harold Washington when named mayor of Chicago, and Carol Moseley-Braun when she became a U.S. senator from Illinois.

Although each of these individuals was closely identified with by black citizens and recognized as a leader by the larger black community, Stokes, Bradley, Washington, Dinkins, Wilder, and Moseley-Braun were all political activists whose successful elections were facilitated by a coalition of both black and white supporters.

In spite of the fact that the elections of Dinkins, Wilder, and Moseley-Braun relied on a great deal of financial and voter support from nonblacks, many blacks still considered these politicians to be their "black leaders": not just leaders who happened to be black, but black politicians who were expected to speak out on behalf of black issues and to espouse, support, and favor *black* views over all other views. They were different from Edward Brooke, the black man elected to the U.S. Senate by Massachusetts in 1966. Since he served as a Republican when most blacks were supporting the Democratic Party and the liberal civil rights legislation of Kennedy and Johnson, few blacks looked to Senator Brooke for leadership and assistance on their problems. Politicians like Bradley, Dinkins, Wilder, and Moseley-Braun were the champions who were going to be held to the highest possible standard of blackness.

This was an unfair standard for any black politician. And it proved to be an insurmountable burden for several. Mayor David Dinkins in particular. No matter what he did in the area of increased minority hiring, greater minority vendor set-asides, or even his reluctance to criticize blacks who staged an extended and unpleasant boycott of a Korean store in Brooklyn, Dinkins was consistently faulted by black residents for showing favoritism toward Jews and other white New York residents.

Just one month before the 1993 election, the *New York Times* ran an October 4 front-page story entitled "Disappointed Black Voters Could Damage Dinkins's Bid," which foreshadowed the injury that complacent, dissatisfied, spoiled, or petty blacks would inflict upon the city's first black mayor by failing to vote on election day. Blacks around the city gave their opinion on Dinkins's candidacy. According to the *Times* article, a manager at a financial services company said Dinkins was not attentive to black communities in New York: "He's trying to please one group in the city at the expense of his core constituency: the African Americans." The article pointed out that there was a feeling among black voters "that in his effort to be seen as an impartial steward . . . Dinkins has catered more to white constituents."

Placed in the awkward position of needing to prove his loyalty to his own people without jeopardizing his alliances with the white public that he was also charged with representing, Mayor Dinkins was criticized by all. Eventually, white conservatives, many of whom were Irish or Italian voters from the Bronx, Queens, and—in particular—Staten Island, blasted him for caring only about black issues.

Even New York's premier black paper, the *Amsterdam News,* questioned Dinkins's loyalty to his black constituents. In 1993, numerous letters and op-eds suggested that black citizens rightfully expected Mayor Dinkins to serve them first. It became clear that many black voters had overlooked the contributions that Dinkins had made: his creation of coalitions between different racial and ethnic groups, his support of multicultural issues in the schools, his increased appointments of blacks and women to judicial and executive positions, and his insistence that the city and any vendors working with the city be required to maintain a higher percentage of black and minority employees.

Ungrateful, many blacks failed to realize the kind of "black-issue support" they could get—and had been getting—from Dinkins, and therefore failed to enthusiastically support him in his 1993 reelection bid. Many, including liberal black newspaper columnist

Bob Herbert, blamed Dinkins's loss by a forty-four-thousand-vote margin on black people's failure to come out and vote. In virtually every black neighborhood in the city, including central Harlem and Bedford-Stuyvesant, black voter turnout was down from where it had been in the prior mayoral election. It hovered somewhere around a dismal 60 percent. In the end, black residents lost the most when they deserted him at the polls and allowed the conservative Rudolph Giuliani to become the first Republican in twenty-five years to be elected mayor in the mostly Democratic city. With Democrats outnumbering Republicans five-to-one in the city, the election was an embarrassment to the Dinkins camp. When Giuliani abolished the Office of African American Affairs, shut down the personnel department's Office of Equal Employment Opportunity, announced a group of cabinet appointees that were mostly white, then promised to dismantle various affirmative action programs that aided minority vendors, it took little time for black people to recognize how much Dinkins really had done for us.

This example bears out the need for black people to learn how to utilize and understand black politicians who are elected by non-blacks and who are elected to serve more than just an all-black population. To begin with, we must stop trying to gain these black leaders' support for our issues by merely appealing to them on a purely racial level. Instead, we must appeal to them on moral, ethical, legal, intellectual, and economic grounds. By using such approaches, we provide the leader with the arguments that he will use to justify his support of our causes. An example of this was the moral and ethical arguments put forth by Senator Moseley-Braun in early 1994 when she demanded that the Senate stop renewing the copyright on the Confederate flag. By arguing that the flag represented a shameful period of this country's history, she convinced her fellow senators to vote in the way that black citizens would want, yet she avoided turning the vote into an "us against them" racial battle.

Similarly, we must recognize that we cannot approach a black official who represents multirace constituencies and demand that he act as an advocate only for black people any more than we would want a white official to aid only the white segment of his black and white constituents.

Furthermore, we cannot hold black elected officials to the same standards that we hold the heads of black civil rights organizations. Civil rights leaders have a mandate to espouse those views that advance the "black cause." Elected black officials, however, must balance the views of diverse groups.

And finally, we must accept that, like white politicians, black politicians who serve a multirace constituency are going to be most responsive to those citizens who have the greatest impact on that politician's political success. While politicians will hopefully be guided by their own moral compass and their own political ideology, they will also be greatly influenced by the voices of citizens who vote and who contribute time and resources to that politician's campaign. When blacks fail to demonstrate their voting and economic power, their voice becomes eclipsed by others who attempt to influence the politician.

Whites are often attacked as racist when they accuse blacks of being lazy for not voting and of being impractical for not contributing funds to politicians. Can we still call them racist when the politicians that we are failing to support are black or are extremely supportive of black interests?

Many of my white friends were surprised when they saw me volunteering for and contributing to both Jesse Jackson's 1984 and 1988, then Bill Clinton's 1992 presidential campaigns, and when they saw me write checks for the campaigns of Carol Moseley-Braun, Dinkins, Mark Green, and Mike Woo—candidates I couldn't even vote for, since I was never an Illinois, New York City, or Los Angeles resident. In all honesty, I wasn't upset that my white friends were surprised. I was, however, disturbed by the response of my black friends: people who were well educated, savvy, and high-salaried.

"I can't believe you actually give money to politicians who don't even represent your district," a black banker friend said to me. "I've never even given to Dinkins and I *live* in New York City."

How familiar this sounded. For years, we blacks have complained that we lack power and influence because we lack money and representation. My banker friend earns in excess of a hundred thousand dollars. But like the less affluent black man who claims he can't afford to contribute ten dollars to a local black or white politician who supports black causes, my friend won't contribute either. Is it because he's stretched to his financial limit? This can't be the case because I know he contributes to black political activist groups. I believe it is primarily because he can't fathom how his contribution to a single candidate—one with multiracial, multiethnic supporters—will ever translate into a direct benefit for him, the black citizen. His is a shortsighted and naive analysis of the political process—one with which blacks seem to be stuck.

We must acknowledge that most black leaders—even those who are elected by a mixed-race constituency, can have a role in advancing black causes. We may have to alter our approach or our pleas for assistance, but we should not overlook these individuals simply because they have gained the appeal of people outside our race.

Factor 4: **Blacks expend too much effort placating an arrogant white media and public that want us to select a single leader who speaks for the entire black race.**

There is no single leader who speaks for all Irish Americans, Jews, Italian Americans, Hispanics, Asian Americans, or women. And there is certainly no one leader who is proclaimed to speak for all white people. So why is there an ongoing struggle in my community to convince the white press and white public that there is no single black leader who speaks for all black people?

The fact that black leadership is dominated by individuals who come from the working-class and grass-roots movement is already a complicating factor, but what makes matters even more complex are the attempts by whites to reduce millions of black voices into one message and one spokesman who speaks for all of us.

The April 4, 1994, *New York* magazine cover story typifies white America's approach to black leadership. An analysis of black leaders in New York City, the cover story featured a photo of Rev. Al Sharpton. As the table-of-contents page explained, the story was intended to address the question, "Who will speak for New York's black community in the post-Dinkins era? There's no clear successor." Note the singular form of "successor."

White people and the mainstream media approach blacks in America as though there were, or should be, one spokesperson for us and, hence, just one spokesperson for them to look to in order to gain an understanding of what "all black people are thinking today." In the past, at one time or another, that anointed person has been Roy Wilkins, Martin Luther King, Malcolm X, Whitney Young, Fannie Lou Hamer, Stokely Carmichael, Shirley Chisholm, Vernon Jordan, Julian Bond, Bill Cosby, Benjamin Hooks, Spike Lee, and others. Whether the media were to choose Rev. Jesse Jackson, former DNC chairman Ron Brown, minister Louis Farrakhan, the Rev. Al Sharpton, Senator Carol Moseley-Braun, former Congressional Black Caucus head Kweisi Mfume, or Wyatt Tee Walker, the dynamic pastor of Harlem's powerful Canaan Baptist Church, the selection reveals nothing more than the media's complete disregard of and lack of respect for the diverse messages offered by individual activists and individual civil rights organizations.

More than a few reasons explain the white public's disregard of our diverse messages. By choosing to anoint and focus on just one of us—sometimes the most vocal of us, and at other times, the most powerful of us—they can eliminate the effort it would require to learn the subtleties and nuances of our diverse people and our diverse opinions. Using this approach, they can rely on general impressions—and for a significant percentage of the white public, an "impression" about blacks is a satisfactory threshold for them to reach.

They are the proverbial Martians landing on earth, with ray guns pointing. "Take us to your leader" is their only request. It seems that neither Martians nor white people have the time or

inclination to converse with powerless beings whose words, however thoughtful, might reveal a group's varied opinions or subtle
differences in attitude.

Some of the whites who insist that the black community
choose a leader to speak for it secretly hope that the process has
the result of marginalizing certain black leaders—particularly ones
whites find especially offensive or threatening. And if that doesn't
happen on its own, some whites are more than willing to step in
themselves and anoint a leader who is either powerless or inept.
The result of this, of course, is to undermine the power of the
more willful, independent, and capable. With this impression
reflected in the press, the public (whites, and sometimes blacks as
well) soon begins to ignore these "unchosen" black (unchosen by
whites, that is) leaders as well.

And if any black voices dare to challenge that individual's
selection, the white media's paternalistic declaration has the additional effect of making us seem petty, divided, and unwilling to
accept the obvious. And it is because we are seen as such a mono-
lith that whites can't imagine that we don't all agree with what
we've been told is best for us.

White people sometimes speak nostalgically of a time "when
black people were better controlled" and when we were peacefully
unified under "the direction of one reasonable black leader—Dr.
Martin Luther King, Jr." In actuality, even at the height of his pop-
ularity in the national white media, Dr. King was never a welcomed figure in the white mainstream, and blacks were always a
part of the myriad groups led by people such as Malcolm X, A.
Philip Randolph, Ralph Bunche, James Farmer, Whitney Young,
Adam Clayton Powell, Roy Wilkins, and later, Stokely Carmichael
and Eldridge Cleaver, to name a few of the well-known blacks
who held the respect of members of the black community at the
same time as King.

Perhaps what is more offensive than white people bullying us
into choosing a single leader to represent our community is the
notion that whites can actually enter the black community and

select the black individual themselves. Such brazen behavior on the part of whites often gives rise to white-bossed-and-bought black leaders who not only fail to advance the causes of black people but who serve to reinforce negative black stereotypes and enforce a white political agenda. In the past, white conservatives have invested a great deal of money in fringe blacks who are eager to use their black skin as a passport to a political future. Such was the case in the spring of 1967, when the New York State Republican organization went looking for a black Harlem candidate to oppose Adam Clayton Powell's candidacy for an additional term in Congress. The state Republicans approached and supported James Meredith, a black man who had become famous for integrating the University of Mississippi yet who had no true connection to the Harlem community or to black people's concerns in the New York area.

White political and media representatives continue to assert their power and influence over black people in more subtle ways as they attempt to advance their own notion and image of the black leader. Such an act was recently committed by Morgan Entrekin, a bright and popular white book publisher, when he published the 1993 autobiography *Monster,* which told the story of Kody "Monster" Scott, a formerly violent black Crips gang leader who was serving a prison sentence after having been convicted of robbing, shooting, and dismembering victims in south-central Los Angeles. Entrekin launched the book with an announcement that *Monster* may very well be "a primary voice of the black experience." *Monster*'s author photo shows Scott shirtless, with sunglasses, bulging muscles, and a machine gun. Although Entrekin was to later revise his statement and apologize to civil rights leaders who were justifiably offended by this white man's suggestion that uneducated, violent social deviants could be labeled as "a primary voice" in the black community, this remains an example of white people's desire not only to select our spokespeople but to also characterize us as a group fit to be represented by criminals.

Similarly, in its attempt to declare leadership spokespersons among the black community, the white press resorts to the most inappropriate black celebrities to represent or comment on the black experience. For example, *Esquire* magazine commissioned articles from prominent American writers for its October 1993 "Sixtieth Anniversary" issue. Among the group was William F. Buckley, George Plimpton, Norman Mailer, Jimmy Breslin, and other writers and intellectuals. The only black author represented among this prominent group of writers was, ironically, not a writer at all. *Esquire* had selected none other than the crude rap artist Ice-T, who had gained national prominence with his song "Cop Killer," which glamourized the killing of white police officers. The first few sentences of this rap star's *Esquire* article (which was entitled "Sometimes a Woman Can Be One of the Boyz") were as follows:

> Yo, listen up. They figured out the game.
> A 90's woman is out hawking sex just like you.
> You ain't playing her no more. She's playing
> you. She will dump you, just like a dude will.
> She will fuck you and not call you back. She
> will mess with your mind . . .

With all of the black writers and spokespeople available today, it was disturbing that a national magazine would have settled on this crude singer and a barely literate 250-word slang-filled essay as the only representation of the mood of the black community.

It is indeed disappointing to watch as the larger white public rewards the most deviant members of the black community. The message being sent to white America and to the black middle and upper classes is that an African American person is not authentically black, and will not be permitted to speak for or about the black community, unless he was raised in the projects, dropped out of school, spent time in prison, experimented with drugs, talks jive on the street, and bore a child out of wedlock.

Even today, there are white intellectuals who shamelessly attempt to reach into the black community to select and anoint unlikely role models for black citizens. In a surprisingly presumptuous March 25, 1992, *Wall Street Journal* essay entitled "Up From Dependency," the conservative writer Dinesh D'Souza not only suggested that the black community select a black voice to direct its approach to problems, he went so far as to reach back in history and select a leader that he believed would best serve black people in the category of role model: Booker T. Washington.

"In frustration," says D'Souza, "many young blacks are today turning to the rage of Malcolm X. But for a more constructive outlook, they and the NAACP would be wiser to turn to the rejected wisdom of Booker T. Washington."

One of the most influential black leaders of his time, and the only one to gain the almost unqualified respect of powerful white leaders during the late nineteenth and early twentieth centuries, Washington moved into white circles because he told whites what they wanted to hear: that black people should blame themselves for their inability to advance in society. In an environment where blacks were being lynched at dramatic rates in the South and kept unemployed and uneducated in virtually every pocket of the country, Washington's remarks were peculiar at the very least. Washington, at worst, sold out black people (by his acceptance of segregation) in order to get close to whites who would provide him a platform and financial support. And at best, he was too deluded to see the folly in his arguments. Himself born a slave, he made the bizarre argument in the late 1800s that recently freed black slaves who lacked an education, jobs, self-esteem, and the right to vote could get wherever they wanted if they worked hard and gained "the respect and confidence of their neighbors." This statement was clearly disingenuous in an environment where both the laws and the public sentiment worked to keep blacks unskilled, uneducated, and unemployed. Leaders and their remarks have to be taken in the context in which they were born—and it is absurd and disingenuous to state that the misguided Booker T. Washington and his leadership style has somehow become more palatable with age.

When W. E. B. DuBois and other truly committed black leaders suggested that Washington was an apologist who gave intellectually dishonest white people the opportunity to assuage their guilt, they were on target. So it is not a surprise when conservatives like D'Souza—who know virtually nothing about black people of any socioeconomic class—would today advise that we look to the ghost of—or some reincarnation of—Booker T. Washington, the consummate "sellout," as a model for our modern-day leader.

What D'Souza and many white conservatives appear to be asking us to do is surround ourselves with black leaders who either: (1) absolve white people of all responsibility, knowledge of, and involvement in black people's problems, or (2) lead in such an ineffective manner as to render black people powerless, silent, and out of the way of white people. While such attempts by white conservatives are arrogant and calculated, they are nonetheless another factor in the erosion of black leadership.

As a white, more conservative America challenges us to select a single black leader whom it can approve of, we must remember that the only group we need to satisfy when selecting black leaders is ourselves.

Factor 5: **After a generation of black people have seen whites unfairly vilify responsible black leaders, American blacks have become cynical and distrustful of any white scrutiny or legitimate criticism of our leadership.**

The cynicism that developed among us as we watched white Americans undermine the most responsible and compassionate of black leaders cannot be ignored. I believe that this cynicism and later reluctance to accept findings of corruption in our own people are the result of years of unfair attacks on our most prized leaders, dating back to the 1940s with Paul Robeson and continuing through the mid-1960s with Congressman Adam Clayton Powell.

Beginning in 1941, the FBI, under the direction of J. Edgar Hoover, maintained a program of ongoing surveillance and finally a campaign to discredit actor, attorney, and activist Paul Robeson, one of black America's most popular and most accomplished heroes. Already a major singer and stage and screen actor in the United States and Europe, Robeson used his star power to speak on behalf of liberal organizations to criticize the second-class treatment of black Americans and to encourage blacks to spend less energy on World War II and more on gaining their civil rights within the U.S. borders. Hoover's anti-Robeson campaign was aggressive, divisive, and calculated to not only undermine the influence that the eloquent Robeson was exerting over blacks and other liberals but also make him appear unstable and unpatriotic.

While Robeson had many friends who belonged to the Communist Party, he was never a member of the Communist Party. That did not stop Hoover from launching an aggressive campaign to convince white and black Americans not only that he was a Communist but that he was also eager to endanger the advances that black people had already made in the United States. In fact, Hoover's attack was so successful that the media often openly referred to Robeson as an anti-American Communist. When the Associated Press misquoted full sentences from a Paris speech that Robeson gave in April 1949, he was certified as anti-American because of the news organization's fabricated anti-American remarks that it attributed to Robeson. Although his speech criticized the U.S. military's rules of segregation, the Associated Press reported his speech as stating that blacks should never fight on behalf of the United States or defend it against the Soviet Union.

Unfortunately for Robeson and even more unfortunately for the black cause in general, Hoover's scheme caused white and black admirers to strongly repudiate him and his alleged comments. Hoover's ability to raise questions among prominent business and civic leaders, to encourage suspicion wherever Robeson performed or lectured, and to persuade the press to print negative fabricated accounts of Robeson and his views worked to damage the man's reputation. Even prominent blacks such as Roy Wilkins of the NAACP, Congressman Adam Clayton Powell, Jr., and Mary McLeod Bethune of the National Council of Negro Women joined liberal whites in lambasting Robeson for his alleged Communist ties and anti-American views. Because of Robeson's intellect—he was class valedictorian from Rutgers College and a graduate of Columbia Law School—charisma, compassion, and ability to guide blacks and other disadvantaged people, his repudiation was a devastating and calculated blow to the black community's future. It was not until long after the damage was done that the black press and black community discovered how Robeson had been unfairly smeared.

This pattern was to repeat itself in 1963 when many in the black community turned against one of the most powerful and successful black politicians the country had ever seen. After being elected to office in 1944, Rep. Adam Clayton Powell, the first congressman from Harlem, rose in seniority to become the powerful head of the Education and Labor Committee by 1962. A combination of Powell's confrontational style and his aggressive challenge of many white businesses' labor practices caused the press, government, and the white community to launch various attacks on Powell. These attacks were unsuccessful because his black constituents refused to listen to his white critics—at least until 1963.

White critics were finally able to sway black leaders in the black community once the white press offered evidence suggesting that Powell had not only misused public funds for personal use but that he had also publicly and unfairly accused an elderly grandmother (Esther James) of illegal gambling in New York. When the New York media ran negative reports about Powell, Roy Wilkins and the NAACP joined in by announcing the problems that they, too, had with Powell. While most black citizens in Harlem were aware that Esther James was, in fact, a numbers runner in the community, and while they indicated their support of Powell and all that he had done in pushing through legislation that aided blacks and other disadvantaged people, prominent black leaders like Whitney Young, Ralph Bunche of the United Nations, and James Farmer of CORE stood by silently and watched the media and white members of Congress strip Powell of his committee chairmanship and even drive him out of his congressional seat. Because of later reports that vindicated Powell and Robeson in the black press and because of some twenty-twenty hindsight among a formerly guileless black population, the black public realized they had misjudged their heroes. Their recognition that they had misjudged black leaders such as Powell, Robeson, and many others taught blacks to develop a strong cynicism toward the white media and an unofficial yet collective resolve within the black community to resist chastising or even believing negative evidence about black leaders who had previously done right by blacks. Virtually no amount of evidence would sway blacks from their spokespeople after this.

By the time U.S. government organizations like the FBI and various white groups stepped up their anti–Malcolm X and anti–Martin Luther King campaigns in the mid- and late 1960s, the black community was ready to stand its ground and defend these leaders against criticism. Armed with a great deal of cynicism and the opinion that white racists and conservatives would try anything to undermine black leaders, the larger black community learned to give little heed to negative stories that the white press reported on these men. It was for this same reason that blacks immediately supported Malcolm X's daughter Qubilah Shabazz in January 1995 when the FBI accused her of plotting to kill Nation of Islam leader Louis Farrakhan.

With the revelations—during the 1960s and 1970s—about the FBI campaigns to discredit high-profile blacks, as well as eventual assassinations or assassination attempts on the lives of countless local and national black leaders such as Medgar Evers (1963), Malcolm X (1965), Dr. Martin Luther King (1968), Chicago Black Panthers (1969), and Vernon Jordan (1981 attempt), the black community became even more distrustful of the white public when it came to questioning the integrity of any black person in the public eye.

But along with this steadfast loyalty has unfortunately also come a stubborn myopia whereby we refuse to acknowledge that our black leaders can actually ever perform dishonest or outright criminal acts. We have viewed them with a selective scrutiny and an intellectual dishonesty by not holding them to any standard other than requiring that they have black skin. The naive notion of creating and encouraging "because-I'm-black-you-should-trust-me leaders" is one that was born out of white racism yet continues today in situations even where white racists have no involvement. But we cannot allow that history of a white, racist, manipulative press to blind us to the fact that there are such things as corrupt black leaders and spokespeople who get away with unethical behavior simply because we are unwilling to criticize and denounce them.

Perhaps all of this explains why we blacks are reluctant to cut loose our support of the very worst black leaders and spokespeople of all—worse than the uneducated or ill-equipped Mike Tysons, Sister Souljahs, and other entertainers, and worse than the politicians who were once good and then went bad like Washington, D.C., mayor Marion Barry. Perhaps this is why we hold on to the most dangerous ones of all—the Leonard Jeffrieses, the minister Farrakhans, and the Khalid Muhammads—the ones who preach hate and bigotry, the ones who make their appeal to us on an emotional or intellectual level—the deepest penetration of all.

The black community would be better served if we applied the emotion of black pride and tempered it with intellectual honesty, recognizing that while no leader is flawless, we should still not tolerate messages of hate or acts of corruption or malfeasance from any leader or spokesman. Because of the myriad news organizations that police government agencies as well as each other, today's media has decreased the likelihood of ad hominem smear campaigns and inaccurate race-driven news reports.

Factor 6: **Because of certain forces in the black community, the black public ends up placing almost no value on the characteristics that make up a good leader, instead embracing poorly educated and untrained figures who are "real blacks" and holding on to leaders who have proven themselves to be hateful, unethical, and criminally corrupt.**

No group seems to be more willing to recruit ill-equipped and unqualified spokesmen to argue its own cause than black people. Overlooking well-educated, thoughtful, and responsible activists, attorneys, professors, and businesspeople, we consistently turn the reins of black leadership and "spokesmanship" over to rap artists, athletes, entertainers, hatemongers, and former convicts simply because these people have asserted themselves as the only "authentically black people" in America. This sixth factor is particularly complex because it addresses both the manner in which we choose new leaders and the way in which we hold on to old leaders who have gone astray.

Too frequently, black America demonstrates its willingness to throw its support behind self-proclaimed leaders who lack the training, intellect, and discretion that are required to give direction to a people. One example of this took place in 1992 when a little-known black rap artist, Sister Souljah, burst onto the political scene by making a controversial remark to a *Washington Post* reporter about crime in the black community. Taking issue with her comments, then presidential candidate Bill Clinton addressed an audience at a conference sponsored by Rev. Jesse Jackson and quoted Souljah as saying, "If black people kill black people every day, why not take a week and kill white people?"

Once the remark was repeated by the press, the theretofore virtually unknown rap singer was launched into the mainstream media. Calling herself a community activist who "reserves the right to put pressure on white America, to be angry with white America and to organize against white supremacy and racism," Souljah (born Lisa Williamson) found herself on the covers of *Newsweek* (June 29, 1992) and several other publications. Though many black people had never heard of Souljah, many others including Jesse Jackson attacked Clinton for criticizing this woman, who was quickly assuming her role as the newest self-proclaimed spokesperson for disenfranchised blacks.

Souljah's bravado surprised many in the black community. To begin with, even if Souljah had the potential to one day become a responsible leader, her alleged remark about killing white people had already demonstrated her irresponsibility. Those blacks who had blindly come to her defense revealed a dangerous naïveté. But her political career blossomed, and her invitations to speak on college campuses about black leadership increased exponentially. Black students, in particular, wanted her advice and direction. White students and the white media wanted her to tell them what black people—her followers—were thinking.

That the black community is oftentimes willing to make leaders out of irresponsible and thoughtless black celebrities is a character flaw that could continue to undermine our ability to progress beyond media grandstanding and move to a point where our leaders provide intelligent analyses of and practical solutions to our problems. What made Souljah famous was a reckless remark and then an irresponsible debate with Bill Clinton in the media. The end result was that black people spent time deciding whether to defend a rap star whom they had never heard of, but who nonetheless was black, or to stand behind the white Clinton, who had possibly manipulated this opportunity but who was nevertheless correct to argue that it was irresponsible for blacks to endorse the killing of any group of people.

Few would believe that this was the best use of our time. Unfortunately, it is at this level where we spend a great deal of our energy when we allow the proliferation of irresponsible leaders. There is a pattern here: We expend energy and resources to support a black who is unqualified to speak for us. Once the spokesperson becomes overwhelmed in a political debate and conducts himself or herself in a reckless and irresponsible manner, we are embarrassed and are forced to decide whether to defend or censure the spokesperson (who never should have been speaking for us in the first place). If our egos are so sensitive that we refuse to acknowledge when our leader has stumbled, we end up reinforcing negative behavior and losing sight of where we wanted our leaders to take us in the first place.

Other examples of black people's fixation on recruiting ill-equipped spokespeople onto the black leadership bandwagon are found in the way so many black individuals and black publications like *Jet* magazine or the *Amsterdam News,* New York's black weekly paper, cite the instruction and "wisdom" of Mike Tyson, the prize-fighter who was imprisoned after a 1993 conviction for raping a black beauty-pageant contestant, and Ice-T, the rap star who encouraged black backlash on police in his "Cop Killer" album.

I have enjoyed Tyson boxing matches, as well as Sister Souljah and Ice-T albums. But I recognize these people to be nothing more than entertainers. I expect nothing more from them than amusement.

So why is it that these rather unsophisticated, violence-espousing individuals have been launched by both the white and the black media as valuable spokespeople within the black community?

Giving space on editorial pages of respected black publications to convicted rapist and boxer Mike Tyson is an insult to our own people's intelligence and suggests that we have no better black advisers in our moral and political arsenal.

Growing up poor, becoming a juvenile delinquent, dropping out of school, earning millions of dollars as a heavyweight champion, and going to prison for rape are not experiences that particularly qualify an individual to discuss weighty black issues. Quite the contrary. A large segment of black America has allowed years of racist typecasting to convince them that poverty, lack of education, and criminal behavior are the necessary elements for honest-to-goodness blackness, and that anything less makes one an inauthentic African American. The black community would be better served to honor its black educators, social activists, physicians, and business owners.

It is time we begin to redefine the term "black leader" so that it necessarily includes those who are educated, thoughtful, compassionate, and responsible.

Just as we have demonstrated a weakness in applying correct standards to select or anoint our new leaders, we have failed in applying proper standards to judge the black leaders we already have, and yet who have failed us. Caught up in semantics and physical camouflage, we overlook their poor behavior and instead convince ourselves that they are still good for us because they are still fluent in our black slang, still clothed in our African or black American attire, and still offer a sanctified reputation by attending our black Baptist churches.

Following many years of rumored abuses against his office, three-term Washington, D.C., mayor Marion Barry finally stepped down in disgrace in 1990 after undercover police secretly video-taped him smoking crack cocaine. Although the evidence was incriminating, although he served time in prison, although his response to the crime and charges was abrasive, undignified, and unrepentant, Barry was able to hold on to many of his black followers. In fact, even after humiliating front-page stories of his divorce, drug addiction, government corruption, and womanizing, Barry was still able to make a political comeback on the city council just two years later. The formerly corporate-looking Barry made his reappearance in 1992 with all the carnival flair of a P. T. Barnum. He tossed out his conservative business suits as he left the prison walls and reintroduced himself to his black constituents, outfitted in a dashiki, kente-cloth shoes, and an African crown on his head. Angry at a system that had rightfully put him away, he came back to us in the form of a militant reformer—as a man clothed in righteous indignation, wildly manipulating Afrocentric symbols to overcome accusations that he was too corrupt to serve as a responsible black leader. With his new clothing and superficial Afrocentric references, he was ready to convey the message that he was a new man irreversibly committed to the causes of black people.

Even if the voters in the city's Ward Eight believed that Barry had given up his old ways, to think that he could be an effective representative in a city that no longer trusted his word or his judgment was at the very least shortsighted. These residents ended up turning their back on an incumbent that the October 5, 1992, *Jet* magazine described as the "civic-minded, four-term black councilwoman and attorney Wilhelmina Rolark, considered a pillar of the city's society [and] supported by newspapers and civic groups." Not only had the current mayor, Sharon Pratt Kelly, endorsed Rolark over Barry, but so had all thirteen of the other city council members.

Still, reluctant to look at the dismal facts surrounding Barry, a guileless black public took the arrogant and unrepentant Barry back. Unable to accuse the press or the judicial system of unfairly prosecuting him with a racist agenda, most of the black citizens were unable to explain how they could give up a bright and accomplished incumbent for a recently released convict who had been imprisoned for bribery and who had smoked crack on video shown on national television.

Clearly, Barry recognized that we black people rely on and sometimes even look for the most superficial symbols to help us confirm that a man who tells us that he cares about blacks actually does. And he had good reason to believe they'd respond positively to his appeals for them to elect what he presented as the most authentic black: He had gotten them to do it ten years earlier in 1982. In that year, he ran against the bright and accomplished black attorney and Carter cabinet appointee Patricia Roberts Harris. Throughout the campaign, Barry hinted to black voters that Harris was not "black enough" to represent their needs. Focusing on her success in law and government, as well as her prestigious corporate board positions, he was able to persuade black voters that this woman, who had graduated from Howard University, served as dean of its law school, worked as executive director of the black sorority Delta Sigma Theta, and headed important committees at the Washington, D.C., NAACP and Urban League, was not really black enough. He had made her success synonymous with nonblack attributes.

So strongly were black residents swayed by Barry's ghetto jive and "blacker-than-thou" posturing that Harris found herself giving speeches and interviews that attempted to defend and prove that she was, in fact, just as Afrocentric as Barry. The very accomplishments that should have made her an ideal leader for the black community—she had been appointed ambassador to Luxembourg at age forty by President Johnson and had served in the Carter cabinet as secretary of housing and urban development and of health, education, and welfare—were interpreted by Barry and the black residents as liabilities. In essence, they had been convinced by Barry and years of poor self-esteem that to succeed in America was to also somehow become less black.

As an incumbent who had worked the streets since his days as a chairman of the Student Nonviolent Coordinating Committee, Barry knew the value that the large number of less affluent black people would place on his darker skin, his street savvy, and a seeming lack of polish. (Although Barry was himself ambitious, smart, and well educated—he had a master's degree in chemistry—he played down these qualities.) So, in contrast to Harris, he was able to portray himself as being ahead in all those categories about which the large black population cared. And in running for, and eventually winning, the seat, he made these characteristics define what a committed black leader was all about.

The politician was to repeat history in the fall of 1994 when he defeated *Washington Post*–endorsed city councilman John Ray and incumbent mayor Sharon Pratt Kelly, an accomplished black woman who had been a successful attorney for many years prior to entering public office. Although Kelly was a respected mayor who won acclaim as a conciliator between the black and white communities in the district, and although Councilman Ray was endorsed by the *Washington Post* and others, Barry (who had recently married for the fourth time) was once again able to portray himself as an advocate of the underclass running against another articulate, well-educated, light-skinned black woman (Kelly) and a well-connected black political insider (Ray) whom *he* portrayed as friends of the white establishment.

Even more chilling than black people's refusal to repudiate corrupt leaders like Marion Barry is our occasional reluctance to criticize black leaders who preach hate. Recent years have seen us support the rise of some of the most hateful black leaders in the twentieth century. Nation of Islam leader minister Louis Farrakhan, his former aide Khalid Muhammad, and New York's City College professor Leonard Jeffries had all enjoyed the attention of blacks prior to their most recent heightened notoriety of the last five or six years. Jeffries was noted as a scholar who headed the African American Studies Department at City College and who advanced the application of the multicultural curriculum in New York City public schools.

Both Farrakhan and Muhammad had the respect of thousands of Nation of Islam followers, who saw them as religious leaders and role models who taught black men how to take responsibility for their mistakes and give up drugs, alcohol, and criminal activity. It was not surprising that individuals teaching such self-restraint would have gained respect from large segments of black America.

Unfortunately, though, these three intelligent leaders began to alter their course and aggressively adopt hate messages in their teachings and presentations. In 1990 and 1991, Jeffries offered speeches about whites and Jews that countered the antiblack rhetoric advanced by Jewish professor Michael Levin, Jeffries's colleague at City College. Jeffries made statements suggesting that Jews had not only financed the black slave trade but also worked together with the Mafia in Hollywood to create negative black stereotypes in films. During this same period, Farrakhan stepped up his negative remarks about whites and Jews, referring to the Jewish faith as a "gutter religion" and implying that Jews were taking over the United States for their own gain. A further example of Farrakhan's vitriol for Jews is expressed in a book published by the Nation of Islam. The pseudoscholarly text, *The Secret Relationship Between Blacks and Jews,* examines Jews, who made up just under 2 percent of the slave traders, and "credits" them with being responsible for the whole nasty business.

With these three—and many other fallen leaders'—careers, one can find a point in time when they communicated positive and responsible messages to constituents. Examples include Jeffries's support of multiculturalism and Farrakhan's support of black-male responsibility. But at some point—sometimes months, sometimes years—after the leaders' rise to prominence, one notices a pattern of behavior that turns unethical, hateful, or, perhaps, even criminal. Our mistake is failing to criticize these leaders when we first recognize their hateful and destructive messages. We must criticize them—not because the Anti-Defamation League or the local white-owned newspaper asks us to respond—but because we know that by having acted as our advocates, these men have also become our spokespeople.

The lesson we need to learn from our conflict with fallen leaders is that as long as they speak for us, they can do us both help and harm. We can't applaud them for aiding us and then remain silent as they misrepresent us and harm others. We also cannot excuse their behavior by pointing to reprehensible white figures like the disgraced Oliver L. North, who lied to Congress and then later ran for a Senate seat in Virginia. We must learn to cut loose those reckless and corrupt black leaders who don't deserve the forum and the attention that we have given to them as black followers. Before they do too much damage to their own reputations, our own future and our relations with others outside the black community, we must release them from their powerful positions.

Gaining control of our black leadership is not an impossible task for black America. By dividing our interests along socioeconomic lines, getting our two oldest and largest black organizations to select a course that is relevant to our people, making proper use of those black leaders who represent mixed-race constituencies, halting our willingness to appease conservative and possibly bigoted white interests, learning to scrutinize our own black leaders, and appreciating the characteristics that make up good leaders, we can get where we want to be. And where we want to be is the position where we can solve our own problems rather than trying to respond to others when they ask us the question, "Who's running this race?"

8

THE BLACK LUNCH TABLE
IS STILL THERE

D URING A RECENT visit to my old junior high school in
Westchester County, I came upon something that I never
expected to see again, something that was a source of fear and
dread for three hours each school morning of my early adolescence: the all-black lunch table in the cafeteria of my predominantly white suburban junior high school.

As I look back on three decades of often being the only black
person integrating such activities and institutions as the college
newspaper, the high school tennis team, summer music camps, our
all-white suburban neighborhood, certain eating clubs at Princeton, or my private social club at Harvard Law School, the one scenario that puzzled me the most then and now is the all-black
lunch table.

Why was it there? Why did the black kids separate themselves? What did the table say about the integration that was supposedly going on in homerooms and gym classes? What did it say

This piece appeared in the *New York Times* on February 3, 1991.

about the black kids? The white kids? What did it say about me when I refused to sit there, day after day, for three years?

Each afternoon, at 12:03 P.M., after the fourth period ended, I found myself among six hundred twelve-, thirteen-, and fourteen-year-olds who marched into the brightly lit cafeteria and dashed for a seat at one of the twenty-seven blue Formica lunch tables.

No matter whom I walked in with—usually a white friend—no matter what mood I was in, there was one thing that was certain: I would not sit at the black table.

I would never consider sitting at the black table.

What was wrong with me? What was I afraid of?

I would like to think that my decision was a heroic one, made in order to express my solidarity with the theories of integration that my community was espousing. But I was just twelve at the time, and there was nothing heroic in my actions.

I avoided the black table for a very simple reason: I was afraid that by sitting at the black table I'd lose all my white friends. I thought that by sitting there I'd be making a racist, antiwhite statement.

Is that what the all-black table means? Is it a rejection of white people? I no longer think so.

At the time, I was angry that there was a black lunch table. I believed that the black kids were the reason why other kids didn't mix more. I was ready to believe that their self-segregation was the cause of white bigotry.

Ironically, I even believed this after by best friend (who was white) told me I probably shouldn't come to his bar mitzvah because I'd be the only black and people would feel uncomfortable. I even believed this after my Saturday-afternoon visit, at age ten, to a private country-club pool prompted incensed white parents to pull their kids from the pool in terror.

In the face of this blatantly racist (antiblack) behavior, I still somehow managed to blame only the black kids for being the barrier to integration in my school and my little world. What was I thinking?

I realize now how wrong I was. During that same time, there were at least two tables of athletes, an Italian table, a Jewish girls' table, a Jewish boys' table (where I usually sat), a table of kids who were into heavy-metal music and smoking pot, a table of middle-class Irish kids. Weren't these tables just as segregationist as the black table? At the time, no one thought so. At the time, no one even acknowledged the segregated nature of these other tables.

Maybe it's the color difference that makes all-black tables or all-black groups attract the scrutiny and wrath of so many people. It scares and angers people; it exasperates. It did those things to me, and I'm black.

As an integrating black person, I know that my decision *not* to join the black lunch table attracted its own kind of scrutiny and wrath from my classmates. At the same time that I heard angry words like "Oreo" and "white boy" being hurled at me from the black table, I was also dodging impatient questions from white classmates: "Why do all those black kids sit together?" or "Why don't you ever sit with the other blacks?"

The black lunch table, like those other segregated tables, is a comment on the superficial inroads that integration has made in society. Perhaps I should be happy that even this is a long way from where we started. Yet I can't get over the fact that the twenty-seventh table in my junior high school cafeteria is still known as the "black table"—fourteen years after my adolescence.

9

THE UNDERSIDE
OF PARADISE

BEING BLACK AT PRINCETON

"The road has been hard. It began about as tough as I ever had it—in Princeton, New Jersey, a college town of southern aristocrats, who from Revolutionary time transferred Georgia to New Jersey. My brothers couldn't go to high school in Princeton. We lived for all intents and purposes on a southern plantation. And with no more dignity than that suggests—all the bowing and scraping to the drunken rich, all the vile names, all the Uncle Tomming to earn enough to lead miserable lives."

WHILE THESE WORDS very nearly describe my experience as a student at Princeton University in the early 1980s, I cannot claim them as my own. This is Princeton as seen by Paul Robeson, the political activist and actor, who spoke of it in a well-received speech in New York City on June 19, 1949. While he was to graduate as valedictorian from neighboring Rutgers University and from Columbia Law School, Robeson was one of the many accomplished blacks who never forgot Princeton's denial of his admission to the two Princetons—both the school and the town—purely on the basis of race.

Last among the Ivies and one of the last universities in the North to admit blacks, Princeton University and the affluent community that surrounded it remained as Dixie as those once segregated southern colleges in states like Arkansas, West Virginia, and Georgia well into the 1970s. Most often compared to liberal establishments like Harvard and Yale, in my experience this school— whose most famous twentieth-century president (Woodrow Wilson) was unwilling to denounce Ku Klux Klan atrocities—has a closer kinship in racial terms to the separate-but-equal Ole Miss. While the racism expressed itself not in unseemly shouts and lynchings but in genteel murmurs and rejections, it was every bit as intractable.

My childhood had taught me that it was possible to live with a foot in two worlds: one black and one white. What I found at Princeton was a campus, a student body, a faculty, and a community that had no tolerance for black students who wanted an integrated experience. Regardless of your background or your views, you were compelled to choose between black and white. *My* mistake was trying to change the rules.

CLUB LIFE

"Larry, you really should consider joining Cottage," the sandy-haired twenty-year-old member announced as we both focused on a group of wooden cubbyhole shelves that lined the wall near the formal dining room. Hal found the square wooden hole with his name, reached in, and then pulled out a starched white cloth napkin for dinner.

"Well, gee, that would be something," I answered, feeling both flattered and horrified by the notion that I could spend the next two years dining alongside members of Princeton's most southern, white, male eating club.

I sat down at the large wooden table and looked around a dining room jammed with about one hundred Princetonians. Although I'd been at the school for a little over a year, not one of these white male students looked familiar to me. But membership was open only to juniors and seniors, and I was still just a sophomore. Perhaps it was only age and not race that was creating the chasm between me and the rest of the room.

The waiters didn't help. Although they seemed to be around my age, somewhere between sixteen and twenty years old, none of them had familiar faces either. Briskly, almost nervously, they scampered in and out of the kitchen, quietly slipping plates of hot broiled chicken and vegetables underneath the arms and between the broad shoulders of students who were pulled up close to the table. As each waiter served a plate, he retreated with what looked like a swift bow of the head and a polite and simultaneous bend of the knee and waist—almost like a curtsy. Although none of them stood still long enough for me to lock eyes, it soon became apparent that they all shared one distinguishing characteristic: Each was a dark-complexioned black.

Amidst this boisterous roomful of white students, swarming with fastidious and swiftly bowing and curtsying dark-skinned servants, I was the only upright black Princetonian in the dining room—and, perhaps, in the building.

Hal, my genial host, gave me a fraternal shake on my right arm and leaned in close toward my plate of steaming chicken with his Pepsodent smile. "Now, if you're worried you wouldn't get in—or even *fit* in here," said Hal, "let me tell you, you're just the kind of guy that we'd actually *like* to have around Cottage."

"Really?" I asked with an air of nonchalance.

"Yeah, and you wouldn't be our first one *either*."

I toyed with the notion that Hal was merely cajoling me with his own brand of corny racial humor. After all, this was 1980—several years before college political correctness was in vogue. But Hal's expression revealed no deeper agenda, and I therefore had to wipe away the phony grin that had been drawn across my face.

"I'm serious," he added.

Hal *was* serious. I really was his "kind" of black. Imagine, after knowing me for only fifteen minutes, he had already determined that I was his type: safe, predictable, respectable, tame, docile—the kind he could understand and whose actions could easily be anticipated. I was the sort of black that didn't live in Princeton Inn—the down-campus dorm where many of the nonintegrating blacks lived. I was an up-campus black, the kind who understood the nuances of black-white relations. The kind who saved black slang for those deep and gritty personal moments with my own people. The kind who roomed with white guys yet didn't date white girls. The kind who would volunteer time to help plan the club's monthly parties yet not insist on attending or bringing black friends to them.

"Excuse me, sir," whispered a voice as I watched a slender brown-skinned arm reach over my shoulder and place a saltshaker on the table.

"Oh, certainly," I answered with a smile. I looked up at the young black woman. She looked to be around sixteen years old. Her hair was pulled into a matronly bun. "Hi, how are you this evening? The dinner looks great."

The teenager stared at me blankly, and then looked at Hal. As he touched me on the arm, he directed her back to the kitchen with a slight nod of his head.

"You know, you shouldn't feel obligated to speak to them. They're all townies," my host explained.

After dinner, Hal took me on a tour of the three-story building. Like the twelve other eating clubs on campus, Cottage's clubhouse was an ornate mansion that sat on roughly a half-acre parcel along tree-lined, suburban Prospect Avenue. The street, which was known for its clubs, created the eastern border of campus.

Like the four other selective clubs at the university, Cottage was guarded by a massive brick wall that ran across the front property. I was told by a woman from another club, Cap & Gown, that the easiest way to remember which clubs were selective was to look for a front wall. Open clubs, which accept all applicants, have no more than small bushes at their street borders. The exception was Quadrangle, which was not quite open, since it had a petition system for admissions—and a lower wall that you could almost step over. Cottage was located in a redbrick Georgian that Hal estimated was built in the early 1900s when Princeton was, in his words, "a very different place." Founded in 1886, Cottage was the second oldest club—right next to Ivy, Princeton's premier club for WASP men.

"I think you'd really find acceptance at Cottage," Hal offered as he led me up the wide sweeping staircase.

"Really?"

Hal flashed those teeth again. "And you're the kind of guy who would make everyone feel good about your membership. You're articulate, good background. And somebody told me you play tennis, right?"

"Right, and I used to teach it too."

"No shit." Hal beamed. "Larry, I can't speak for everyone, but I'd bet you're just the kind we want here. What the guys are afraid of is that angry militant or apartheid stuff. And that's obviously not you, so there's no way you'd get hosed."

After Hal walked me through the ornate, cathedral-ceilinged three-thousand-volume library, he pointed to the graceful gazebo and fountain in the backyard. Whether he had been pressured by others or he had decided on his own, Hal was making it quite obvious that he wanted me in this club. I'd never met him before, but it was obvious that he knew about me and my chances of admission. "Larry, you'd have no problem getting through the bicker process here. Three days of interviews and all you need is a two-thirds vote. I can't imagine many who'd object. There's just no *way* you'd get hosed."

As I looked out a wide window in the back of the mansion and peered down below to the ornate patio, I thought about all the F. Scott Fitzgerald stories I'd heard since arriving at Princeton. The alumnus who brought us Jay Gatsby and *This Side of Paradise* knew of what he wrote. The place was seductive. Intoxicating. The dark wood, the thick carpet, the smell of old leather, Hal's booming confidence like a siren's song. How could I not want to be a part of it? I would have been apprehensive, but he made it seem so easy for me. To be black and to be accepted into surroundings like this—in some sense, it was the ultimate accolade I could receive at Princeton.

As we walked back down the stairs to the large foyer, I went to the coatroom to find my jacket. I glanced over at a framed collage that featured photos of all the current members. There were several recognizable last names, sons of politicos or business leaders. Finding my way through the alphabetized names, I saw where my name and photo would be placed if I were to become a part of the collage. I could almost imagine my pose—smiling proudly with blue blazer, white shirt, and club tie. The thought made me all at once feel giddy, light-headed, and superior.

Moving away from the framed collage, I turned back to the coatroom. Standing next to the doorway was the same black waitress who had served me earlier in the dining room. No longer nodding and bowing at the table, she was now looking through a telephone book and popping a wad of bubble gum. I felt, at first, too embarrassed to look her in the eye. Although I'd been cordial to her, I now wondered what she thought of my sitting at that table, laughing with Hal for the past forty minutes and grinning ear-to-ear like a Cheshire cat? Her image of the 1980s black sellout.

"Have a nice evening," I finally said with a cordial wave. "The dinner was really terrific."

The young woman rolled her eyes at me. "Gimme a break," she answered, then returned to the pages of the New Jersey phone book.

When I came back to the foyer with my coat, Hal was smiling broadly. He held the door for me as I walked out onto the front steps and slapped me on the back.

"It was great meeting you," I said while waving good-bye and walking down the walkway toward the street.

Just as I reached the tall brick wall at the edge of the property, Hal called out to me in the brisk fall evening air, "Hey, Larry!"

"Yes?"

"Do you like steak?"

I turned back toward him with a huge grin. Lying, I gave him the answer I assumed he wanted. "Sure, who doesn't?"

"Man, have we got steak! Every Saturday night at Cottage."

I gave Hal a corny good-old-boy thumbs-up gesture that should have gotten me kicked out of the black race on the spot. "Awesome!"

His white teeth glistened in the dark. "See, I knew you'd fit in here. Later!"

Just as I passed the brick wall separating Cottage from the public sidewalk, two tall white students dressed in black wool Princeton jackets brushed past me. One of them kicked a small amount of gravel at my feet and said something that sounded like "niggers leaving out the front door."

By the time it occurred to me what those words meant, the speakers were well past me. Turning to see which club they were headed for, I saw them climbing the very same steps I had just left—toward the front door of Cottage Club. As I turned to cross the street, I looked up above the club's white wood-and-stone doorframe. Flapping lightly in the evening breeze at the end of a short pole was a Confederate flag. It was 1980.

A History of Blacks at Princeton

"For 200 years, this University has pursued its policy of excluding Negroes from its campus. Can we not hold on to this one distinction which sets Princeton above the average college? Ever since slavery days, the Negro has lacked initiative. . . . As for us, we hope the day will never come when Negroes will wave their hats with our sons 'in praise of Old Nassau.' "

So read a letter appearing in the *Daily Princetonian* on October 5, 1942, and signed by W. Kennedy Cromwell, Charles C. Fenwick, Kenneth Gorman, and Harry Stack, four members of the class of 1946. While it reflects their personal views, for me it crystallizes the entire sordid history of black admissions to Princeton.

Founded in 1746 as the College of New Jersey, Princeton's antiblack policies very quickly began to stand out as an aberration among the top colleges in every segment of the United States except the South. While many other leading universities such as Harvard, Yale, Amherst, and Brown began accepting blacks in the early and mid-1800s, Princeton pursued a three-tier strategy to ensure that blacks would not enroll, and was so successful that it accepted a black student exactly a hundred years after Harvard and eighty years after Yale. First, Princeton strictly enforced an unwritten rule of rejecting all black applicants; second, it denied having such a rule in the face of growing criticism; finally, it utilized "deflection" rejection letters directing high-profile black applicants to apply to other schools rather than explicitly denying admission; this was designed to deter those who might publicly protest their rejection by the school.

Reflecting Princeton's obsession with decorum, these polite letters of deflection were written in a uniform format developed by Princeton's thirteenth president, Woodrow Wilson, just three years before he was elected president of the United States. The University Archive in the Seeley Mudd Library reveals a letter that begins, "Regret to say that it is altogether inadvisable for a colored man to enter Princeton. . . ."

In an impressive display of early-twentieth-century political maneuvering, Wilson never signed these letters, but instead had his secretary send them out with his own signature with the polite closing line, "I would strongly recommend you to secure your education in a Southern institution or, if you wish to attend a Northern institution, I would suggest that you correspond with the authorities of Harvard, Dartmouth, Brown. . . . Yours Very Truly . . . "

As Princeton's administration became increasingly surrounded by prestigious universities and liberal arts colleges that admitted blacks (its neighbor and football rival, Rutgers, had been admitting blacks since the Civil War), it continued to hide behind its unwritten, but well-enforced, no-blacks policy, and also implemented the final stage of its policy on blacks. This involved forwarding the applications of black Princeton applicants to nearby Lincoln University, a school founded in 1854 by several Princeton alumni for the purpose of educating blacks exclusively. Providing a "separate-but-equal" alternative for unwanted black applicants put an ironic spin on the university's famous motto, "Princeton in the Nation's service."

The Princeton tradition of "discouraging" its black applicants was ostensibly developed to spare the feelings of black students who might be unhappy or unsuccessful at a predominantly white campus. Certainly, another driver was the conviction of the Princeton admissions committee that no black could be academically qualified to be accepted. This logic was undermined when black applicant Bruce Wright, who went on to become a New York State Supreme Court judge, was accidentally accepted in 1938 because his race was not indicated in his application, then summarily rejected on the first day of classes by administrator Radcliffe Heermance once the admissions office discovered that Bruce was not white.

Princeton was finally integrated—under pressure—in 1944, when the United States Navy set up an ROTC program on campus and brought with it, unbeknownst to Princeton, four black students.

Letters apologizing for the new blacks on campus were immediately sent by various Princeton administrators to alumni and benefactors. An October 2, 1945, letter sent by Princeton administrator L. G. Payson to J. M. Barr of the First National Bank in Louisville, Kentucky, explains, "The U.S. Navy asked to establish an ROTC on campus and we agreed. When the personnel arrived, its members included, unbeknownst to us in advance, four Negroes. If Princeton were to stand against the Negroes who were admitted under the Navy War-time ROTC, the Trustees would be in a very difficult spot. . . . One of [the Negroes] has already expressed a desire to transfer to the University of Pennsylvania, and his wishes will be aided by whatever help Princeton can give him."

The university was to spend the next twenty years dodging black applicants with its unwritten no-blacks policy (virtually no blacks were admitted to the classes of 1950 to 1959—and only seven were on the 3,500-student campus by 1962), and the next forty years encouraging or permitting the separation of the races in campus activities and dormitories.

The school's history is even more troubling because Princeton still refuses to acknowledge that it had a rule and refuses to address the rule's impact on the university's politics today. While Harvard openly acknowledges its old "Jewish quota," Princeton archives reveal dozens of letters sent by alumni, scholars, and journalists asking the university if it ever had a policy against admitting blacks.

One query was sent by Lawrence T. May, a research associate from Brandeis University's Lemberg Center for the Study of Violence, on March 3, 1969, to the Princeton librarian. The researcher's query letter says, "The present record seems to indicate that Princeton College did not allow Negro students to be admitted until 1944." Then it asks, "Was this exclusion a deliberate policy rule of the College or University administration?"

Princeton's archives reveal that a curt, almost cryptic two-sentence unsigned letter, dated March 6, 1969, was written in response. It read: "Dear Mr. May: In July 1945, four Negroes were sent here by the Navy on the V-12 program. One of them, Arthur Jewell Wilson, Jr., graduated A.B. in June 1947 as of the Class of 1948."

So in 1969, at the height of the campus civil rights movement, Princeton was no more willing to acknowledge its policies than it had been a hundred years before.

The first blacks who got into Princeton had been grudgingly accepted. Arthur Wilson, the first to graduate, told me that he and the other three black students sent by the navy were pretty much insulated from the negative attitudes of other students because they lived together with the naval unit in a separate dormitory. "There were a few students at Tiger Inn, one of the eating clubs, who reached out to me and asked if I wanted to join," Wilson explained, "but once the alumni found out, they insisted that the students withdraw the offer and keep me out of the club."

Once there, Princeton's first black students were ushered out by whatever means (early graduation, transfers, dropping out) were available to the school. Princeton's admissions practices were not to change fundamentally until the early 1970s, and its treatment of blacks on campus was to remain substandard well into my tenure there.

THE ROAD TO PRINCETON

Of course, I had no hard proof to substantiate Princeton's rumored history when I decided to attend. My parents threw secondhand stories at me, and others repeated second- and third-hand tales. I knew lots of students and alumni of other Ivy League schools, but I'd never personally met anyone who was a Princeton student or alumnus. I only knew I wanted the best. I wanted the stereotypical pastoral setting. And I wanted a place that history had recognized: I thought that the college of Wilson, Fitzgerald, Adlai Stevenson, and Bill Bradley was it. I had my reasons for not applying to one of the many top black colleges, including the fact that they were not listed in the "Most Competitive" category of the *Barron's Guide to America's Colleges,* and because my need for white approval at that time was extremely important.

The only people I socialized with in my high school were white honors and advanced placement students. Besides myself, there was only one other black guy in the group. My black friends outside of high school were also honors and AP students. We were all terribly ambitious and all planned to attend a school in the Ivy League. That other black guy from high school wanted MIT—and that's where he was to go.

My parents knew not to suggest a black college to me because they knew, at age seventeen, I cared about doing only those things that were considered to be "the best" in the broadest sense. Attending the best black college would not have been sufficient. The only time I ever thought about a black college was the April afternoon during senior year when I told a neighbor that I would probably attend Brown University. When the woman's face remained expressionless, I was immediately offended.

"You know, Mrs. Kramer," I said with worry in my voice. "Brown University in Providence?" The sticker had just been put in the back windows of our Buick station wagon and BMW sedan.

"Brown?" she asked.

Mrs. Kramer, a white middle-aged divorcée who had spent most of her time fund-raising for local charities, had lived down our street all my life. I had never taken her to be a scholar, but surely, I thought, she must have known this school. It was 215 years old—one of the seven Ivy League colleges. One of my cousins had gone from Phillips Exeter to Brown and was then in his final year of medical school. It seemed like a good route to me.

"You know—in Providence. Brown University."

Then her eyes lit up with a sudden sign of recognition. "Oh, right. Right, one of those *black* colleges."

And that's why, at the last minute, I decided to go to Princeton.

In spite of pleas from my parents, who cited the experiences of New York State judge Bruce Wright, Paul Robeson, and other blacks who had tempted fate at Princeton, and pleas from a high school guidance counselor who hardly knew me yet still argued the anti-Semitic and antiblack past of the school, I decided that race relations couldn't possibly be as bad as they had once been.

"And even if they are," I insisted, "I've always been able to maintain strong friendships with whites and other blacks."

I'd done it before, so I'd do it again.

REJECTED ON THE LEFT: FELLOW BLACKS AT PRINCETON

Being black at Princeton should not have been an extraordinary experience. After all, we made up 10 percent of the 1,020 freshmen in the class of 1983. But despite these numbers and the school's academic excellence, the university continued to demonstrate little vision or courage in the area of race relations. When I arrived on the 2,600-acre New Jersey campus, I found a college environment that had made no genuine progress from its troubled racist history. Instead, through benign neglect, Princeton had allowed *de facto* segregation to develop. Subtle but strong, it divided the campus as surely as Jim Crow laws had divided the South. The very first contact I made with a black student at the school confirmed this for me.

"So, how'd you end up with a white roommate?"

Of all the questions I had anticipated from my fellow freshmen, this was the last one I had expected on my first day on campus. Walking alongside me as I left my dorm for the school store was a heavyset black woman I'd never seen before.

"I don't think we've met," I replied. "I'm Larry Graham. I'm a freshman."

"Yeah," she answered. "I'm Shirlene Watkins [not her real name], from Nashville. "So, how is it you got yourself a white roommate?"

I was already deep into my first-week "happy-talk, I'm-trying-to-make-friends-not-set-the-world-on-fire" mode, and I got the distinct impression that this question and this girl were working against me.

"I don't know," I answered. "The housing office just put Steve and me together, I guess." I immediately wondered how Shirlene knew my roommate was white and what she planned to do about it.

"Well," she persisted, "did you tell 'em you wanted to live in Princeton Inn?"

As we walked up campus toward the store, I listened to the woman's humorless and derisive remarks about the school and our fellow students. (They ran from "This place is so white, I could scream" and "Somebody oughtta shake these kids up" to "You think they'll ever get a Black Panthers chapter here?") Her smart-ass comments and questions seemed so over-the-top, yet familiar, I felt like I'd met her someplace before. Then it came to me.

Shirlene was a slightly grown-up version of Dee, the young black sister from the 1970s sitcom *What's Happening?* She was at once funny, mean-spirited, and charismatic. She was that seventh-grade bully who found a perverse pleasure in making or breaking your reputation before anyone else got to meet you.

Shirlene had obviously decided I was a suburban black man in need of conversion, so I chose my words carefully and feigned ignorance. "Princeton Inn?" I asked.

"Yeah, the *black* dorm," she snapped.

I was well aware of Princeton Inn, the stately colonial-style former hotel that had been converted into a large student dormitory overlooking a country-club golf course at the edge of campus. During the spring of my senior year in high school, I had actually come to campus to look over student housing. I'd heard that Princeton Inn was popular among blacks who favored a down-campus dorm that featured some all-black lunch tables, all-black hallways, and all-black rooming situations. For those reasons, I specifically requested that I *not* be put in Princeton Inn, or PIC, as it was usually called. Neither its location nor its segregated nature appealed to me.

"Well, I didn't know I could pick a dorm or a roommate."

Shirlene looked unconvinced. "Hmm. Well, most of us are in PIC. And if not," she added in a reproachful tone, "we have black roommates. You could have found somebody like I did—and requested them. Instead of rooming with some peckerwood."

"Gosh, I wish I'd known."

As Shirlene veered off to the west side of campus, I thanked her for the advice.

"Yeah, well, I'm going over to the Third World Center," she announced. "You should get yourself over there this week."

As I watched Shirlene's purposeful stride take her down McCosh Walk, I had a sinking feeling about race relations at Princeton. Was it a coincidence that the first black I met just happened not to like white people? Given that this was Princeton—a university rated "Most Competitive" by the Barron's bible, a school that my neighbor Mrs. Kramer both recognized and approved of—prestigewise—I had just assumed that the blacks I'd meet there would be just like me—ambitious, upper middle class, and well assimilated.

Though it was difficult to assess how much damage I'd done to my reputation with my remarks to Shirlene, I could tell that she was one of those down-home, self-righteous blacks who didn't like white people—and cared even less for blacks who were willing to give them a chance. Having already been pegged as a black suburbanite in a white dorm, with a white roommate, I sensed that Shirlene would walk through the front door of the Third World Center and immediately add my name to the file folder of black students who needed to be watched.

And since that was the case, it was probably a good thing that I had lied to her. Not only had I specifically asked the housing office that I not be put in PIC, but I'd also specified the kind of roommate I wanted. Determined to enjoy an integrated Princeton experience, I had drafted a request that could have delivered only a white suburbanite or the kind of integrated black person who frustrated people like Shirlene.

My freshman year, I ended up being assigned to a dorm with a smart, well-liked, white, Catholic Eagle Scout, who had been president of his class and a Boys State representative from his school in affluent Cherry Hill, New Jersey. Steve was to eventually become our sophomore class president, chairman of Princeton's Honor Committee, a member of Ivy Club, and a graduate of Georgetown Law School. In other words, he was the all-American white guy. The kind of roommate who—because of his stellar credentials—could only get me into trouble with most of the blacks on campus.

About a week after classes started, three white friends from my dorm and I were coming into Firestone Library on our way down to the reserve room. As we approached the stairwell, I saw Shirlene coming in my direction. My friends stopped abruptly as she walked up to me.

Dressed for battle in dark green army fatigues, a black TWC T-shirt, and a black leather bag over her shoulder, Shirlene spoke up before I could dodge her stare. "Hey, you! Mr. Suburbanite."

My eyes begged her not to embarrass me.

"Mr. *White* . . . Plains," she added, drawing out her reference to my New York suburban hometown that was listed in the class face book.

"Oh, hi, Shirlene," I answered with a grimace.

"I haven't seen you at TWC yet."

When I saw the three white guys look strangely at me (they didn't yet know that TWC stood for Third World Center), I told them to go on downstairs. I could already anticipate the accusation she was to lay at my feet.

"They can listen," she said without glancing in their direction. "I was just upstairs in the Afro-Am library talking to some folks about how the black freshmen should be working to empower OBU and helping to mobilize the antiapartheid movement on campus."

"Oh?" I hadn't the slightest idea of what she meant.

"Yeah, I was telling Darsha, Waltrina, and Rasheed."

"Right," I answered, then turned in relief when my three white companions grew impatient and waved good-bye.

"Do you *know* them?" Shirlene asked testily.

I forced a smile. "Oh, sorry. That was Peter, Craig, and—"

"No, not the white boys," she interrupted. "Darsha, Waltrina, and *Rasheed.*"

My mind drew a blank.

"Of course you don't. Instead of assimilating yourself so much, you should help us out over at TWC."

Feeling both bullied and ashamed, I lied. "Well, I've actually already been by TWC."

Shirlene eyed me suspiciously and then pulled at an uneven curl in her Afro. "Really? When?"

"A few days ago—uh, Monday."

"When Monday?" she snapped, while stepping closer.

"Monday afternoon—sort of late."

Unconvinced, Shirlene poked me repeatedly in the ribs with her finger and laughed. "Look, Mr. Suburbanite, [*poke*] why you gonna lie to me? [*poke*] The sooner you wake up, [*poke*] the better off you'll be. These peckerwoods don't give a shit about you. White folks'll eat you up and spit—you—*out*! [*poke,poke*]"

"Shirlene," I interrupted finally, "it's obvious you don't like me, so why don't we just drop this?"

As I began to turn away, I saw two black women and a black man in a beard coming down the stairs to where we stood on the busy main floor. Though I'd never seen them before, I had a sense that they were going to somehow be drawn into this confrontation.

"This is the one I was telling you about," Shirlene said to the approaching threesome.

"Hi, I'm Larry Graham." I forced a smile and calmed myself with a silent promise to never again speak to the troublesome Shirlene. The three students were dressed unlike anyone I'd seen on the Princeton campus. Like almost everyone else during the height of the preppy movement, I was in beige corduroys, white turtleneck, and light suede shoes. These three were covered head-to-toe in black and army green surplus. I reached out to shake the man's hand, and he nodded. I missed the grip entirely.

"Yo!"

One of the girls smiled and held out her hand. "Hi, you have to excuse Shirlene. She comes on a little strong for a freshman. Since the rest of us are almost outta here, she's just trying to help us get the freshmen involved in OBU."

"Oh, I see." I didn't see.

"You know, the Organization of Black Unity," the woman explained. "Shirlene just wants you to get involved in TWC. You should listen to her because you can't trust these white folks around here."

"That's what I told him," Shirlene snapped indignantly. "Trying to straddle the fence with his white friends. He can't have it both ways."

The other woman smiled again—almost apologetically. "Just stop by when you can."

As the four students walked away, I stared at the loose-fitting green army fatigues that were cinched at Rasheed's and Shirlene's waists. The two senior women wore heavy work boots. The back of Rasheed's jeans jacket had a large upheld fist and forearm outlined in red paint. Above it was stenciled the word FIGHT!

As I leaned against the green marble wall, staring across the two-story library floor and watching them walk against the after-dinner crowd of incoming, preppily dressed pastel white students, the four blacks looked like a 1960s anachronism. Angry, loud, and resentful, their clothes and attitude were more ghetto than Ivy League—more ghetto than I'd ever encountered.

"FIGHT!"

"FIGHT what?"

This was all I needed to convince myself that I'd been meeting the wrong blacks on campus. I'd spent enough time with the militants who resented me and my background. It was now time to find blacks like myself: ones who came from suburban, middle-class backgrounds and held no objections to my friendships with white people.

The first thing I did after returning to my dorm room was to close myself up in the bathroom and begin my search for like-minded blacks in the pages of *The Freshman Herald,* our class face book. With marking pen in hand, I opened the ninety-nine-page book and began with the As. Underneath each postage-stamp-sized photo was the student's name, a home address, a high school name, and a birthdate. Immediately eliminated from consideration was any black student pictured with an oversized militant-looking Afro or cornrows. Next I crossed off any black students from southern towns that I knew to be semisegregated. Then I also canceled out students who were photographed in basketball uniforms, who'd attended large or notoriously all-black high schools in inner-city areas like the Bronx, Newark, and south-central Los Angeles, and just about anyone who was an apartment dweller. When I was done with my review, I had eliminated more than 75 percent of the blacks—including Shirlene and her buddies. As slim as it seemed, the remaining group still left me with a few possibilities.

The group appeared to be suburban, middle class, and from a cross-section of integrated or mostly white communities and public or private schools. I was sure I could find some black friends in that group. I was certain I'd meet other integrated blacks like myself. So I tried.

First there was Jack Felton (not his real name) from Maryland. After meeting him at a lunch table in Commons, I mentioned that I was going to start dropping by TWC with the hopes of meeting some of the black girls on campus. When I asked if he'd ever been, he said that I'd be better off coming to an EST group meeting that was taking place on campus. "Now there's where you'll get to meet all those fine blond California babes—they love that EST stuff." Jack, who was on an endless pursuit of blondes, told me that he'd never date a black girl. "They're too angry," he explained.

Then there was Tiffany Rogers (not her real name), who lived in my dorm and had come from a private school in Boston. After seeing her on the stairwell and in the laundry room, I introduced myself. Tiffany did not meet my stare and did not bother to shake my outheld hand. This medium-complexioned black woman, whose hair became more and more blond each month, responded quite bluntly to my question about TWC. "I don't even know where the Third World Center is," she said. "And don't really care." Four years were to pass, and I was never to see Tiffany talking to another black person.

Next was Cindy Jefferson (not her real name) from a New York suburb, who not only distanced herself from black people but seemed to display a particular distaste for relatively successful black students like myself. After graduation, she was to eventually return to work as an administrator at the school. And although I was always kind to her in school, she is now the only classmate who consistently shores up my writing career with mean-spirited letters sent to the publishers of magazines where I've been published. Even though I give consistently to Princeton, my guess is that she will use her epistolary skills to ensure that my kids never get admitted to Old Nassau.

Finally, there was Donald Herbert (not his real name), from a midwestern suburb, who was assigned to a seat next to mine in a freshman French class. Every day, as we approached each other in the classroom or on campus, Donald's head swung away at a ninety-degree angle. If he was without his white friends, he would smile and say hello. If he was with them, I would get a distracted nod.

In the end, I was to make three "integrated" black friends who lived like me and balanced a social life between black and white classmates. Though I was to find many more close black Princeton friends after graduation, my struggle to find integrated black friends in school introduced me to a long succession of Oreos and self-loathing black teens who'd been taught that assimilation with whites was a greater goal than identifying with one's own.

REJECTED ON THE RIGHT: WHITES AT PRINCETON

It was the first time I'd ever been in an all-white cafeteria. It was the second month of freshman year, and I had wandered into Upper Eagle, one of the four dining halls that made up Commons, after realizing that my friends from my resident adviser's group had already eaten lunch and vacated Madison Hall, our regular Commons dining location.

Eating in Upper Eagle gave renewed meaning to the old black southern expression, "If you're light, you're right. But if you're black, get back." Located at one end of the all-male Hamilton Hall dorm, it felt as private as a country club. After standing in line for my food and then finding a space at a long wooden table populated by fourteen or fifteen very WASPy-looking men and women whom I'd never seen before (virtually everyone in the room was blond), I put down my tray of food and walked back through the crowded room to get a glass of milk.

After getting the milk and turning back toward my table, I realized I'd just missed a round of musical chairs. Except for my green tray and the knapsack on the back of my high-backed wooden seat, my entire table was empty. The people, the trays, the knapsacks, even the chairs—except mine—were now gone.

As I stood there, glass in hand, contemplating the now vacated table, it occurred to me that more than a few people were amused by this scene. A few students at the table across wore embarrassed grimaces, but several of them—particularly the ones that were now double-parked with their chairs up against a nearby table—were looking at me defiantly. It was 1980. We were in New Jersey. The school was at least 8 percent black. I had to remind myself that everything really was okay.

It was a year before I would return to Upper Eagle. Situations like this remind me of how stupid I was to object to the all-black lunch tables at PIC.

Although I was able to maintain serious and close friendships with four or five white students in Princeton, most other relationships that I formed were superficial and short-lived. Having come from an integrated high school where I was a popular student, this was an extremely painful exercise. One student vilified me in a class essay that was put on reserve in Princeton's Firestone Library reading room. Our professor, the nonfiction author John McPhee, had paired each of his students with a classmate and asked us to write biographies of each other. If my memory serves me correctly—and I doubt I'll ever forget it—the essay written about me opened with the sentence, "When Lawrence Graham gets up from our interview in the Chancellor Green student center and fails to throw away the plastic wrap from his cupcakes, he reminds one that he really is overwhelmingly middle class. . . ."

In a place like Princeton, at the height of the Reagan period and preppy movements, where manners and decorum were essential, profiles like this made one quite unpopular. Even my roommates made a special trip to Firestone for a glimpse. Ironically, the classmate who wrote about my frighteningly bourgeois, un-Princetonian manners and background had just told me about the day he came home from junior high school and learned that his father had walked out on his family and left them virtually penniless. I'd asked the classmate if he'd rather I not reveal this in an essay that would be on reserve for the whole school to read.

One of my Princeton acquaintances, whose father had attended the school in the 1940s, brought me back to his dorm room one evening freshman year and treated me to some of the most bizarre and still mystifying moments of my first semester. Lonnie said he wanted to show me some of the Princeton paraphernalia that his father had saved and passed down to him. Hanging from the ceiling was a giant orange-and-black Princeton cloth banner indicating a class from the 1940s. Next to that was a Jimi Hendrix poster and a hook where Mardi Gras beads hung in long loops. Nailed on the wall just above Lonnie's desk was a small glass-and-wood frame. To give me a closer look, he twisted the swivel neck of a floor lamp so that it threw a yellow spotlight on the picture frame. Inside the glass was a creased and decaying yellowed sheet of paper. At first I thought it was one of those fake, design-your-own-headline newspapers that would read, "Lonnie Smith Discovers Cure for Cancer." But, in fact, it was a news article from the *Daily Princetonian* with a date sometime in September 1942. It spoke of a campus debate taking place that evening and being sponsored by a student organization, American Whig–Cliosophic Society, a Princeton debating group that I myself had just joined.

The topic of the debate: "Should Negroes Be Admitted to Princeton?" Standing there in the yellow light, my eyes pressed up closely to the faded letters, I glanced over to the nearby 1979–80 football calendar mounted on the wall. What's going on here? I wondered. Not only was this a bizarre article to put behind glass and hang on a wall, but he was bizarre to think I'd find it interesting. I hardly knew Lonnie, but I was confident that something was wrong with this picture. Was this the kind of memorabilia white alumni passed to their kids? Was this guy, who fancied himself too cool to wear socks, trying to make some kind of statement to me? Like I'm black, he's hip—so let's be friends?

"Is this real?" I finally asked.

"You bet," he answered without the slightest bit of discomfort. "My folks were always obsessed with the fear that Negroes would come here. Can you believe it?"

The inscrutable Lonnie kept talking, droning on and on—something about South Carolina, rights of association, desegregation, mongrelizing, citizens councils, and mulattoes. I didn't hear a single complete sentence that came from his mouth as I tried to get through the rest of the article. Slightly repulsed and thoroughly confused, I finally excused myself, edged my way back into the hall, and left. As I jogged back to my room down campus, I wondered if this is how "cool" white people get "deep" with blacks. I never understood why they felt the need to share this with me, but Lonnie was not the last alumni child to remind me that their fathers had been proud to attend an all-white university.

THE TWC PARTY

Weeks had passed. I had systematically introduced myself to what I felt was every "suitably integrated" black suburban freshman in the book—seventeen of them—and not a one seemed to be interested in attending TWC parties or joining OBU gatherings—much less talk to blacks who belonged to such groups. I, on the other hand, needed to be connected to the black community, so I continued to throw myself into the fray.

One Friday night in October, dateless and black-companionless, I put on a pair of black corduroys, a gray herringbone jacket, black loafers, a white button-down shirt, and a black tie with orange tigers on it. My roommate asked me where I was going.

"Oh, just to some party."

"In the dorm?"

"No." I paused nervously. "Off campus."

Steve looked up from his open books. "How do you know anybody *off campus*?"

Steve must have known I was lying. At Princeton, there was no such thing as a party "off campus." There were dorm parties and there were club parties. That was it. Nobody lived outside the gates of the two-and-a-half-square-mile campus. But I was pretty certain that from where Steve stood, the worlds of TWC and OBU were as off campus as they could possibly be. Even though he was probably among the more thoughtful students, he must have seen them as minority, militant, and counterculture. Neither I, nor university politics, had attempted to portray them any differently. And I was as mainstream as a black roommate could be. Dressing head-to-toe in alligator-covered apparel (even the socks), fretting over my declining tennis game, and bragging endlessly about my parents' new BMW and Buick station wagon, I'd worked hard to advance my nonthreatening integrated black-male, middle-class, suburban persona. So why undo all that hard work with a confession about my evening plans?

Winding my way through the dark campus walkways, lined with rhododendrons and pine trees, I was giddy with the prospect of meeting some new black friends at the party. All my life I'd had both black and white friends, yet here, I'd felt alienated from so many of the blacks on campus. It seemed like I'd met only militants and Oreos. Maybe, I thought, TWC's first party would introduce me to blacks in the middle—people like me. The kind who could do what Shirlene said was impossible: have it both ways. God only knows why they'd be at TWC, since they'd been no other place so far. Still I was hopeful.

And still, though, as I walked across the dark campus, I found myself looking over my shoulder as groups of white students approached. While unashamed of my desire to make black friends, I was still terrified that I'd run into white friends on the way to TWC. How would I explain my interest in the group? Already I had the sense that TWC had a militant reputation—and that white students misunderstood the need for self-selected all-black gatherings or organizations. They certainly wouldn't have thought I'd be a part of that.

As I jogged, eyes down, past oncoming white people, I thought about Shirlene and my roommate, Steve. I was going to manage this. I was raised in both worlds, and I could walk that tightrope again.

As I reached the edge of campus, at the beginning of Prospect Avenue, I saw groups of loud white students walking up and down the sidewalks in front of the clubs. Coming toward me, dressed in jeans and T-shirts with cups of soda in their hands, were two white guys from my dorm.

"Hey, Graham," Craig called out. "What's with the jacket and tie?"

Reluctantly, I mumbled that I was going to a Third World Center party.

"Third *World*?" Peter asked. "What the hell is that?"

"Blacks and minorities, you asshole," answered Craig, as he slapped Peter on the arm.

Peter was intrigued. "Oh, wow. Can we go? None of the clubs will let us in without a pass."

I paused. While the three of us had spent the first month of school going out to parties and meals together, it was at that moment that I realized things were going to eventually change for us. Yes, I could get into their parties and yes, they would even get into some of the black parties, but they'd always be waiting for me to side with my own, and I'd always be expecting them to form their closest friendships with whites. It was sad to see that we were already reaching this conclusion about one another. For a second, I almost considered loosening my tie, removing the jacket, and joining them on their club crawl, but I changed my mind. There was no use prolonging the inevitable.

Craig interrupted. "I don't think they'd really want us. Is that right, Larry?"

I looked at Craig's Grateful Dead T-shirt and Peter's Top-Sider shoes. And no socks! They just screamed "white boy!" Everything about them reminded me of the vast cultural gap that stood between the blacks and whites at Princeton. Politics were the least of it. Different music, different clothes, different slang, different heroes, different hometowns. It made me realize how ill equipped I was in solving this problem. Craig was right, but I didn't have the courage to tell him. "You're actually not dressed up enough."

"Yeah, but we wouldn't be allowed in anyway, right?"

Craig was pushing me. "I don't know—" I said almost apologetically. "I really don't know."

The two looked at me regretfully and walked on.

Ahead of me, just across the street, was an eight-foot-high red-brick wall. Behind it was the large two-story brick-and-wood-frame house that served as the Third World Center. Before I hit the wooden steps, I could smell reefer wafting from behind the bushes at Elm Club. Inside the TWC building was the heavy beat of Patti LaBelle singing, *"Voulez-vous couchez avec moi ce soir?"* Black, sexy, and hip. Except for a strobe light that reflected off a mirrored ball, the activity room was pitch-black and jammed full of people writhing to the latest dance—one that I, Mr. Suburbanite, didn't recognize.

It was everything that I hated about young black parties—loud, dark, crowded, and filled with attitude and the latest sexually suggestive dance step. All rhythm and no melody. Although it lacked the seedy beer smell and drunkenness of white parties I'd gone to, it was nonetheless an environment that I never felt comfortable in—and it was completely counterproductive for meeting the people and making the friends I was seeking.

Passing two black guys in dark sunglasses and dark double-knit slacks and polyester "freak" shirts buttoned halfway down their chests, I swallowed hard and tried to make eye contact through the dark room. After circling the room, recognizing no one, I finally escaped to the temporary safety of a well-lit kitchen. "How could Princeton be like this?" I wondered. Looking around and not seeing any of the "middle-of-the-road suburban blacks" I'd been expecting to meet, I had no idea how I'd ever fit in here. I felt like an oddball in a building full of people who looked just like me. Except clotheswise, of course. My jacket and tie were screaming "OREO FROM THE SUBURBS." I guess I should have known better, but wasn't this what a black at Princeton was supposed to look like?

Giving it another chance, I felt my way through the dark hall leading back into the party. At the punchbowl, a small lamp lit a six-foot radius. In the background was some sexy amplified voice screaming suggestively, ". . . You gotta ring my bell—ll—ll, ring my bell, ding-aling-aling." Even Mr. Suburbanite could figure out that this black songstress wasn't talking about her front door buzzer.

With palms sweating profusely, I shoved my hands into my pockets, until finally I recognized a woman from my psychology class. She was standing with a guy and another woman in the dark shadows of the corner behind the punch.

"Hi, I'm Larry Graham."

"Hey," one of the women replied.

The guy turned to me but said nothing.

The other woman pulled down her sunglasses and stuck them in her oversized Afro. She looked at my tie and pants. "Are you sure you're in the right party?"

Oh, to be black and unhip. It's among the worst possible social crimes to commit among my race. But, as embarrassed as I was, I played it off fairly well. "Oh, these clothes? Yeah, I had a meeting."

Two of them snickered. Miss Sunglasses rolled her eyes.

After twenty minutes more of the party, I walked out. A roomful of black people and I didn't stand a chance. Whether it was the fault of Shirlene, my clothes, my inability to dance, my slang, or my timing, I was on the outs with blacks at Princeton. Stuck between the Oreos and the militants, I didn't know which way to run.

With only a few exceptions, blacks and whites at Princeton did not socialize, date, live together, eat together, or study together. And the university seemed to think this was appropriate, for the administration never did anything to change it. The situation was apparent to all—particularly evidenced by the rooming arrangements in PIC. In the 1960s, when Princeton finally began to admit blacks on a regular basis, the housing office always assigned incoming black freshmen to single rooms on the top floors or basement floors of dorms. Claiming to be making these assignments in the best interest of the blacks "who would probably not want to live with whites," this exclusionary practice was ironically adopted by black students. The blacks would take over full hallways and sections of dorms, finally limiting themselves to certain sections of particular down-campus dorms like PIC and New Quad, the dreadful area that I'd been assigned to as a freshman. It was as if they were creating a black college in the midst of a white one—an echo of the Lincoln University transfers that Princeton had facilitated thirty years earlier. Not surprisingly, the university did nothing to counteract this voluntary segregation.

The eating clubs were another symptom of this problem. Most white students belonged to them; only a handful of blacks did. It was as if the black and white students were attending separate schools.

Not once do I recall the president or dean speaking out on the racial situation on the campus. Not once do I recall the president offering to visit the Third World Center to discuss ways to solve the problems that were apparent to all. The fact that there was a Third World Center at all may have been part of the problem. Many universities like Harvard never allowed the establishment of separate ethnic centers for just this reason.

As bad as relations were with whites, I realize that the covert nature of racism at Princeton was easier to tolerate than the vicious, overt bigotry that occurs on college campuses such as

Michigan State, University of Michigan, or Rider College, where the fraternities sponsored a 1992 "Dress Like a Nigger Night" and paraded around dressed like black slave mammies and butlers. Princeton was a polite place. Few would ever call you a nigger to your face. Maybe behind your back. Instead, they treated you like one. They ignored you. And if you pointed out their bigotry, they called you oversensitive. Formality and politeness were the rule. Perhaps that was why it was so hard to fight—because, like smoke, it was hard to get your arms around it.

I remember attending a rare campus race relations workshop during my junior year. As we sat discussing race issues in one of the classroom bowls of the Woodrow Wilson School of International Affairs, I heard one white woman from Louisiana explain that she wanted to befriend black classmates, "But I don't know how to do it. I just don't know what to say to them."

A few of the blacks in the room rolled their eyes at her remark, but then immediately tried to work with her. She reminded me of one of my two white sophomore roommates—stuck somewhere between good intentions and a total ignorance about others. Her candor was actually endearing, and I wished other whites—and blacks, too—had been as honest with their feelings and as aggressive in asking for moral direction on this issue.

"Talk to us in the same way that you'd talk to your white friends," I suggested to the woman. "Stop trying to speak to our black skin."

"Yeah, I hear you, but I always get the feeling you're laughing at me," she said. "It's like you've got your own code between you."

I persisted. "If you're sincere in speaking or even just saying hello, black students will do the same. I don't copy your southern accent, so you don't need to learn black slang. Most of us don't even use it."

For the next eighteen months during my junior and senior years, I passed this woman on campus and going to and from meals at our respective clubs on Prospect Avenue. Every time I would open my mouth to say hello, this woman who had argued, with great conviction, that she had wanted to befriend black students decidedly dropped her head or abruptly crossed the street to evade my salutation. It occurred to me that she was willing to be candid in that meeting when none of her white friends were present but unwilling to practice what had been preached to her once she was outside with the white friends who might not have appreciated her desire to mix with blacks.

She needed some white person—some white leader—to give her permission to do the right thing. But no one was there to do it.

APARTHEID MARCHES AND BLACK ANGER: TRYING TO BALANCE BLACK AND WHITE

Bowen! Bowen! Tell us why—
You let James Mange die!
NCR made the sale—
Where Steven Biko died in jail!

We blocked the walkway that ran down the middle of the Princeton campus—just between Cannon Green and the back of Nassau Hall. It was early April 1980, the spring of my freshman year and the height of the college antiapartheid movement, which called for divestiture in South Africa. I shouted angry, catchy phrases, carried large hand-drawn placards, shook my fist, and marched around the gravel path in large circles with twenty-five to thirty other black students.

We had a rhythm to our chant and a purpose to our step. While most of the marchers wore work boots, sunglasses, dark jeans, and army fatigues, I was, as always, in corduroys, suede Wallaby shoes, an Izod pullover, and a light blue crewneck sweater that I'd gotten monogrammed at Bergdorf's. I was a suburban black man on a rampage and I was mad as hell.

The rage that had brought me to the antiapartheid movement, though, had little to do with Steven Biko, James Mange, the jailed

African National Congress leader Nelson Mandela, or the plight of the people in South Africa. Ending all-white rule in South Africa hardly compared to my own self-centered cause of finding black friends and getting even with the white people at Princeton University—the ones who ignored me in the dining halls, who changed direction when they saw me approaching on the same path, and who had made me feel like an outsider since the day I had set foot on campus.

One evening after returning from an afternoon of anti-apartheid marching, I returned to my room and was confronted by my white roommate, the Catholic Boy Scout from suburban New Jersey. He mentioned that he had seen me marching out near Nassau Hall earlier that day.

A very sincere, compassionate guy, Steve broached the subject in his usual diplomatic manner. "Larry, I was sort of surprised to see you out there marching."

Of course he was surprised. I'd spent the first six months of the year cultivating my image and trying to prove to him and every other white student that the only thing black about me was my skin color. I explained that I and the other marchers wanted the administrators and students to know that the United States and its institutions were inherently racist and they perpetuated this racism by investing in corporations that operated in racist South Africa.

Steve nodded politely. "I heard what you were saying out there, about how Americans shouldn't support and invest in places like South Africa. Please don't get offended by this, but do blacks really think Americans are so terrible, and that things are so racist and unfair in the United States?"

Well, why wasn't I surprised to hear this? Although I knew Steve was open-minded and friendly to black people, I always thought that most other white people secretly wished that all black people would disappear, taking our problems and their guilt with us. It had taken me eighteen years to get mad at white people. And eighteen years to get mad at blacks. Of course I was opposed to apartheid, but that's not why I was marching. I was marching because I needed to express my anger with white Princetonians. And my anger at blacks. I wanted to bond with them, but they didn't want me. The self-loathing Oreos wanted nothing to do with black people or the black causes that affected us, and many of the other blacks wanted nothing to do with whites or with the blacks who talked and socialized with the whites. People like Shirlene said I had to choose, but I couldn't do that. So instead I tried to earn their love by championing their causes even more than Shirlene and her friends championed them. It was the first time I had ever done something to cause my white peers to say, "Oh, so he *is* just like the rest of them."

I was a mixed-up version of the old adage, "Talking black, but sleeping white." I had always "talked white" in the sense that I played it safe, thus making white people feel comfortable and making black people feel nervous about my commitment to black causes. And I had always "slept black" in that I had always placed my greatest loyalties, respect, and trust in black people and our causes.

It annoyed me that Shirlene and her crowd were even less accepting than so many of the blacks I encountered at the all-black table in my junior high school cafeteria. In junior high, one could at least befriend the kids at the black table even if one didn't sit there. Here, in college, though, the only way to win acceptance into the group was by offering a persona that was as Afrocentric, as hip, and as strident as Shirlene's. At first I thought I wouldn't be able to do it.

SENIOR YEAR: WORKING IT OUT

By the time I was ready to graduate, my Princeton experience had taught me to become an expert at straddling the fence that ran between blacks and whites. With my antiapartheid activism, the militant blacks forgave me for rooming with whites. With my published books, talk-show appearances, conservative clothes, and club affiliations, the bigoted and not-so-bigoted whites made me an exception to their rule of not socializing with blacks.

By the early part of senior year, I had terrific grades and was well liked by many on campus. I had joined one of the selective eating clubs and had found a small but solid clique of friends. Even though I had no idea what I stood for, even though I was incensed by the racism I saw continuing on campus, I had no one to pull me aside and tell me the moral thing to do. So I kept my mouth shut.

I wanted the university to give me and my classmates guidance on race issues, but it never did. The only black male role model that I tried to reach out to was uninterested. He was my only black male professor, a teacher of Afro-American history. He not only gave me my lowest grade at Princeton but also somehow made sure to put distance between himself and my need for a black role model and mentor. Ultimately, this man was to divorce his black wife and marry a young white student.

So I had to do it on my own. And the only way I found to succeed in my situation was by expecting nothing, standing for little, and getting people to like the person they thought I was.

And I came to be rather good at it. Desperate and insecure, I learned the importance and methods of pleasing just about any person I encountered: skeptic, snob, athlete, artist, Republican, Democrat, racist. Whatever they wanted from me, I felt that I had better discover some way to find it and give it to them. (One of my sophomore-year white roommates, a guy whom I will call Oscar, here—not a prince like Steve from freshman year—seemed to be the greatest test of my skills at dealing with borderline racists.) Insecure and afraid of being rejected, I managed to dig deep and give white people what they wanted of me. Some of them I liked and some of them I didn't. It usually didn't matter. In the most humiliating of circumstances, my experiences at Princeton—a school where manners mattered most—taught me how to enter rooms crowded with faces that hated my people and then leave with them liking me—the crowd-pleasing, integrated black man. I taught myself to approach white bigots with a smile and warm words, present my "act" of informed obsequiousness, find something in common, share some deep thought, then walk away with the prize in hand—all with great modesty and gratitude, convinced that I had gotten a bigot to like me and no longer caring about whether he or she liked black people.

This was that schizophrenic game of "crowd pleasing" that I, as an integrated black, was required to play at a school that never set a standard for people who wanted to address the race problem.

Even though I was to eventually quit the crowd-pleasing game, my desire to break the color barrier at Princeton caused me to hone and perfect my skills at winning white acceptance from people who shouldn't have mattered.

THE UNIVERSITY AS MORAL COMPASS

The best American universities have always been laboratories for the social and political changes that sweep the country from time to time. Ideally, a college campus provides a haven where students, with newfound freedom from the intellectual and social boundaries drawn by their parents and childhood communities, can safely confront different types of people and radical ideas. The best universities provide an environment conducive to such challenges. And yet they stand *in loco parentis* with the authority and responsibility to provide parental direction for the student body. An eighteen-year-old freshman, whether arriving on campus from Topeka, Beverly Hills, or Newark, needs the university and its administration to act as both provocateur and moral compass.

Race is a subject that desperately needs the informed and authoritative voice of the college community. Most black and white students leave their homogeneous communities and arrive on campus curious, intimidated, or even repulsed by students of the other race—and this is true at more places than just Princeton. Filled with doubt or, even worse, derogatory stereotypes regarding the other, they are at a loss about how to treat or identify with those different from them. Without guidance or a higher moral vision from university leaders, the course of least resistance for a student is to re-create that homogeneous community on campus. Unless a university instills a vision of diversity as somehow better, more desirable than homogeneity, a campus naturally begins to mimic the outside world, with its sturdy, racially defined barriers. With well-organized racist militants and demagogues flooding college campuses from groups like the Aryan Nation and the Nation of Islam, it is not surprising that black and white college students have become more racially polarized than ever.

What force other than activism on the part of university administrations can stem such a tide? Certainly, individual students will find their own way toward greater tolerance. But the vast majority will need to be led. College administrators have the ability and obligation to act as moral compasses for their students. To lead by example. For, if they do not, they create a leadership vacuum that can be easily filled by the voices of separatism and racism. Universities should establish moral policies and be willing to back up those policies with moral courage—a courage that acknowledges the existence of a racial problem, but then challenges bigotry and encourages dialogue and interaction between the races.

This is what I needed from Princeton in the early 1980s but what the school had always failed to offer. I needed Princeton's leaders to acknowledge its past and more recent racial problems, accept its obligatory role as a moral leader, and find a vision that could be respected and heeded by its student body. My own experiences suggest why universities like it will continue to fail black and white students who want to do the right thing in this racially polarized society.

As it approaches its 250th anniversary, the Princeton of more recent times seems to be lurching toward becoming a university that is more willing to acknowledge racial problems and devise responsible solutions. But its progress has been unsteady. All of the eating clubs have finally become both racially and sexually integrated, and there is no longer a dormitory where most of the blacks live. There is an NAACP chapter on campus, and there is finally a significant number of high-profile blacks on the faculty, including Toni Morrison, Nell Painter, and Arnold Rampersad. There are now minority affairs advisers in the dorms who act as counselors and mentors on diversity issues. In the spring of 1992, when the Los Angeles rioting erupted, nearly six hundred students, faculty members, and town residents gathered in front of the campus library to speak out against racism on campus and elsewhere.

But even with this new willingness to speak out, there remain problems on campus for black students. For instance, after black students complained about being harassed by campus police, a university report commissioned by the provost found that many campus police officers "harbored prejudicial attitudes that influenced their treatment of black students and staff."

A spring 1992 survey performed by two graduate students and a member of the class of 1992 found that nearly two-thirds of black and Latino Princetonians have witnessed racial problems at the school.

The problems continue at an even more rapid clip beyond the immediate borders of the campus. For example, Professor Cornel West, the outspoken professor who headed the university's Afro-American Studies Program from 1990 to 1993, abruptly announced in late 1993 that he would leave the school and move to Harvard, where he would join the staff of an already established African American Studies program. Given the fact that he has moved to a school where he will be a mere member of the program—and not the head—some have wondered what caused the sudden move. Black Princetonians have speculated that it was his treatment by the town of Princeton. Many articles, including a February 1994 profile of West in *The New Yorker*, have commented on the frequency with which West was stopped by local Princeton police—usually with the complaint that he was driving too slowly. Assistant Dean of the Chapel William Gipson told the *Princeton Alumni Weekly* in late 1992, "The most explicit examples of prejudice and racism I've experienced and learned from others have happened in Princeton Borough." At one point, things got so bad for black students that they drafted a statement for local store owners to sign, which read that they would pledge "to treat all customers fairly and equally regardless of ethnic heritage or racial origins." The local newspaper, the *Princeton Packet,* reported that many merchants were unwilling to sign the pledge.

But nothing was as disappointing as the university's handling of the 1989 speaking invitation to minister Louis Farrakhan offered by students from the Organization of Black Unity. While announcement of the invitation drew resentment from white and Jewish students who objected to Farrakhan's controversial remarks on race and religion, the Princeton administrators remained typically silent—neither voicing support of free speech nor criticism of Farrakhan's racist views.

In a move to appease the whites and Jews on campus, yet still not address the racist nature of the upcoming speech, the university acted to silence the speech by first telling OBU that they had to pay the school $3,000 for security. The school then waited two weeks to change that number to $8,000. According to OBU organizers and the findings of the *Daily Princetonian,* the school gave OBU only two days to raise this additional $5,000 or Farrakhan could not visit. Not surprisingly, the students were unable to raise the money on such short notice and had to cancel the speech. Two days later, President Harold Shapiro made a disingenuous announcement. He told the campus paper, "I am sorry they weren't able to complete their plans. Maybe it can happen another time." The university missed an ideal opportunity to take a stand on the issue of racial problems on campus and beyond. But instead, it took the easy, passive-aggressive route that it always has. It said nothing about the nature of the speech but used a shopworn ploy to prevent it from happening.

In spite of these incidents, I continue to contribute each year to Princeton's Annual Giving fund drive. I am obsessed with the school because I so desperately hope to see it progress into an environment that works for its black students as well as its white students.

I am also obsessed with replacing some of the memories that I left with. One of them involved a meeting I had set up with the dean of students a few days following an incident that I believed to be an insult to minorities on campus. A fraternity had been trying to gain a foothold on campus, and for its initiation, it required its pledges to urinate on the front door of—where else?—the Third World Center.

Breaking my rule of never speaking out on race issues or appearing controversial, I contacted the dean of students and met with him in what became a five-minute confrontation. When I asked the dean—himself a white Princeton alumnus—if there was anything he could do to address this clear racially based affront, he responded with a remark I will never forget:

"What do you want me to do—go scrub it off the door?"

When I told him that I hoped he would write an open letter to the student body or take out an ad in the paper deploring such bigoted acts, he called the meeting to an end.

Breaking my no-controversy rule once more, I made one final attempt to address this issue. I wrote a rather innocuous three-sentence letter to the editor of the *Daily Princetonian* asking students to use this time to address racial problems at the university.

Three days later, a letter was published in response to my own. It was filled with resentment and self-righteous indignation. It stated that I was the real racist for suggesting that it was an act of bigotry for white students to urinate on the front door of the Third World Center.

The letter was signed by Oscar, my white, sophomore-year roommate.

10

BLACK MAN WITH A NOSE JOB

How We Defend
Ethnic Beauty in America

Dad, slow down some."

The relentless spring breeze finally calmed as my father let up from the accelerator and swerved us into a right-hand lane.

This man, who was normally quite solicitous of his youngest son and who almost never drove above fifty miles per hour, was suddenly sighing indignantly over my interference with his driving speed.

"What's wrong?" I asked.

He stared straight ahead, occasionally glancing at the stream of cars that were now passing us by. "Nothing," he answered.

As we reached the Henry Hudson tollbooths that would take us out of Manhattan, three young black faces peered into the side window.

A portion of this essay appeared in *New York Newsday,* June 4, 1990.

"What the hell happened to *you?*"

"Somebody fucked his shit up—look at that shit!"

Three black guys in their early twenties looked down from their Jeep into my open window and shook their heads with perverse amusement.

Determined to get a response, the driver finally asked, "You get shot?"

Dad moved us up another car length as I put the ice pack beneath my eyes and moved into a reclining position.

"Extra token and a receipt."

"My goodness—is everything all right in there?" the blue-jacketed toll woman asked as she stared into the backseat at my head: an oversized bowling ball of white gauze, plaster, and hospital tape. Unbeknownst to me, melting ice was quietly transforming the gauze-covered bloodstains, making them a more prominent red color and giving them a surreal, almost tie-dye-like quality underneath the white material.

I think I nodded faintly.

"Just a nose job," my father answered while retrieving his change.

"Really?" She seemed surprised by my father's air of nonchalance.

Or was it an air of contempt?

As I lay reclined, with my head practically in the backseat of the little maroon BMW, I wondered what my father thought of me now. A man of a different generation—born and raised in the segregated South—educated and trained in an almost exclusively black world where the concept of an oxymoron readily included such things as a black man with a nose job.

For my entire life, until yesterday, I had displayed his same nostrils, bridge, and profile. Tomorrow I wouldn't. Tomorrow I'd look like someone else. Staring up at the back of my father's head, I realized that the success of my operation would be measured in direct proportion to how much differently my nose looked from his. It was a shameful contrast to make with someone I loved so much, but when looking at my sketches, it was an accurate one nevertheless.

. . .

"This is the one I want," I had said while handing the opened magazine to Dr. Wilson.

"Which?" he asked.

I scanned the well-lit Upper East Side office, then crossed my legs with an air of affected nonchalance. "I actually don't care. Any of those would do."

This black plastic surgeon—one who had been practicing on the Upper East Side for longer than my time on this earth—had no doubt met my kind before: that overly anxious patient who displays reckless confidence in the miracles of modern medicine. Walking the streets with desperation in our eyes and portfolios under our arms, we young, well-to-do seekers of cosmetic enhancement bear a strange resemblance to professional models, except that inside *our* portfolios is a lifetime supply of dog-eared photos and print ads depicting *other people's* faces, features, and body parts that we wish *we* had been born with and that we hope can still be affixed—Mr. Potatohead-like—onto the various appendages and extremities of our bodies.

Having torn more than fifty or sixty shots of sharp-nosed, square-jawed, model-handsome, near-black-looking or practically black-looking men from some of the best store catalogs and hippest fashion magazines in New York, I felt I'd done more than my share of the legwork. I was now ready to pay whatever it cost and submit myself to whatever tests, X rays, computer imaging, or painful surgical procedures were necessary.

Dr. Wilson* flipped ahead with a ruffled brow. "What magazine are these pictures from?"

I leaned over his desk and looked at the pages. "That's the Brooks Brothers catalog. But I've got lots of other noses and faces mixed in from other catalogs and magazines."

The good doctor—I'd been told one of the best in New York—had no idea of how long I'd agonized over this project. I'd

---

* This name has been changed.

been saving noses and profiles for the prior three years, tearing out pages from magazines, catalogs—even stealing a poster from a Boston red-line subway car one Sunday afternoon—all in the search for the right features. I stuck all this into a bulging April 1987 issue of *Ebony*.

"Mr. Graham," the sensitive doctor began as he reached for my chin and turned my head to either side. "There is only a certain amount of alteration that is possible, or even desirable, for any one nose."

"I know what you're going to say," I interrupted. "That you can't make me look like those guys because they have white noses. But if you notice, those are all *black* men on these pages I've given you. They're all *black*."

"Hmm."

The least black-looking collection of black men either one of us had ever seen compiled.

"Even if I *could* do this—and it would be unlikely—such a long thin prominent nose wouldn't work on your face."

"Okay, then what about this one?" I showed him a page from a nine-month-old *Sports Illustrated*.

The good doctor shook his head.

"But he's black too." Yeah, black and something else.

"Umm."

"What about this one?" I showed him several shots of a brown-skinned model in a *GQ* layout. Probably a black Cuban.

He waved me on.

I pulled out a recent issue of *Essence* and turned to the first of the paper-clipped pages, which featured models who were suddenly displaying darker skin and wider, flatter noses. "How about that?" I pointed to the *Essence* man who stood holding an elegant glass of whiskey.

"Why don't I sketch out what I think we can consider."

But I wasn't giving up yet. "Wait—let me just show you this last one. I got this tourism ad out of *Ebony*. You must at least be able to do *that*."

He looked down at the brownest of all my men. "Mr. Graham, that nose would never be in harmony with your lips and chin. They would never work together."

"My lips and chin?" I asked. I had to pause a few seconds and consider the significance of his remark. "Then change them," I finally howled. "Change them. I'll pay whatever it costs. Change them. Just change them!"

Sometimes it takes very little to send some of us down the slippery slope toward black self-hatred.

Eventually I entered a hospital on Manhattan's Upper West Side to undergo that common surgical procedure we all call rhinoplasty. While this procedure is performed nearly a hundred thousand times each year, I had the feeling that my case was different. It was shortly after being wheeled into the large, brightly lit recovery room that I became certain that I had just launched an assault on my identity and my people. But now it was too late to go back. I was, forever, a black man who had gotten a nose job.

Although I'd grown up in a white neighborhood where male and female adolescents got their noses narrowed, chins and cheeks enhanced, and skin chemically peeled as a coming-of-age ritual during junior high and high school vacations, I had never seriously considered plastic surgery for myself. Yes, I wanted to be thought of as more handsome, but no one in my family had ever undergone cosmetic surgery. For these white friends and classmates who had undergone surgical changes, their explanations focused simply on cosmetics: They wanted to look "better." Not surprisingly, no one ever seemed to impute any other motive or to psychoanalyze the real meaning of "better." For me and my family, physical appearance and its alteration were issues of ethnicity and heritage. Black people had wide nostrils, thick lips, protruding mouths, and dark skin—and any desire to change those features was, by definition, a negative commentary on our people and our own racial identity.

For the most part, I never even compared my looks to those of the white kids or white adults around me. During my adolescence, I did, however, draw contrasts with the young blacks in my own world of black professionals and their families who socialized in our black social clubs and vacation places. There were numerous occasions as a child, and later as an adult, when hosting summer cookouts in Sag Harbor, Long Island, or Oak Bluffs, Martha's Vineyard; attending our Jack & Jill family gatherings; or partying at the Sisters of Ethos all-black dances at Wellesley College, when I'd run into dozens of well-to-do, light-skinned, straight-haired, thin-featured black childhood friends. After returning to the security of my own bedroom mirror, I would critique my features against those other blacks in my life who had "sharper," "nicer," "finer" (all words that meant more attractive and less Negroid) physical characteristics.

I would flatten my thick lips against my teeth, protrude my chin, and try but fail to attach a wooden clothespin on the wide fleshy tip of my nose. The pain of this primitive procedure was outweighed by the satisfaction I got from capturing a glimpse of longer, thinner nostrils.

Except for those occasions when I flipped through men's magazines or passed by some daytime or nighttime TV soap opera, it was rare that I ever compared my features to whites around me. Unlike young girls, I was fortunate that as little boys, my brother and I weren't saddled with trying to find our image and, hence, our self-worth, in the similarities we shared with the face and features of a white Barbie and Ken doll. In spite of the ambivalence that I once had about my looks, I've always felt that black boys are far luckier than the black girls who get ambushed by white girls in school and summer camp who tell them, "You'd be really pretty if it wasn't for that black nappy hair of yours."

My color ambivalence manifested itself in many different ways during my adolescence. I'm reminded of the Hasbro G.I. Joe army and astronaut set I used to play with. One afternoon I put brown shoe polish all over my 1967 G.I. Joe astronaut's entire pink body and later melted his tiny nose away with the heat from my Mattel

"Creepy Crawlers" cooking iron. I don't know if I can ascribe my actions to black pride or a desire to punish Joe, but I never took him out in public after that.

Finally, after considering hundreds of magazine and catalog layouts and doctor's sketches, after writing a check for $4,000 to a black surgeon, and after having the operation, I still sometimes feel like I've upset the standard of blackness that I'd been raised to accept and appreciate.

When I told a former black classmate about my operation, she accused me of trying to pass out of the black race. It was hardly the sympathetic response I had expected from an intelligent woman who had been one of my first friends in law school. In fact, her contempt was so great and questions so numerous, I really began to wonder if she was right about my motives.

Did I have this operation in order to become less black—to have features that were more white? Had I bought into the white definition of beauty—the sharp nose, the thin lips, the straight hair? Did I think that my less Negroid-looking black friends were more attractive than me?

My wife says my decision is personal and that I shouldn't feel compelled to defend it or explain it to anyone else. I'd like to think she is right. Maybe she's right about not needing to justify my acts to white coworkers or white neighbors. But what about my black relatives, my black friends, my black coworkers, my black secretary? Don't I owe them an explanation? Don't I have to let them know I wasn't saying that I wanted to be white when I pared down my wider, rounder Negroid nose?

Of course, I could take the easy way out and tell onlookers that one's racial identity is not embodied in one's nose. It certainly should be obvious in my case. After all, my dark brown skin and curly black hair are still intact. A different nose won't make me look white. But that's really not the point I need to address, is it?

For two years prior to my operation, I agonized over the ethnic ramifications of cosmetic surgery. According to the American Society of Plastic and Reconstructive Surgeons, 640,000 cosmetic procedures were performed in the United States in 1994. Since the preponderance of those patients were white, I am fairly certain that many of them felt no obligation to justify their surgery to members of their ethnic group.

All of this leads me to conclude that my defenses are a wasted effort. While my white friends have guiltlessly selected profiles and implants with their surgeons, I was making a futile attempt to validate my ethnic loyalty by developing arguments to prove that a nose job would not make me less black.

I shouldn't have to defend my surgery any more than those 640,000 patients who pass under the scalpel each year—or for any person who makes any type of cosmetic changes in his or her natural appearance. After all, an Italian person rarely feels guilty for turning his brown hair blond. Few Jewish people apologize for having their noses shaved down. Not many Asian people have to justify putting waves into their straight hair. Many people, in fact, are surprised to learn that in both Japan and Korea, as well as in the United States, it is quite common for male and female Japanese and Korean people of all ages to have their eyes done (for less than $1,500, a surgeon creates a more westernized eye by creating a fold in the eyelid that makes it appear rounder) and their noses enhanced (for about $2,500, a surgeon creates a more Caucasian nose by raising the bridge and tip by inserting a plastic or cartilage implant). With so many other groups undergoing the same procedures, it is ludicrous for black cosmetic surgery to be taken as a form of heresy against the race.

I am discovering that many whites as well as blacks perceive a black person's cosmetic surgery as a sign of self-hatred or the desire to be less black—an accusation often aimed at singer Michael Jackson, who in spite of his claims about rare skin diseases and naturally changing bone structure, pinched his nose, bleached his skin, tattooed his eyes, enhanced his chin, and straightened his hair. Even black talk-show host Montel Williams felt compelled to explain his nose job to his viewers. His claim: He'd done it because he'd had difficulty breathing. Whether we believe his explanation or not, none of us have the right to challenge such a decision.

An equally presumptuous attitude prevailed a while back with regard to colored contact lenses. No one objected when white actors, models, and consumers wore the cosmetic lenses, but when black talk-show host Oprah Winfrey wore them on TV, there was an immediate avalanche of attacks from both whites and blacks who could not understand why a black person would wear green contacts. White people seemed to be threatened by the notion that black people could actually avail themselves of cosmetic advances and appropriate the beauty characteristics that white people had theretofore defined as exclusively their own. Black audiences, too, looked at rich, powerful, and famous Oprah and feared that she was somehow about to "buy" herself out of the black race and leave us bereft of one more black heroine and role model. In the end, when the host held her ground on her black identity, black and white viewers wised up and realized that the ever dedicated and down-to-earth Winfrey wasn't going anywhere she didn't belong. Colored contacts weren't going to change her.

Black plastic-surgery patients or lens-wearers should not have to address the issue of ethnicity any more than white people who go to a tanning salon or get a collagen shot to thicken their lips—as so many white actors, models, and fashion-conscious citizens are doing today. Black people who get their hair straightened each month should be able to do so just because they want to sample a noncurly style.

Because I've narrowed my nose, some of my black friends say I have sought to deny my ethnicity, and oddly enough, some of my white friends—even those who have had nose jobs themselves—say I'm representative of the young black professional who wants to assimilate into the white culture. Perhaps it is true that the media images and the white kids who surrounded me as a child sometimes caused me to judge my own attractiveness on some other group's standard of beauty, but I dismiss the suggestion that any black who seeks to alter his natural physical characteristics has turned on his people and attempted to "pass" as a member of some other race.

Once the bandages were finally taken off (a few years ago), friends discovered that I am no less black than I was before the operation. I still had the same black friendships, still supported the same black causes, and still maintained the same black consciousness. As my father, the stoic black southerner, was able to do, my friends continue to allow me to take pleasure in my new appearance. For them to view this as anything more than a cosmetic procedure would be to suggest that the culture, feelings, and history of black people are awfully superficial.

11

MOVING FROM "BLACK RAGE" TO "BIAS NEUTRALIZING"

A NEW PARADIGM
FOR AFFIRMATIVE ACTION

Ever since April 15, 1979, the day I received my college admissions notification letters, I have been an unapologetic supporter of affirmative action. Unfortunately, for a large part of that time, it was for the wrong reasons: I felt resentment toward, and wanted revenge against, those who I felt would never respect me.

That afternoon, I was sitting in my high school's student newspaper office helping some of the junior reporters review and proofread incoming stories for our biweekly paper. As eleventh-graders, they were all a year away from recognizing the significance of this day—a day when, like my fellow seniors, I should have been running home to open my mail. Instead, I was fulfilling my duties as editor in chief.

"Larry. It's your dad," one of my coworkers said after picking up the heavy black telephone.

This was it. The mail had come, and at that moment, I felt the weight of every test, book report, class project, and school activity that I'd ever been associated with being lifted off my shoulders—either to come crashing back down on me or to be held as evidence that hard work leads to admission to a respectable college.

"Son, good news," my father began. "You got into Dartmouth, Princeton, University of Pennsylvania, Brown. . . ."

It was everything I had hoped for. I repeated the list of schools to the students who sat there editing. One cracked a smile and gave me a thumbs-up sign. Another said, "Wow." The rest of them remained silent.

"Hey, did you guys hear me? You're supposed to say congratulations."

Finally, one of the eleventh-graders broke the silence. "Give me a break. How could you *not* get in? You're black."

Another one looked up from his proofreading. "No offense, Larry, but with affirmative action, you end up taking *our* places and we get screwed. Now, if one of *us* got into Princeton, *then* I'd be impressed."

The five white faces smiled faintly and nodded at each other in agreement.

Here I was, clearly the most powerful person in the room—the head of the paper and on top in the hierarchy. I was a senior; they were juniors. I was the editor; they were reporters. Here, after receiving what I thought was one of the best honors of my life, I was left feeling like the "bad guy." Suddenly, I was left feeling that I should be apologizing for accepting an honor that I didn't deserve or a respect I hadn't earned. I then remembered a conversation that should have prepared me for this moment.

A year before, on a May afternoon in 1978, I sat in the same office. At the time, I had only been editor in chief for four weeks, and the first issue edited by our new staff had just been published. The staff of fifty-some students—all white, mostly middle- and upper-class Jews—divided the five thousand copies, slapped on mailing labels, and collated them by zip code. Three or four of the senior editors read through the paper, congratulating ourselves on the issue.

"I bet David will be impressed with *this*," I said to the feature editor, a girl I'd been friends with since the third grade. We both looked over the front page as I thought about David, the outgoing editor in chief, who was then on his way to Harvard and who would eventually win a Pulitzer as a reporter at the *New York Times*.

"Well, even if David *is* impressed, you'll never be respected like him," she said almost nonchalantly.

As I stared down at the newspaper that lay across Rona's (not her real name) Gloria Vanderbilt jeans, I thought about the substance of her remark. Coming from someone who was rather superficial and who was not among my more articulate friends, her comment sounded oddly sophisticated and out of character. She was not a mean person, but her almost rehearsed delivery of the remark had a very mean edge to it. It was almost as though she had heard someone else say it and now wanted me to feel the brunt of it.

I didn't know exactly where the conversation was heading, but with the false modesty that I'd come to believe was necessary to affect in order to maintain the unchallenged loyalty of my all-white teenaged staff, I added, "Rona, I'm not competing with David. I know that nobody's a match for his braininess."

"I'm not talking about braininess," the sixteen-year-old said curtly from behind her glasses and long mop of brown hair. "I know you're smart. I'm just saying nobody's ever going to *respect* you."

There it was again. I could hardly believe what I was hearing. Had somebody told her to say this to me? Was this liberal Jewish girl—in tight jeans, a halter top, and straightened hair—trying to hurt my feelings or just letting me in on what others had said about my role here?

"Rona, what the hell are you talking about? I've taken more honors classes, written more stories, and gotten better grades than—"

"Larry," she said while nonchalantly cutting me off and jumping from the top of the large wooden table. "I didn't say you weren't smart. I'm just saying that no matter what you do, no matter what you say, we're never going to *respect* you."

My adolescence was sufficiently littered with thinly veiled racially motivated remarks like this from brazen and resentful white kids for me to come to the conclusion, by the age of eighteen or nineteen, that winning respect from white people was not only painstaking, it was, in some cases, absolutely futile.

Given these disturbing experiences, I relished the idea of personally benefiting from, and getting other blacks and minorities to benefit from, affirmative action: Finally, here was our chance to take something from them—a chance to stick it to those who had overlooked our accomplishments and had stuck it to us.

But how wrong I was.

From Affirmative Action to "Black Rage"

On September 24, 1965, President Lyndon B. Johnson signed Executive Order 11246 establishing the practice of affirmative action both in the federal government and for any contractor wishing to conduct business with the government. In recognizing that blacks had historically been discriminated against in education and employment, Johnson implemented a mechanism that he felt would make up for past discrimination and help blacks reach parity with whites in these areas.

While many whites opposed affirmative action, arguing that blacks would have no problem catching up to whites since *de jure* segregation of jobs and education had already ended, the president stated in his famous June 4, 1965, Howard University commencement speech, "You do not take a person who, for years, has been hobbled by chains and liberate him, bring him up to the starting line of a race and then say, 'You are free to compete with the others' and still justly believe you have been completely fair."

Through the actions of the federal government—specifically the Department of Labor's Office of Federal Contract Compliance Programs (OFCCP)—affirmative action policies came to be defined as specific and result-oriented procedures that would be temporarily in place to aid minorities in order to make up for past discrimination.

On December 7, 1993, a thirty-six-year-old black man named Colin A. Ferguson boarded the crowded 5:33 P.M. Long Island Railroad commuter train heading for Hicksville, New York. As the train left the borders of New York City and entered Nassau County, Ferguson took out a gun and began walking down the aisle of the train shooting passengers at point-blank range. Before he was wrestled to the floor, he had killed six people and wounded nineteen others. Through notes found in his pockets and a subsequent confession, it was revealed that Ferguson had intended to kill as many white people on the train as possible in order to exact retribution for the discriminatory treatment that he felt he had received from whites in the past. A few months later, New York defense lawyer William M. Kunstler revealed that he and his partner, Ronald Kuby, would be defending Ferguson with a plea of "not guilty." Although Ferguson had confessed to the shootings, he had conceived a new legal basis on which he would declare his innocence: the black rage insanity defense.

Kunstler said that he would argue that Ferguson should be found blameless because as a past victim of antiblack discrimination, he deserved some form of dispensation for his anger, and hence, his crime. The state should excuse Ferguson for the shootings as a way to compensate him for past injustices done to him and other blacks.

When I first heard of this black rage defense strategy, I was appalled. The idea of giving blacks—or any other group—the legal right to get away with murder was unconscionable. Like many blacks, I was shocked by this defense strategy (and its implicit view that blacks need not be held to the same standard of human moral behavior as whites). But I soon learned there was another group that, while also offended by the theory, was not the least bit shocked to hear it being articulated: white people. Many whites claimed publicly, on television and in print, that they were not surprised that our legal system had come to this because, in their eyes, the country had started down a slippery slope in 1965 that led inevitably to this point: How far of a leap was it from giving a black man a job because of past wrongs to letting him get away with murder?

As a black man who strongly supports affirmative action and its goal of ensuring equal opportunity for blacks, I was deeply troubled by the cynicism of whites who take this egregious example of "compensatory justice" as the logical outgrowth of affirmative action.

I was equally troubled by the large percentage of black people—68 percent, as reported in a June 1994 survey by the *National Law Journal*—who support the black rage defense and the anti-white, retribution-driven theories that justify it. My guess is that many of these blacks would rationalize this new defense with the same rhetoric they have come to use in explaining affirmative action: We're just taking back from those who once took from us. I once felt the way they are feeling, and I had at least a few kids from the high school newspaper to thank for that.

All of this suggests that affirmative action—or at least the rhetorical justifications for affirmative action—has done a great deal more to damage black-white relations than most of us realize. It has taught whites that blacks and the government are intent on punishing them in perpetuity for crimes their white forefathers committed. And it has taught blacks that they are completely justified in seeking any form of retribution or revenge—displacing a more competent white employee at work, displacing a more qualified white college applicant, committing "justified" criminal acts against whites—because white people once proudly endorsed antiblack discrimination.

I would like to offer a new paradigm for affirmative action—one based less on entitlement, retribution, and punishment and more on ensuring equal opportunity and neutralizing biases. For some very obvious reasons, I call this paradigm "bias neutralizing." My belief is that our approach to affirmative action has been entirely misguided. While I strongly support its goal of offering increased opportunities to blacks and others, I believe that it was incorrectly built upon and designed around theories and rhetoric that create resentment among whites and vindictive antiwhite attitudes among blacks, while also serving as an ineffective, backward-looking method for increasing the opportunities available to blacks and other minorities.

Instead of using remedial, backward-looking, punishing, retribution-driven affirmative action programs that are put in place temporarily, this country needs forward-looking, bias-neutralizing programs that are corrective and that, in a permanent way, work to neutralize the inherent antiblack biases that are otherwise impossible to eradicate in white-dominated institutions.

A COMPENSATORY JUSTICE POLICY SPECTRUM

To better understand how most white people currently interpret affirmative action and other racial preference policies, one needs to imagine a spectrum simulated by a footlong horizontal line. At the far left end—the beginning of the line—is a point labeled "Ending *De Jure* Discrimination Against Blacks." Here we would place the acts that overturned laws preventing blacks from voting, attending white schools and universities, and patronizing public establishments—laws that existed before the 1954 *Brown v. Board of Education* Supreme Court decision that finally struck down the "separate-but-equal" legal doctrine. At the far right end of the line is *"De Jure* Punishment of Whites." This is where we would place laws excusing physical assaults on whites: legal theories such as the "black rage defense," by which blacks are exculpated for their homicidal attacks on whites. Somewhere around three-quarters the length of the line—at about nine inches—is a point labeled "Affirmative Action." One inch to the right of that point is "Racial Quotas."

The spectrum displays the various legal approaches that have been utilized to increase the opportunities of blacks. Although some would characterize the spectrum as a range of potential legal measures to increase black opportunity, whites who follow the popular interpretation of affirmative action would call them encroachments on white people's rights. These whites would call this the "antiwhite retribution/impediment spectrum," and this is why, for them, the actual practice of affirmative action appears so far down the line, closer to "*De Jure* Punishment of Whites." As opposed to looking at this spectrum as a measure of black people's access to opportunity, most whites perceive this more like a spectrum measuring the degree to which they are penalized for being white. They see each point after that as one more proposal requiring them to surrender a legal right to blacks because of what whites unfairly did to blacks in the distant past. While almost all whites (with the possible exception of white neo-Nazis and other extremists who would push back to the point where they could act beyond the law in penalizing blacks) would agree that ending *de jure* discrimination—with the 1954 desegregation of schools and passing of Title VII—was fair, many would draw a bright line on the spectrum there, with anything that would reduce *de facto* discrimination as being inherently unfair. I believe they are wrong to interpret it this way, but this response is not surprising. It is the inevitable outcome of the rhetoric of punishment and retribution attached to affirmative action thirty years ago.

And just as many whites accept this analysis of affirmative action, many blacks accept it as well. They see affirmative action, quotas, reparations, the black rage defense, and any policy allowing them to act beyond the law as representing the spoils that black people have finally taken away from whites. And not surprisingly, as whites push to move society toward the left on the spectrum, blacks are simultaneously pushing in the opposite direction, trying to move society to the right on the spectrum, closer to where they will be permitted not just more opportunities for themselves but also more opportunities to deprive white people. At one end, whites are the losers, and at the other end, blacks are the losers.

Often pitched in the rhetoric of what white people must give up, what white people should be penalized for, what white people must do to compensate for having discriminated against minorities in our history, affirmative action has consequently been portrayed as the white man's persecution. This has always been the language of affirmative action. One example is Charles Silberman's 1962 essay, "The City and the Negro," which focused on the guilt of whites and the debt they owed blacks. He stated that black people's loss of opportunities should be made up for by white people. "These are sins for which all Americans are in some measure guilty and for which all Americans owe some act of atonement."

At the Georgetown Conference on Poverty in January 1964, the Swedish social scientist Gunnar Myrdal spoke out against the anticipated affirmative action policies because he suspected that poor whites, who competed for jobs with blacks, would be further embittered if they were told to give up their own opportunities to aid blacks. White resentment inevitably followed.

Equally inevitably, many blacks have appropriated this same retribution rhetoric so they could justify more far-reaching racial preference policies.

Responsible black leaders from yesterday and today have made remarks pointing out the need for white people to give up something in order to repay blacks for what was taken from us. Many have similarly characterized the recent efforts by Reverend Jackson, Michigan congressman John Conyers, and others to pass legislation that would give blacks financial reparations for the enslavement of their ancestors. A Jackson, Mississippi-based black civil rights group suggested that twenty thousand dollars should be paid to each black American. And who should pay these reparations? Some have suggested that they be paid by any white person descended from a white slave owner.

Some blacks have taken a different but equally negative path in defending affirmative action by focusing on the many private networks that effectively provide affirmative action for privileged whites.

ACKNOWLEDGING "WHITE-SANCTIONED AFFIRMATIVE ACTION"

A discussion of 1965-style affirmative action would not be complete without an analysis of those programs (formal and otherwise) that exist to favor a predominantly white and affluent group of beneficiaries. The arguments for or against affirmative action often focus on such issues as compromised standards, merit, the stigmatization of black beneficiaries, the significance of diverse views, as well as the standards and predictors of success.

When our neighbors and teachers discuss and excoriate affirmative action, they are typically referring to these aforementioned issues in the context of programs mandated—in 1965 or at other times—by the federal government or by the private sector to meet slated government goals—what I have been referring to as 1965-style affirmative action. These mandates and goals have historically been designed to benefit minorities and the underprivileged.

The benefits that I would like to turn to for a moment are those accorded by that rarely discussed but often utilized body of programs I call "white-sanctioned affirmative action." These are programs and policies that are put into place to—whether by design or by accident—succeed in giving a disproportionate number of white people preferential treatment, particularly in the areas of educational and employment opportunities.

Although many of my affluent white childhood friends had been lifelong beneficiaries of white-sanctioned affirmative action, the sophistication and systematic nature of the process was not apparent to me until I was well into college. The person who introduced it to me was Andrew (not his real name), one of my close friends (one of those same friends, I might add, who complained that blacks had an unfair advantage in society because of affirmative action) from high school.

Early in the tenth grade, both of us began our search for summer jobs by applying to personnel offices at the same local headquarters of *Fortune* 500 companies. About a week into the application process, Andrew's parents told him that he wouldn't have to continue with the applications or try to seek interviews, since several high-level executives of these companies belonged to their country club and could provide him with a summer job without going through the normal channels. For the next three summers in high school—tenth, eleventh, and twelfth grade—Andrew was employed by each of three different *Fortune* 500 companies, on each occasion by having his parents call directly to high-ranking executives who belonged to their club and who offered jobs to the kids of friends who also belonged there.

Although I went through the normal application process at these companies and was only once offered a position (after freshman year in college), I accepted—with some degree of envy—that Andrew would often get ahead simply because of contacts. Although I saw the pattern repeated each year, I never equated this practice with the affirmative action programs that Andrew used to criticize for awarding benefits based upon an accident of birth. I was envious, but never looked down my nose at him for it. In fact, he bragged so much about his inside connections that they became a source of pride.

My competition with him for academic advancement was similarly thwarted. Throughout high school, we were both in the same accelerated classes. We studied hard, but because of Andrew's family wealth, he was able to hire math, science, and French tutors throughout high school. He also received several weeks of tutoring for the nationally administered PSAT.

When our senior year arrived, Andrew informed me that his father (a Duke graduate) and his mother (a Cornell graduate) assured him that with their own alumni status and their friends at the club and elsewhere, they could assure his acceptance to a school no worse than Duke or Cornell. I am still amazed by his (and probably their) outrageous terminology: "no worse than Duke or Cornell."

Over time, I had grown accustomed to Andrew's approach to virtually any competition or application process. His first response was to run home and ask his parents, "Who do we know at such-and-such a place?" Andrew was confident that for virtually any selective process he faced, a special system would enable him to circumvent the traditional rules and requirements of merit.

After receiving ten weeks of SAT tutoring, he and several other kids from his club hired a professional admissions consultant—a former college admissions officer—to help write his college applications and essays and coach him for the admissions interviews. Two years before, by their own admission to me as I sat at their kitchen table, his parents had stepped up their own personal contributions to their alma maters and then later called on friends and club members who were alumni donors and had them write letters on behalf of Andrew's applications. Since Andrew and his father would script the letters of recommendation with the consultant before passing them on to their alumni friends to retype and sign on personal or business stationery, the letters were full of hyperbole and misstatements about his accomplishments and his relationship to the letter writer.

As he kept me informed with almost daily updates—also letting me in on the identity of other students in our class who followed the same practice—I realized how unprepared I was for the application process. In the end, Andrew's alumni connections worked, as he was later admitted to these schools yet rejected by less competitive colleges where he had no alumni connections.

With this account of Andrew's method for landing employment and educational opportunities, I have taken the long way to say that, like my friend, many white people are beneficiaries of white-sanctioned affirmative action. In his case, Andrew availed himself of a whole set of unofficial programs that were put in place to help well-connected white people receive a benefit without being placed under the same scrutiny as others. And I am not blaming him for taking advantage of the special treatment, because as I sat across from him in the lunchroom listening to how his father had just landed a letter from an alumnus who was also president of a major foundation, I quietly wished that my parents knew somebody who had some clout and could pull some strings. What I blame Andrew for (and what I blame myself for—at that age) is the unwillingness to recognize that he was availing himself of the same preferential treatment that had supposedly earned his ire with regard to 1965-style affirmative action.

While a subset of arguments supporting 1965-style affirmative action is based on the notion of fairness, too much of its rationale relies on theories that are grounded in retribution, punishment, and revenge. In the 1960s and today, we see such theories put forth by both white and black proponents of affirmative action. And the spectrum that they have created is one that is destined for trouble: one that would have blacks pushing in one direction and whites pulling in another. This is an analysis that leads blacks not merely to seek opportunity for themselves but, taken to its logical extreme, justifies senseless revenge against white people. It helps no one.

A Better Approach to Affirmative Action

Taking a twelve-inch line similar to the one described above, I offer a different and better spectrum to analyze the options for increasing opportunities for blacks. It has the same starting point—ending *de jure* discrimination against blacks. But it has a very different end point as its goal. The end point that society should target is what I referred to earlier as "bias neutralizing."

The end point is labeled as such because this spectrum's approach is to characterize and apply affirmative action as a means to prevent others from limiting black people's opportunities—not as a means to penalize white people. As opposed to viewing affirmative action policies as one more point earned by blacks against whites in a zero-sum game, this bias-neutralizing approach sees affirmative action policies as a means to improve black equality of opportunity by counteracting or neutralizing white biases and white interference with black advancement. A benefit given to black people, therefore, does not necessarily translate into a loss for whites. The goals for both groups in this paradigm are the same: to reach a point where no bias exists in either group.

With bias neutralizing, the goal ceases to be revenge by blacks against whites; it becomes making opportunities equally available for both races and maintaining an approach that neutralizes bigotry of any type. Bias neutralizing assumes that although *de jure* discrimination has ended, the workplace will never quite rid itself of *de facto* discrimination—of white bosses who choose to mentor white employees rather than black ones, of white bosses who bring white managers instead of black managers into their country-club networks, of white bosses who promote white employees faster and farther than black employees because the white ones just "somehow seem to make them feel more comfortable," and of white bosses who just honestly believe, in their hearts, that blacks are slightly inferior to whites.

Bias neutralizing is a stronger, more consistent, and longer-lasting response to discrimination than is Lyndon Johnson's 1965 affirmative action. Bias-neutralizing policies give blacks and other minorities increased opportunities but do not unfairly penalize whites. They can be employed easily in the academic as well as the employment context and can neutralize the effect of a biased employer and of a biased environment.

Recently, I was contacted by a senior manager at a fast-growing, medium-sized accounting firm that wanted to increase the number of black college seniors that his firm hired for entry-level positions.

"The problem," explained the white human resources manager, "is that we use a standard minimum grade-point average to determine who we will interview for jobs. And we are almost never able to find black seniors with this rather high GPA at the schools where we recruit."

Upon questioning the manager, he revealed that of the ten colleges where the company recruited, only one had more than a 2 percent black population. I made note of this fact because the first bias-neutralizing policy I would recommend was that he broaden the list of colleges on his recruiting schedule so that he visited some schools with larger black populations. "There are many top-quality universities that have much larger black student populations than the ones you visit," I explained.

He was intrigued. "But are they as good as the ten colleges we selected?"

I looked at his list and realized that his schools—two or three moderately prestigious and the others not at all—were scattered around the South and Midwest, with one in the Northeast. "To begin with," I explained, "each school in the Ivy League has many more black students than any of your ten colleges. And there are literally dozens of other top colleges like the University of Virginia, Howard, the University of Michigan, Spelman, Duke, Morehouse, Wellesley, and Georgetown that have many top black students."

He nodded and smiled at the simplicity of this idea. "You know, we've always gone to the same ten schools, so I never really thought about the fact that we could have a bigger pool of blacks if we picked different schools."

I was incredulous that this was the case. "Well, where did you get this ten-college list from?" I asked. "It's an uneven list, and they are not even geographically close to any of your offices."

He smiled sheepishly. "We just end up going back to the colleges where our most senior directors went. We sort of like having an alumni connection to our target colleges."

It was probably obvious to him at this point in our conversation, but I explained that he and his directors would never get the best candidates—black or white—if they picked their target universities (and hence, target students) based merely on the directors' alumni status. "If you insist—with all due respect—on interviewing at mediocre universities that happen to be 99 percent white, all you will ever hire here are white mediocre students who have an alumni connection with your firm." The ultimate old boys' network.

He nodded, then I explained that his firm had unintentionally set up a bias that worked against the possibility of hiring black college graduates, since the firm missed the schools where black students could be found in decent numbers.

Next, we dealt with the company's process in selecting those white and black students it actually interviewed.

"I should add," he continued, "that the white directors at my firm neither feel compelled to, nor want to, implement an affirmative action program where we would have a completely different set of standards for the blacks that we actually get to interview. They want me to use the same GPA standards, even though I keep telling them that we'll never get any blacks if they remain firm on that issue. They just don't think it's fair to eliminate white students who have the right credentials and take blacks who don't."

I asked the manager if he had ever considered why black students' grades were lower. He said that it was not because the blacks took harder courses. "As a matter of fact," he explained, "of the few blacks that we see, most are taking the same courses as the white candidates."

I then asked if it was possible that although both blacks and whites were taking the same classes, the whites had been better prepared for college because of their high school education.

"Well, I've actually considered that," he said. "Most of the blacks we have seen went to poorer, inner-city schools whereas our white applicants went to far superior suburban public schools or private day or even college preparatory boarding schools."

After asking a few more questions about the students' transcripts, I learned something else from the manager.

"I've noticed," he began, "that the biggest barrier for the black students getting offers from us is their particularly low freshman grades—lots of Cs and even Ds during the first, second, and occasionally, the third semester. After that point, their grades are substantially similar to those of white students we hire."

"Then you think that the grades that black students are earning by their junior and senior years are close to those of the white students?" I asked.

"Actually they're indistinguishable."

Since the manager explained to me that his firm was hiring only graduating seniors and that the applicants always took accounting-related courses during the junior and senior years, I offered a second bias-neutralizing hiring policy for his recruiting office to implement:

"Since you recognize that the black students are mostly coming from less competitive high schools when they enter college, and since you are not hiring them until four years after that point, you might get a fairer assessment of black students and a more relevant assessment of both black and white students if you focused your evaluation of them on their transcripts from sophomore, junior, and senior year, as opposed to all four years. Using this approach, you can maintain your GPA standard and apply it equally to blacks and whites. You could get your fellow employees on board with this policy because you would not be setting a lower standard for black recruits and you'd be turning your focus on the most relevant of a student's grades: those from more recent semesters."

The new hiring practices I devised for this accounting firm (albeit a stodgy company, but not uncommonly so for its industry) were simple ones. Yet they took into account some of the existing biases that work against many minority students (their absence from many middle-tier colleges where older white men hail from, their poor primary and secondary education) and neutralized them by finding a point where blacks could be aided without setting up lower standards that would unfairly penalize whites. In this situation, it was obvious that the black student pool could be enhanced simply by adding a few new appropriate colleges to the recruiting list. It was also obvious that many of the black students were able to overcome their disadvantaged secondary educational experience and catch up to their white peers by their third or fourth semester. Unfortunately, these black students could be forever penalized because this employer was averaging all grades during the four-year college experience, regardless of the fact that the most relevant grades would be those that appear toward the end of a student's college tenure.

Bias-neutralizing policies can work to counteract employer biases, environmental biases, and historical biases that have a direct and traceable negative effect on an individual's present situation.

A PERMANENT SOLUTION

In addition to its being grounded in theories of white retribution, I am troubled that affirmative action has always been defined as a *temporary* solution to racial discrimination. As Johnson's 1965 policies were interpreted, affirmative action would be defined by temporary programs and practices to undo bias. The problem is that the type of bias that keeps blacks from being hired, retained, and promoted in jobs is not temporary; it is permanent.

Lying somewhere beneath the discriminatory acts of an employer or staff of white employees are inherent biases that cannot be undone or compensated for with temporary measures. Even if a black manager gets past the discriminatory hiring practices of a racially biased personnel officer, he will still have to confront the biases of his white boss, coworkers, and clients. By no means is racial bias limited to a single act or relegated to a time frozen in the past. Whether whites believe it or not, even the most well-meaning institutions have continuing racial bias simmering just beneath the surface.

Take, for instance, what has happened recently at such well-respected organizations as AT&T, The Four Seasons Hotel in Boston, and Miller Brewing Company. These examples illustrate the depth of the racial bias both among workers and in the work *environment,* hence supporting the assertion that workplace discrimination lasts well beyond the day that an employer agrees or refuses to hire a black person. It is not only advanced by individual coworkers, it can also be part of the very environment—in the form of company newsletters, policies, and even the images employed by the corporation.

At The Four Seasons Hotel, as hotel management prepared for the May 1994 visit of the prime minister of India, hotel management announced that only white employees would be allowed to serve their special guest. All minority staff people were required to exchange their responsibilities with white coworkers during the visit. When the hotel's policy became publicized and widely criticized, the hotel apologized to the Massachusetts Committee Against Discrimination and followed up with an apologetic gesture to two of its bellmen—one Hispanic and the other black. Each of the two minority workers was given $179.

In September 1993, AT&T—which has long been known for its commitment to affirmative action—published three hundred thousand copies of its monthly employee magazine with an illustration that offended thousands of black customers and employees. Using a cartoon illustration of the world globe, it showed caricatures of people around the world, dressed in their native clothing and holding an AT&T phone to their ears. On Europe stood a man with a French beret and a long mustache. On Russia stood a woman in Soviet dress and a babushka on her head. On North America stood a white man in jeans and pullover shirt. On the continent of Africa, also with a phone to its ear, stood yet another AT&T customer: a hairy gorilla with a grin. Following thousands of complaints about this portrayal of people of African descent, AT&T apologized and announced that it fired the artist who had drawn the illustration for the publication.

At Miller Brewing Company's upstate Fulton, New York, plant, it was reported in 1993 that black workers were being harassed by white employees with blatantly racist practices. Black managers complained of whites filling black employees lockers with chicken bones and erecting mock gravesites—with named markers—on the property to symbolize the impending deaths of the black workers. One black supervisor, Harold Thomas, had been taunted so severely with harassing and humiliating antiblack announcements over the companywide paging system—he was often paged as "Harold—the Ape—Thomas"—that he sought psychological counseling and took time off. Upon his return, the paging system announced to all two thousand workers at the plant, "Welcome back, Harold, but you're still a nigger." As the FBI began the second of two investigations into the racial harassments—which led to broken windows at Thomas's and other black workers' homes—Miller announced it would close the plant in early 1994.

Within a few weeks of each other, in July 1994, two prominent white New York–based executives apologized for making outrageous and unkind references about blacks and watermelon, in one case, and blacks and monkeys in the other. A barely contrite deputy mayor to New York City's Rudolph Giuliani gave a bizarre explanation for having made references to watermelon when talking about a black woman who owned a brokerage firm that had won a city bid. Only days later, a white male vice president of the New York Yankees was forced to resign after a magazine reported that he had referred to young black residents in the Yankee Stadium neighborhood as unruly "monkeys" that hang on basketball hoops.

At many other widely respected U.S. corporations, such as Texaco, Denny's, and Shoney's restaurants, alleged discriminatory remarks and treatment against blacks and other minorities have been widely reported by the media, and the number of discrimination claims is so high that one is reminded of the types of egregious behavior carried out thirty years ago. "Temporary remedies" still haven't changed many of these organizations.

Prior records of black hiring often fail to reflect the true racial attitude and atmosphere of an organization, because even those employers who have a respectable percentage of blacks working for them oftentimes still permit subtle (and not-so-subtle) on-the-job discrimination. As it has been practiced, 1965-style affirmative action is only a temporary policy solution. It was designed to be temporary because the common understanding of discriminatory employment practices was that they could be measured by examining a company's hiring statistics. If a company was in need of a 1965-style affirmative action program, it was because it had been demonstrated that the company had too few black or minority employees. This was the standard for 1965-style affirmative action—a particular threshold number of minority people.

Unfortunately, this also came to be the standard for measuring the existence of bias. If an employer had at least a certain minimum number of black employees, it was no longer considered to be a racist organization. Unfortunately, as the aforementioned company experiences demonstrate, racist activities occur in even the most integrated of populations. And this is why affirmative action policies must go farther than their 1965 temporary approach.

Equating blacks with monkeys and apes, creating policies that suggest blacks are not fit to serve dignitaries or wait on white fast-food customers, making inane comparisons between blacks and watermelon; these racist acts—and the mentalities behind them—can't be ascertained by looking at the number of blacks or other minorities hired by that employer during the previous two years. There is no particular number of recruits that necessarily reveals or exposes the day-to-day bigotry in an organization. And such behavior isn't going to be changed with $179 payments, closing a plant with no admission of guilt, or by firing low-level artists who have, no doubt, simply followed directions and received final approval for their racist caricatures from more senior and more culpable managers. There is a mind-set that is acceptable in the employer's environment that tolerates these biases and encourages them to continue. And this mind-set can create an environment in which it is impossible for blacks to do their best work, and therefore impossible for them to be promoted based on merit and achievement. I believe that addressing this mind-set is the deeper, and hence, more realistic challenge for people who are trying to combat discrimination.

Supporting these discriminatory acts are strong inherent biases. These inherent biases—so deeply ingrained—reveal white people's honest belief that black people truly are inferior. And this belief is not ever likely to change. Certainly no law, governmental, or enforcement agency (short of some twenty-first-century thought police) can change it. Modern-day affirmative action has become a numbers game, triggered by a specific prior record demonstrating poor numerical hiring and promotion of blacks. It is not cognizant of inherent biases—and its ultimate premise is that someday these biases will go away.

Most people are surprised to learn that during these supposedly progressive times, the number of EEOC suits involving job-related discrimination claims has continued to increase—reaching its second highest number in 1992 since the commission's creation in 1964. Given that in 1994 more than seventy thousand EEOC complaints were filed, with more than 40 percent relating to racially motivated bias, and given that during the nation's last recession (1991) seventy thousand whites, sixty thousand Asians, and fifty thousand Hispanics gained jobs while blacks—fifty thousand of them—were the only group to *lose* jobs, it seems obvious that some deep-seated form of racial bias will always be with us; it certainly hasn't abated in the past thirty years.

As the legal scholar Derrick Bell states in his book *Faces at the Bottom of the Well,* "Racism is an integral, permanent, and indestructible component of this society." Recognizing this, we must move to develop permanent bias-neutralizing programs that will work to counteract ongoing biases. For even if we do increase the number of qualified blacks in some or all of these companies, we still have not altered or addressed white people's fundamental belief that black people should not be there. If we acknowledge that we can't change white people's inherent and ongoing antiblack biases, then we should accept that the very least we can do is implement permanent measures that work toward bias neutralizing. It's a much better solution than waiting for "black rage" to mislead the deprived and frustrated members of our community.

12

HARLEM ON MY MIND

A JOURNEY THROUGH HARLEM
RICH AND POOR

I FOUND AN AD in the *Amsterdam News* for a rooming house, and the woman on the phone told me to meet her outside the building on Lenox Avenue in the 140s. "Which apartment bell should I buzz to get you?"

"God, honey," she said, laughing. "I don't live in the place—I just *own* it. I live in *Fieldston*! Talk to the super, then meet me out front." I told her my name, but I didn't tell her I was a corporate lawyer from New York looking to spend a month writing about what it was like to live in a Harlem tenement-style rooming house. I just said I was a writer and a musician.

"Musician?" she asked.

"Yes, ma'am." The only instrument I'd ever played was an oboe, and I hadn't picked it up since junior year at Princeton.

"You a rapper?" she asked suspiciously.

"No—jazz," I answered, selecting music that suggested a more stable tenant lifestyle. "A jazz *oboist*."

When she said there would be no contract to sign for the

This piece appeared as a cover story for *New York* magazine, September 27, 1993.

seventy-dollar-a-week room, I thought back to the real property classes I'd taken at Harvard Law School. "Oh, so I'd just be a tenant at will," I answered—not quite sure whether I should be revealing my legal background in such a reckless manner.

But she had no idea of what I was saying. "You'll be my tenant if you bring the four weeks' rent," she responded, then hung up.

Staring at what the newspaper ad had billed as a "quaint and well-kept" building, all I could see in front of me now was a walkway smeared with dog feces and strewn with battered metal garbage can lids. Hunks of plaster from the building's façade lay on the ground nearby.

A man who appeared to be asleep sat at the bottom steps of the building. Tied around his ankle was a five-foot leather leash stretched across to the other end of the stairway—completely blocking passage. At the opposite end of the leash was tied a thick-necked, brown pit bull that napped quietly.

Moments later, a late-model orange-colored Mercedes drove up to the curb. I looked down at its two front plates. The decorative one read in gold letters on black background: PEACHES. The other one was an out-of-state plate, even though the landlady had told me on the phone that she lived in the best part of suburban Riverdale. Out of the driver's side stepped a short, heavyset woman with orange high-heeled pumps, a flowery housedress, a white patent-leather handbag, and a cotton kerchief tied over a head full of thick, wavy black hair that gleamed unnaturally in the sun.

"I know I'm late, but I had to get some Sheetrock out in Brooklyn," she shouted while locking a red-and-black Club onto the steering wheel of her fifty-thousand-dollar car.

As I extended my hand, the woman marched past me, stopped at the base of the steps, and looked into the face of the slumbering homeless man.

"Williams!!" she shouted.

The pit bull got to its feet, but the man sat motionless.

"Williams—I said *Williams*!!" she shouted again while clapping her hands into his left ear.

The man gained consciousness.

"Williams, how many times have I told you to keep that damn dog away from here? My tenants have to come and go." The land-lady picked up a tall can of Colt 45 malt liquor from the step and put it into his lap. "Now get on with that dog."

"Sorry, Peaches—sorry."

As we stepped past the disoriented man, I forced a smile.

"Good-for-nothing Williams. Don't mind him, honey. Let's go on up."

As she leaned into the heavy wooden door, we entered a dingy vestibule that smelled of urine and old carpet. She pulled out a handful of keys. "Did he show you 'round?"

"The super?" I asked.

"Um-hum."

"No," I answered. "I waited, but I couldn't find him."

"Couldn't *find* him?" she asked while looking at me like I was some kind of imbecile. "You just *met* him—*Williams*."

As I looked around at the filthy five-by-six-foot lobby of peeled green paint and rotting carpet, lit only by a twenty-watt circular fluorescent bulb mounted up at the top of an eleven-foot ceiling, I had second thoughts about moving into this fourteen-room SRO slumhouse. "Miss—er, Mrs. Pea—"

"Just Peaches," she added while thumbing through a stack of mail on the radiator. Her eye—as did mine—fell on the cover of a spring 1993 J. Crew catalog. She smiled at the blond model on the back page and mumbled something about "a hundred and eighteen dollars." She dropped the catalog into her purse and left the other mail for her tenants.

"Here," she said hurriedly, shoving a single key into my hand. "Third floor, second door on the left."

I looked at the key, then the woman.

"Honey, now I *know* you don't expect Peaches to walk up all those steps. Not in *these* heels."

I showed myself up two flights of rickety, linoleum-covered stairs that seemed to drop inches as my foot climbed to the next steeper step. I came to the second doorknob, inserted the key, and pushed open the heavy steel door.

It was the first time I had ever stared down the barrel of a gun.

"What the fuck you think you're doing?" a voice asked from just behind the door.

I could smell the odor of human sweat mixed with natural gas. My eyes gazed with an almost dreamlike dizziness. The frosty-gray gun was so sleek it looked like a child's toy. But when the man released the safety, I knew I'd better start talking.

"Sorry, wrong door. Please . . . sorry. Peaches gave . . . Sorry— wrong . . . Sorry . . . key. Please."

That's all I managed to say. As I pulled the door closed again, my eyes passed the image of a half-nude woman sitting at the edge of an unmade bed. She had something metal—a pen or a small pipe—in her mouth. I ran down the creaking stairs, still smelling the gaseous odor, and lunged out the front door, ahead of Peaches, who was oblivious to her mistake.

Back outside, she detected my discomfort. "Peaches got some advice," she said while putting the key back onto a giant ring. "You new around here." She glanced contemptuously at my khakis, Ralph Lauren windbreaker, and white Stan Smith tennis shoes. "'Cause you look it. I can see it, and so can they. You gonna last about ten *seconds* in this place."

I peered across the street to a group of six young men dressed in mostly black. Black baseball caps, dark pullover shirts, black leather and vinyl coats, and black or brown baggy pants. My very appearance was screaming "suburban outsider," and quickly attracting attention.

I thanked Peaches, glanced at her car, then ran back to 125th Street, realizing that if I was really going to move into Harlem, I'd better find a different wardrobe and a better address.

Eight blocks away, the demure Ann Watson sits near the black Steinway piano in the foyer of her nineteenth-century town house.

She looks out at her eighteen-foot-deep rose garden through a dining room window. She adjusts the Hillary Clinton–style headband over her near shoulder-length brown hair. At the table underneath the crystal chandelier that hangs from a twelve-foot ceiling, Ann thumbs through some photos taken in the college dormitory courtyard of Lowell House during her daughter's Harvard graduation ceremony the year before.

Ann's husband, Gerald, has just put away the mobile phone after talking to daughter Debi, now an associate with an investment bank in Chicago. He recalls how frantic their lives had been with child-rearing activities when Debi and her older sister were both students at Chapin, the exclusive Upper East Side private girls school: "Raising proper young girls in New York meant that we had to pour all our time into shopping, ballet, sleepover parties, trips to the West Indies—you name it. It was nonstop," says Gerald with a laugh.

But even with the girls gone, their lives aren't any slower these days. Ann talks about her schedule this spring. "Since we have all this space here, one of my friends' sons asked us to host three of his spring art shows in our home. Right after that, *Metropolitan Home* magazine came to photograph some of our rooms for their May issue, and then I had to get ready for a three-week trip with friends to Paris, Brussels, and Amsterdam."

Welcome to the two worlds of Harlem. A world of guns and poverty, of culture and privilege. One of the most famous yet least understood communities in New York City is that 2.5-square-mile area in northern Manhattan that manages to contain a quarter of a million people—most of them black. You ask a Harlem resident about the community's boundaries and he'll tell you it's that area west of Park Avenue between 110th and 155th Streets. Ask someone else that same question and he'll tell you it stretches much farther: "It's anything north of Ninety-sixth Street and south of the Bronx." For many of the whites who live and work in the five boroughs, it might as well be in Siberia. It was written off long ago as a place abandoned to minority crime, drugs, and unemployment.

In spite of the conventional wisdom among New Yorkers, Harlem is not exclusively impoverished and uneducated. Living, perhaps uneasily, alongside a large underclass population is a community of professional and upper-income blacks who have forged a lifestyle different and separate from that of their neighbors. Theirs is a private world—private schools, clubs, cotillions, stores, summer and weekend getaways—even designated places for buying groceries. This group of physicians, dentists, attorneys, entrepreneurs, and educators has its own admission standards and its own means of identification. Its members are found living at one of three Harlem addresses: Strivers Row, Lenox Terrace, and The Riverton.

As a black child of white suburban New York, I often joined my family as they visited Harlem relatives and family friends who lived, exclusively, at these addresses. There was no other Harlem in my mind. It came as a shock to me when, at age ten or eleven, I eventually discovered through news reports on TV and through remarks from classmates and teachers that Harlem was considered to be one of the nation's epicenters for crime, drug use, and poverty. My Harlem? The Harlem where everyone I knew was a well-educated professional? Where all the kids I knew were smart, ambitious, and well behaved?

My introduction to Harlem was the flip side of most other people's. I had less information than those who lived there, and more information than those who didn't. And I was young. For those who live there, they know what lies around them. For those who've never visited, they rely on the broad negative descriptions advanced by the media and the public. The only Harlem I knew was the one with residents who had private garages and doormen to take their packages, and where daffodils, tulips, and maple trees lined the apartment courtyard walkways. Yes, I might have noticed the seedy neighborhood that we passed three or four blocks away when coming or going, but I didn't associate those sections with the ones I knew. With age, I began to comprehend the fact that the Harlem I thought I knew was actually much larger and more diverse. As I discovered the real proximity of these two very different communities—affluent and poor, ambitious and obscure—I was once again astounded.

But what remained unclear to my suburban mind was how or why these relatives and friends of ours would choose to live so close to a group that was so dramatically different from them. In the suburbs where I lived, groups so disparate never lived at such close range. Out there, people saw only the people who were just like them. I began to discover some answers as I ventured into the lifestyle of that other Harlem by moving directly into it.

My plan was to move myself into Harlem for a monthlong period and chronicle the two lifestyles that continued side by side. I didn't want to stay with friends, who would color my impressions of how rich and poor interacted. And I didn't want to rent space on one of the better blocks because I had long been aware of life in those homes. Instead, I wanted to see the two worlds from the vantage point of the less affluent neighbors.

I wanted to live in the same homes, shop at their stores, talk on the same pay phones, dodge the same street-corner addicts, ride in their livery cabs, work for the local employers, get my hair cut at the same barber shops, buy my clothes in their stores, use their libraries, attend their movie theaters, confront their local police, attend their churches, and eat at their restaurants. In a month's time, I could never see or experience what they have learned in a lifetime. But my plan included living their life as I saw it and then juxtaposing it against the lifestyle that I could, from this vantage point, observe of the more affluent Harlemites. During my experience of living in a tenement, I knew that there were at least a few affluent Harlem institutions that would be open to me. Finally, once my monthlong visit was complete, I would then go directly into the homes of Harlem's affluent—friends and relatives of people I'd known since childhood—and talk to them about the lives they really led and their attitudes concerning, and relationships with, the poor Harlem that I'd experienced and that swirls around them every day. With this, I thought I could find a story that explained how these two very different groups survived alongside each other.

My journey began after I had met with a number of landlords who owned single-room-occupancy buildings and had advertised for tenants in the weekly black newspaper, the *Amsterdam News*. After meeting Peaches and three other landlords, I had transformed my résumé, my clothing, and my attitude into one that did not seem so bizarre for my surroundings. And then I moved into the eighty-dollar-a-week rooming house that was owned by a Mrs. Jenkins and managed by a Mr. Willie Edwards. It was a four-story building that sat just off Lenox Avenue in the 130s.

Moving back and forth between the two worlds of Harlem, I found two communities that coexist, yet almost never collide.

It was a Wednesday just after 9:00 A.M. in front of my building.

Willie Edwards* stared at the potato chip bags and empty forty-ounce bottles of malt liquor strewn along the front stoops of the four-story walk-up. Last night, he was responsible for at least three of those bottles. As his lanky six-foot-three-inch frame stood on the top step with a wooden-handled broom leaning against his knee, he waved to a group of buddies who sat at the corner on plastic milk crates and trash cans turned upside down.

"Hey, Willie, whatcha waitin' for?" one of them called while waving a brown paper bag that hid the profile of a bottle wrapped tightly inside. At this hour of the morning, Edwards was usually out there with his friends: six men, aged thirty-five to sixty, unemployed, single, in T-shirts, and all wearing caps—three of them with an *X* displayed on the front.

"Can't go nowhere. Mrs. Jenkins's coming, and I got some cleaning to do."

The men were already in position for the rest of the day—or at least until 1:00 P.M., when they would need to move six feet to avoid the blaze of the afternoon sun. They couldn't hear their

*Certain names have been changed.

friend's response, but it didn't matter. If they didn't see him today, they knew he'd be back tomorrow. As Willie walked up the stairs of the fourteen-person rooming house, sweeping at every other step, he stared down the block, trying to catch a glimpse of the silver Mercedes 300 that Mrs. Jenkins drove in from Forest Hills every third day to pick up rent checks and inspect his work. It was payday, and he hoped she wouldn't make this building her last stop. He'd been her super for two and a half years, and she generally promised to get him his check before David's Check Cashing closed for the afternoon.

Edwards entered the dark foyer of the sixty-year-old building, breathing in the odors of sweat, urine, and cat litter. As he climbed the sagging staircase, past months of grime and oily fingerprints, he could already hear Jojo laughing at a friend's loud complaints. Jojo, a sometime security guard, oftentime coke dealer who lived behind door 13 on the third floor, was cursing loudly because one of his friends had just gotten "padlocked out" of an eighty-dollar-a-week five-by-ten-foot room in another one of Mrs. Jenkins's buildings—for nonpayment of rent.

"Hey, man," shouted the twenty-one-year-old Jojo, "I woulda just gone and capped the bitch if she's lockin' you out anyway."

Edwards passed by quietly and went up the next flight of stairs to his own five-by-ten-foot living quarters. As he opened the door to his room, lit by a flickering forty-watt fluorescent bulb, he looked down at Sadie, his gray-and-white cat, who has been scratching on the door of the refrigerator. Willie gently pushed her into the hallway, and went back to his chores.

"There's no question about it. All the kids on Strivers Row would go to private schools in either Manhattan or Riverdale," says Ann Watson as she thinks about her own children and the other kids that grew up on the two tree-lined blocks of West 138th and 139th Streets between Seventh and Eighth Avenues. "Yes," she recalls, "a few at Fieldston, Dalton, Trinity—and some girls who went to Spence and the Lycée over on Seventy-second Street."

Watson's neighbor, Myron Billings, now a government major at Harvard, attended Dalton from kindergarten through the twelfth grade. "There has always been a network of black students around here who went to the top schools," explains Billings, who was elected student-body president the same year black students held the job at Trinity, Fieldston, and Nightingale-Bamford.

Designated as landmarks in the mid-sixties, the four-hundred-thousand-dollar homes along Ann's two blocks earned the name "Strivers Row" because of the many successful black doctors, attorneys, and affluent entertainers who moved there in the twenties and thirties. The brick-and-limestone town houses were designed and built in the 1890s by the renowned architectural firm of McKim, Mead & White, and two other firms. The quiet, bucolic streets out front have been used as a backdrop in many films, most recently in Spike Lee's *Jungle Fever.*

The Watsons' four-bedroom, four-bath town house was previously owned by Dr. Louis Wright, a black 1915 graduate of Harvard Medical School and the first black physician to hold a hospital position in New York City. (Edward Myers, Jr., a tax attorney and partner in the Harlem real estate firm Myers Smith & Granady, owns a house on Strivers Row and says that the neighborhood attracts many prominent people. "You'll find upper-class blacks who had originally grown up in Harlem," Myers explains. "There is a wide range of interesting people. Everyone from TV news anchors to intellectuals like Booker T. Washington III." Myers's real estate partner, Judith Smith, bought a Strivers Row house soon after they opened their business in 1972.)

"I guess you could call it an oasis, but the group is pretty well defined and most of us live in these three places," says Beatrice Riggs Martin, who first moved into the spanking-new Lenox Terrace in 1960. The six-building complex at 135th and Fifth has private parking spaces, private courtyards with resident keys, front awnings, and uniformed doormen—surprising accoutrements to an outsider in the heart of Harlem.

Martin, who is on the board of the YWCA and the New York Urban League, sits in a spacious apartment filled with artwork purchased during recent trips to Zaïre, Uganda, Taiwan, Portugal, and Greece. Now a widow, she came to Harlem in 1960 with her husband, an attorney and advertising executive. She was an NAACP executive who was often seen photographed in the *Daily News* and other New York papers with Thurgood Marshall, Congressman Adam Clayton Powell, Jr., or Hulan Jack, the first black Manhattan borough president.

"I came to Harlem kicking and screaming," laughs Martin. "Working here was one thing, but to move here, too? I came from a fine family and community in Baltimore, and I just couldn't imagine moving into Harlem, of all places. It seemed so coarse, so noisy. Too much activity and such a mixture of people. How could I raise kids in a place like this? My oldest daughter had been a debutante in Baltimore. How was I going to do that here with two more children?"

To ease her conscience, Martin's husband agreed to maintain a house in Baltimore in addition to the Lenox Terrace apartment. But soon, the couple and their two younger children discovered that they were not alone here.

"Everyone in this building was either a doctor, a lawyer, a dentist, a politician, or married to one. Their kids were in the best private schools, they were ambitious." Martin sits down near one of the large wooden screens that she brought back from a trip to India. She thinks about the people living at Lenox Terrace, a large percentage of them attorneys: Percy Sutton, owner of the Apollo Theater and former Manhattan borough president; U.S. congressman Charles Rangel; and former New York secretary of state Basil Paterson. "These families were from my very same world," exclaims Martin. "Who would have known that all this was in Harlem?"

Martin points to a photo of one daughter's coming-out party at the Waldorf-Astoria. "It was wonderful—tuxedos, roses, white silk taffeta, and tulle—just a lovely ball," she adds. "In our group, the children got the chance to meet other black children who come from families just like theirs. Music lessons, ballet lessons, summers in Martha's Vineyard or Sag Harbor. But if you didn't live here, you really wouldn't know that there is an entire network here." This proud mother makes her point by pulling out a wedding page from the July 17, 1963, issue of the *New York Times*: Another daughter is the only black woman on a page filled with white brides, and she is also the only doctor on the page who is marrying a doctor. "There really is a whole network here."

"Did Sadie come in here?" Edwards asked as I opened the door to my room. This was the first conversation that I'd had with him since I had moved into the building two days earlier.

"Who?"

"Sadie—my cat." The man pushed past me and got down on both knees looking under my bed.

"I haven't opened the door lately."

Edwards stood up and looked in my closet. "You don't need to open the door. She just squeezes through that there hole." The man closed the door and pointed to the three-inch-wide gap between the door and its frame.

The space was clearly wide enough to accommodate a slender animal, and it went as high as the keyhole.

"I guess Mrs. Jenkins told you about the window too?" Edwards asked as he walked across my sheeted bed in his dirty work boots.

Mrs. Jenkins hadn't told me anything about the place I was moving into. Although she was black too, she had looked at me like I was just another black man in Harlem with some temporary source of income. The only interest she had expressed was in getting three weeks' rent in advance.

"'Cause it don't close neither—by about three inches, so get yourself some boric acid for the roaches and some foam for the door."

As he turned to leave, the willowy super gave me a broad smile. "Oh, and give me five dollars—can you?"

It sounded more like a demand than a request. As I fumbled for a response, he pulled out a big ball of silver keys and started thumbing through them. "Yeah, and make sure you use the extra bolt on your lock 'cause although I've got keys to your room and I can usually keep a lookout, other tenants have had money, clothes, food, and you-name-it stolen, since keys sometimes fall into the wrong hands. You know—ex-tenants."

It was obvious where this conversation was going. Either you give me the five dollars now or I'll get it when you're not here. I handed him a crisp bill.

"And Mrs. Jenkins said to tell you no guests, no pets, no smoking, no loud music, no TV, no phone, no parties, no drugs, no guns. And you get one outlet—so watch the wattage."

As I moved around in my new walk-up, it quickly became obvious why so many people in Harlem are out on the streets—particularly in the summer. With no phone, no air conditioning, one electrical outlet (maximum: sixty watts), and not enough floor space to lay out a newspaper, my "apartment" is typical of Harlem rooming houses. My mattress touches three walls, my head is at the window's plastic venetian blinds, and both my sides are "guarded" by brick walls and exposed hot-water steam pipes waiting to take my skin off if I try to "roll" out of bed on the wrong side.

Purring at the foot of my mattress is a twenty-year-old beige Admiral single-door refrigerator. The only other piece of furniture is a three-and-a-half-foot-high dresser. A circular forty-watt fluorescent bulb flickers from the center of the recently painted glossy-white ceiling. Roaches are everywhere.

Like other rooming houses, mine has a community kitchen and bath that I share with twelve others. The kitchen is a yellow five-by-five-foot room with a two-burner gas stove, circa 1958. A squat metal table littered with vacant and occupied Roach Motels stands across from a sink that is propped up with a white stick. The blue bathroom features a cracked but working sink, a toilet with no top on the back, and a tub with four legs. Around the tub, hanging from the ceiling, are three mismatched shower curtains. Roaches and waterbugs slide around together on the soap scum of the tub. The night before, I'd used the shower, but I'd done so with caution. Uneasy about coming too close to the elements, I remained clothed in my red plaid L.L. Bean cotton nightshirt and my white Stan Smiths, stepped in, turned the water on, and lathered up.

Now, Jojo was at my door with large plastic garbage bags and helpful housekeeping tips: "I don't want your roaches, so put your shit in these bags."

As he looked over at my toothbrush, washcloth, paper plates, and box of strawberry Pop-Tarts that sat on my dresser, he shook his head. "And all that stuff—put it in the fridge. Don't leave nothing out. And if you keep the light on at night, the rats and roaches will stay in the walls—pretty much."

"Sure," I said to the savvy twenty-one-year-old whose face and scalp were shaved clean. Although he was only around five eight, his bulging pecs made him seem almost twice my size. He wore a white long-sleeve shirt that was presumably part of his security job uniform.

"I used to fuck the bitch who lived in here," he said while swaggering into my room. "She leave anything behind?"

"Uhh, no."

He laughed while looking into the closet. "Well, watch it, bro—'cause she used to work for me, and she owed a lot of people money."

I mimicked his laugh because I wasn't sure if he was joking or if he was just trying to scare me. "So what's the story on this Mrs. Jenkins," I asked. "She married?"

"Man, folks call her the black widow, but I don't even know the lady's first name," Jojo answered. "Somebody said she's a lawyer or something downtown. All I know is she's one tough bitch. Wants her money, and she wants it yesterday. She'll padlock your ass outta here in a second if you're late or if it's not cash." He laughed quietly. "Yeah, she keeps that Willie hopping."

"But seriously, is she married?"

"No way I can see it. So you got a job yet?"

"I'm sort of a writer and a musician," I said. "But I'm here to *look* for a job."

He laughed condescendingly and dropped the handful of plastic bags on the bed. "You're looking for a job—and you fucking come to *Harlem*? Good luck!"

That night, with nothing else to do, Jojo and I had ribs at Singleton's Bar-B-Q and then found ourselves at Harlem's only movie theater, the Victoria V, which is not unlike most large movie houses. Except that the first thing you see after buying your ticket is a large green sign at the entrance that says: NO WEAPONS. There is a large red circle and an *X* drawn through an illustration of a knife and a pistol.

After hearing about his various legitimate and no-so-legitimate jobs, Jojo and I settled on the movie *Just Another Girl on the IRT,* a new film about a black honors student named Chantel who grows up in the projects, wants to become a doctor, but gets pregnant before graduating.

"This is bullshit," he said as we were buying our six-dollar tickets. "They don't even have *Boiling Point.*"

I hadn't seen the movie, but I'd seen Wesley Snipes's menacing expression and pistol firing out of the *Boiling Point* billboards that decorated vacant buildings and lots throughout Harlem.

At the front of a slow-moving line, we were asked to step through airport-style metal detectors. Something in my pockets or knapsack set off the alarm.

"Please step over here," one of the guards called out, sounding very official.

"Are you carrying a weapon?" the other asked.

"No," I answered. But just as I was about to reach into my pockets, one of the guards lightly grabbed my wrist, patted me down, and then looked in my knapsack.

As Jojo walked through, the beeper went off again.

"Are you carrying a weapon?" the guard asked again.

"What if I am?" Jojo announced defiantly as he was quickly directed back out onto the busy sidewalk.

"It would never cross my mind to go to the movies in Harlem," says Estelle Peters, who lives on Strivers Row and serves as an officer of her block association. "We just wouldn't do it. Even when my son goes, it's always below Ninety-sixth Street. It may be because his schools and friends were always downtown in the Sixties and Seventies, but he's always had a kind of below-Ninety-sixth-Street frame of reference."

Martin and the Watsons agree. Neither they nor their children ever went to the movies in Harlem. "I just prefer to go over to Eighty-third Street—I feel safer," explains Vivian Chapin, a Lenox Terrace resident. And as Myron Billings sits in his Strivers Row living room with two black teenage friends who had gone to private school with him, he admits that a few years ago when he was still in high school, he also went downtown. "I don't think I've ever gone to a movie in Harlem," Billings says while his former classmates listen. The friend, who's now at the University of Pennsylvania, shakes his head in disbelief. His other friend, now at Columbia, has the same memories. While they admit to having played basketball with nonprivate-school Harlem kids, and while Billings has always been very active at the Abyssinian Baptist Church, neither Myron nor his two friends know what public school served the neighborhood kids. "It might be A. Philip Randolph," says Billings, "but I'm not really sure."

"I might go to a hardware store there," says Gerald Watson, but he admits he wouldn't know where to find the Kids Kingdom, Sneaker City, or most other stores along 125th Street.

It seems that very few among this Harlem elite actually patronize the local shops, restaurants, or even grocery stores that line Lenox Avenue, Adam Clayton Powell Boulevard, or 125th and 135th Streets. They never take the subway and only rarely take the buses. Yellow cabs won't travel up that far.

Just as this group passes up public transportation, so do they pass up the Harlem bodegas, Laundromats, haircutters, check cashers, and fast-food restaurants. The grocery stores—many of them cramped, windowless, and overpriced—are saved for emergencies.

"I go to the Grand Union in Fort Lee, New Jersey," says Chapin as she gestures in a westerly direction with a hand adorned by a ring of diamonds and deep blue sapphires. "If I go there or to the Pathmark in Westchester, I'll pay ninety-nine cents for dishwashing liquid. But here in Harlem, it costs me a dollar fifty-nine. I'd get the same markup on meat and produce."

"For clothing and household items, we shop downtown at Bloomingdale's or Saks, or over in New Jersey," says Estelle Peters as she and her husband, Ken, look out at the trellis of roses in front. "And forget it when it comes to buying groceries here. The prices are high and the selection is limited. One of my friends on the block likes radishes in her salads, but it's almost impossible for her to get good radishes in Harlem. So we do our grocery shopping at the Pathmark in Hackensack."

The restaurant selection is just as limited. There is Copeland's on 145th Street; La Famille at Fifth and 124th; 22 West, a diner and lounge across from Harlem Hospital at 135th Street; and of course Sylvia's at Lenox and 126th Street. Owned and run by Sylvia Woods, the well-known soul-food restaurant is patronized by hundreds of black and white New Yorkers seven days a week. Busloads of Asian and European tourists and occasional celebrities, who end up being photographed and displayed on the walls of the crystal-chandeliered green dining room, crowd the place on Saturdays and Sundays.

Chapin admits that if she's not going to Copeland's, she will eat outside Harlem. "I'll drive to Westchester, or go to Tavern on the Green, the St. Moritz on Central Park South, or The Four Seasons with girlfriends." A former president of the Harlem Philharmonic Society, YWCA board member, and New York City school administrator, Chapin has grown accustomed to these quality-of-life survival strategies.

. . .

"Do you know of a good place to get a haircut around here?" I asked Mrs. Jenkins when I saw her coming up the stairs with her Bally briefcase swinging behind her.

She shielded her eyes from the 8:00 A.M. sun and then looked up at the Malcolm X cap that sat on my head. "My," she said, just above a whisper.

"Should I try 125th Street, maybe?"

"Well, I get mine done down in the Sixties," she added as her voice trailed off politely. "But you might try Black Hair Is. They're on 125th and, I think, Adam Clayton Powell. It's probably on the second or third floor, I think." It was obvious that she was not very familiar with the area. Seeing the HP12C calculator that she carried in her bag made me want to ask what else she did for a living, but I steered clear.

"So, Mr. Graham," she asked, gently rearranging the bow that pulled her jet black hair straight back into a small chignon. "Is everything satisfactory?"

"Yeah. Everything's cool," I answered. The place was an absolute dump, but I supposed it was all relative to your initial expectations. "Well, I don't want to hold you from getting back home," I responded, naively fishing for a response.

She glanced at a gold Rolex watch that might or might not have been real. "Oh, I've got lots of other errands before I get to the office," she said, clearly determined not to reveal anything else about her life.

Just as I reached the sidewalk and Mrs. Jenkins was inside the building, I ran into Willie Edwards.

"Larry—this is my big day today!" he shouted with his used-car-salesman smile. "It's my forty-fourth birthday. Can you believe? Forty-four years old *today*!" He paused and stared at me as if I was supposed to tell him that he looked good for his age.

"Congratulations," I replied, making my way to the street.

"So, Larry, give me a few bucks. You know, for my big birthday!"

By now, I'd learned to keep three singles, just for these requests. God forbid I open up my wallet and reveal that I've got charge cards and twenty-dollar bills in there. So I handed him two of the dollars.

"Oh, two dollars," he said while jingling keys and change in his pocket.

I reached back into my pocket and gave him the other single.

"Willie, that's all I've got. Honest."

"I can get me some Thunderbird with this" was his only response as he strolled back around the corner toward the liquor store.

"Yeah—and happy birthday," I said while considering the very real possibility that he may well have been born on some other day of the year.

Next stop was going to be Black Hair Is. The commotion along 125th Street (few people refer to it by the rechristened name, Dr. Martin Luther King, Jr., Boulevard) is relentless. The busy section stretches west from Park Avenue on the east to Madison, Fifth, Lenox (renamed Malcolm X Boulevard), Seventh (Adam Clayton Powell Boulevard), and Eighth (Frederick Douglass Boulevard) Avenues. Except for the old Theresa Hotel at Seventh Avenue, the sixteen-story New York State Office Building, and the Apollo Theater, most of the structures are nondescript one- or two-story buildings that were built in the 1920s and 1930s.

I walked west past the used-furniture stores, and wound my way around mattresses and roll-aways that sat out on the sidewalk on the block between Park and Madison. I passed by crowded Laundromats that stay open from 7:00 A.M. to 9:00 P.M., wig shops, modest storefront churches, produce stands, medical offices, and bars. With only three banks left on the heavily traveled strip of 125th Street, an ATM is virtually impossible to find. And whether it's because of the impenetrable crowds or because they're just not there, one almost never sees homeless panhandlers or policemen on foot.

When I hit the Ben & Jerry's at the corner of Fifth, I looked in the glass window and saw a store being run entirely by homeless men.

"I—I—I can remember when-n-n."

I turn toward the street and see a group of young men walking with giant four-foot-long boom boxes. The opening lines of Mary J. Blige's "Reminisce" screamed out of two different stereos—two different types—in perfect synchronization like ultrastereo.

"Yo!" said one teenager to the other as they walked side by side.

As I got farther west, the music got louder—from every direction: Dr. Dre's "Nothing But a G Thing," Apache's "Gangsta Bitch," Whitney Houston's "I Have Nothing." It's almost like an open party—music, aggressive crowds, and the constant cries from African vendors anxious to sell fake Gucci bags, African kente-cloth-styled head crowns, perfumes, incense, copies of the Holy Bible, paintings of the black Jesus and Madonna, black history books, Karl Kani sweatshirts, collector's editions of *Life* magazine, bottles of boric acid or roach killer compounds, Timberland brand caps, mahogany wood carvings, sunglasses, oversized T-shirts that refer to rap star Dr. Dre, Barney the purple dinosaur or "blunt" (the new slang word for marijuana), a never-ending selection of Malcolm X paraphernalia, pirated black-and-white videotapes of movies that hadn't been released yet, jewelry, diced watermelon in containers, and sweet-potato pies.

"How much are these?" I asked a vendor while looking over a neat arrangement of movie videotapes on a table.

"Fifteen," he said as his eyes darted around nervously.

I bought what was probably a pirated copy of *The Crying Game*. Then I moved on.

Across the street—hanging up near the front door of the Banco Popular building—was an eight-by-ten-foot cloth mural of a character intended to look like Minnie Mouse. She had a red-and-white ribbon in her hair and a pistol in her hand. Over her head in large red letters were the words: DON'T MESS WIT 'DIS BITCH! You could have your Polaroid picture snapped next to her for just five dollars a pose.

On 125th Street, the consumer frenzy seemed to be at its height between Lenox and Frederick Douglass Boulevard. Here, there were legitimate stores—most of them low-end clothing, sneaker shops (including the famous Dr. Jay's), fast-food fried chicken stores (with street-side walk-up windows), hair salons, fruit stands, and combination wig shop/health aids/jewelry stores being managed by Koreans, Arabs, Indians, and a few blacks and Hispanics. There is a large Woolworth's, a two-story minimall called Mart 125, and a high-tech McDonald's where rock-video monitors hang from a metallic ceiling and workers wear kente-cloth hats, vests, and bow ties. These and the African street vendors seemed to make up the legitimate sales.

"Hey, man, you wanna buy a Sony Walkman?" asked a guy in his early twenties dressed in a large sweatshirt and baggy jeans barely holding on to his waist. A street hustler up close. "It's already got the batteries and a—let's see, yeah, a Barbra Streisand tape in it."

"Gold necklaces anybody?" asked another guy, barely slowing down as he walked by.

"Next week's *TV Guide*," whispered a man who walked up with an open corrugated box.

I looked inside.

"Come on, man," he said as I hesitated. "Or this month's *Ladies' Home Journal.*"

Out in the street, walking up to cars stopped in traffic were street hustlers selling uncooked steaks and ground beef wrapped in white paper or plastic.

The street hustlers—most of them between fifteen and thirty years old—can spot a sucker a block away, especially if he acts scared or makes even tentative eye contact. They are oblivious to the well-dressed, unintimidated black and white New Yorkers who hop out of cabs to visit the Studio Museum of Harlem on 125th.

Their prey is the nervous out-of-towner who wants to know how much tickets cost for Wednesday's amateur night at the Apollo. The hustlers wear dark-colored jeans pulled down—almost hanging below their waist—unlaced high-top Nikes or work boots, beepers on their belt loops, and oversized T-shirts with some reference to a rap artist or some form of pot. A heavy gold chain with a gold Uzi pendant, a Karl Kani cap, and a "fade" haircut complete the look. (In order to move comfortably in my building and block, I was to affect the same look.)

As I approached the building that housed the hair salon, I saw teenage hustlers pull out wads of hundred-dollar bills to buy a few batteries or an extra tape for their boom boxes.

"You want me to give you a *what?*" the hairdresser asked as she reached around my neck to button the bib. Her breasts pressed tightly against her black spandex pullover. I breathed in the aromas of fruity shampoo blends and the burning hair that was being relaxed and straightened throughout Black Hair Is.

"I said give me a cut that will let me fit in with the Harlem scene," I said. "I'm a writer and musician from out of town and I need a hip kind of look that'll get me over."

We confronted each other in the large round mirror. With one hand holding a comb and the other hand on her hips, she launched into a tirade with her cornrows flying at her shoulder.

"What do you mean make you look like everybody else?" she asked. "Ain't nobody getting the same exact haircut."

We settled on giving me a "fade" haircut, and I apologized for not being more decisive. She told me her name was Kelly and that she wanted to be a beautician—but for rich blacks downtown.

"Now if I could get a job down at John Atchison's," she said while shaving strips of my hair into my lap, "or even better, at Joseph's on Park Avenue—now that would be something. They do all the whosits' hair. 'Cause you know this place ain't even *owned* by black people. And in the middle of Harlem, no less."

"Are you serious?"

"Like a heart attack," she said. "Hold it a second while I get my oil."

As Kelly opened up the window and reached out onto the ledge of the building for a small container of hair oil, I looked up into the mirror.

"So tell me, Lekeisha," one of the other stylists said to a coworker nearby while combing gobs of white relaxer onto a client's scalp. "You think we should just go on and burn our own neighborhood down? Just to show the white people that we can't be walked on?" (This was during the second Rodney King trial.)

Lekeisha clipped away at a woman's bangs. "Girl, I don't know. I mean, how are we going to get some justice, some respect?"

"I hear you, Lekeisha," the coworker responded, "but why hurt ourselves all over again?"

"Hey," Lekeisha said while examining the evenness of her client's bangs, "they beat that man on national TV—and still got away with it. If they get away with it in this trial too, then hey, we should at least take the riots to Forty-second Street. That's what I'm saying. How much more can we take—and right when we have proof—on a videotape?"

Both the stylists and their two clients shook their heads in exasperation. I paid my seventeen-dollar bill and left.

Every day I was reminded of how hard it is to find a public phone that works in Harlem, and when I did, it was sometimes impossible to finish a call. I did learn that when you're at a Harlem corner phone booth and someone taps you on the shoulder telling you his beeper just went off, you'd better hang up. Fast.

"Yo, man, I gotta use the phone," a voice called out from behind me as I stood near 137th and Fifth.

I ignored the tap on my shoulder and continued leaving a message on my accountant's answering machine. "If you don't mind," I said without looking back.

Before the words left my mouth, my arm was twisted up behind my back, I was on my knees, and the receiver was dangling like a gray pendulum over my head. I never got a good look at my attacker's face, but I heard him loud and clear.

"You see this fucking beeper?" he asked.

How could I miss it? As I sat facing him at just below waist level, he twisted my arm, harder, up toward the base of my neck.

"When I gotta do business, you better get the fuck off the phone! This is fuckin' *business*!"

"Sorry, I didn't see you," I cried while staring at the beeper. I naively persuaded myself that as long as I didn't look at the man's face, he wouldn't feel compelled to hurt me—particularly since it was only ten o'clock in the morning—broad daylight.

"I can get you a twelve-gauge in an hour, but a thirty-eight may take a little longer. Either way, I want twenty-five bucks up front."

That's what one of the regulars who hung out on Willie's corner told me when I found him sitting on one of the red stools inside the Lenox Avenue bar, John's Recovery Room.

The plan was simple. I was to drive to a phone booth on 125th Street off the West Side Highway. Neither one of us would ever touch the gun during the transaction. He would hand me a steel-belted radial for my Toyota. The gun would be wrapped in a cloth inside the tire.

"I'll be in a green Olds Ninety-Eight," the man said as he pulled down his brown Kangol hat. He took another sip from his glass of apple wine. "Drive up nonchalantlike and talk loud and call me Carl."

I looked around us at the darkened bar and thought this was all a little complicated and ridiculous. I liked the fact that I didn't have to go to his apartment, but this still seemed complicated, just to get a gun in Harlem.

"Is all this really necessary?" I asked the old man. "Can't I just give you the sixty dollars and you give me the gun?"

"Carl" took another sip from his glass. I immediately got the feeling I had said the wrong thing. He was clearly from the old school. Aggressive enough to deal in firearms, but old enough to be self-righteous and paternalistic about it.

"Look," he said with a wrinkled brow. "You and your white boys come in here from your Jersey suburbs to buy stuff all the time. Well, if you're gonna come here, then you're gonna buy it *our way.*"

At first, I thought I didn't hear him correctly. Here I was, a black man, dressed like a Harlemite, and he's comparing me to some white boy from suburban New Jersey? I told myself that dealing with this guy was safer than buying from Jojo or some other young unpredictable hoodlum, even if this was slower and painfully methodical.

"So you want light ammo, right?"

"Yeah, light," I said, not sure of what he was talking about.

"Son, light is what you get if you're shooting inside buildings—unless you don't care about stray bullets going through walls and killing other folks."

I hadn't wanted to buy this gun. After a conversation with a Sergeant Morrissey at the Thirty-second Precinct on 135th Street, I was persuaded not to buy a gun—almost.

But living in a rooming house, where ex-tenants and their former associates have keys to your door, can make you feel uneasy. Uneasy enough to want just the threat of a gun—even if it's not loaded—just so you can wave it at an attacker. (Both Mrs. Jenkins and Willie kept promising me a new lock, which never arrived.) I had witnessed a partially chewed rat left on my bed sheets (presumably a gift from Sadie, the cat) and the slow disappearance of my Pop-Tarts, milk, toilet paper, loose change, a sweater, and several hangers.

What's more, three different people had walked in on me after unlocking my door with their own keys! Each one was looking for some woman who owed them money, but I was quick-witted enough to explain—once at 2:00 A.M. with the lights out—that I was not that woman and had no connection to her, romantically or otherwise.

Then I was a witness to two shootings.

The first was around 8:15 P.M. on a Thursday, just as the sky was getting dark. My plastic blinds were already pulled closed.

"So why the hell didn't you step off like I told you to?"

"Shit—why didn't *you* step off?"

Two young teenagers were shoving each other on the sidewalk. Three others were egging them on and pushing them closer.

"I wouldn't take that."

"Man, you heard what he said?"

Through my blinds, I could just see one of the boys, in a shiny white polyester running suit, push another against a car's front fender. I heard the "ping" of metal hitting metal.

"Yo—look!"

"He got a gun." Someone was wearing a pair of LA Gear Light Gears. I saw the red bulbs on his heels as he ran into the street. I instinctively hit the floor.

"Pop, pop, pop."

"Yo!"

I crawled toward the dresser, reaching for a phone I didn't have. How do you call for help? I stayed down there for almost five minutes—hearing only the sounds of cars and buses going up Lenox Avenue. And down on the sidewalk, there was nothing—no gun, no body, no spectators.

Seconds later, I noticed a thin brown hand pushing a yellow Post-it note through the crack in my door. I recognized Willie's handwriting: "Give me three dollars—need to buy cat food."

There was a second shooting three nights later at around 4:00 A.M. Two men and a woman arguing. Something about who had to ride in the backseat of the car that the woman was driving. It happened so fast, and the argument—at least from my window—appeared so inconsequential, it made the single "pop" of gunfire seem almost mundane.

And since so many people have guns, the sound of one is just a small part of the Harlem background noise. Noise that you hear right on up to five in the morning. Yelling, crying, screaming kind of noise—some in anger, but most in conversation. A lot of this loud activity is created because people in rooming houses don't have telephones. They also don't have buzzers or doorbells. So the result is a lot of screaming from the street up to a window—any window that will open and receive a message on behalf of an absent neighbor.

With all this noise, one would imagine you'd have residents opening their front windows—Ralph Kramden–like—and telling the screamers to keep it down out there. But this doesn't happen. Either because it's useless or because the noise brings well-awaited drama into the lives of hundreds of bored listeners. For whatever the reason, no one interferes. Tenants either just listen in and get further caught up in the lives of the people who sit outside their building day after day, or they turn up the television volume and get further caught up in the lives of the soap operas and talk shows they watch from ten in the morning to five in the afternoon.

This was no more apparent to me than on the four days I spent going up and down Lenox Avenue, 135th Street, and 125th Street looking for job openings. I returned each afternoon to my less-commercial neighborhood, passing by windows where people watched well-dressed, well-coiffed soap stars flit through one-dimensional lives of colorful kitchens, picture-perfect patios, obedient children, and thoughtful neighbors who offered fresh flowers and small-town gossip.

I saw whole evening conversations revolve around Oprah's latest guest, Erica Kane's newest hairstyle, Arsenio's funniest spoof, or who got taken to the OR at Harlem Hospital that day. One quickly gets a sense of the boredom, which soon turns into lethargy and, eventually, hopelessness.

"You can work for me," Jojo offered one evening as we sat on my bed swigging from giant cans of Olde English 800 malt liquor and listening to Wendy Williams's "Top 8 at 8" on KISS-FM.

"How can I work for you?" I asked. "You work security."

"Naw, man—I mean *sell* for me." He laughed.

I laughed too. "Thanks," I said, "but I need a *day* job."

I kept plugging on. I started at Frederick Douglass Boulevard and worked my way east on 125th Street. One of the first stops had been the Twin Donuts Shop.

"Is the manager available?" I asked a young Asian woman who stood near the cash register.

"If you want a job, come back in two or three months."

"Can I fill out an application?"

"No applications," she said rather unsympathetically while refilling the coffee machine. "And it probably isn't worth coming back for another three—no, I'd say four—months."

Across the street at Sneaker City, I walked over to the elevated cash register, where there were two men who appeared very distracted.

"What d'ya want?" one asked without looking at me.

"I wanted to apply for a sales or stock boy job."

He finally focused on me. "A what?"

"A job," I repeated.

He waved me away. "No jobs, no jobs—no, no."

I had similar conversations at Popeye's, Martin Paint, Kentucky Fried Chicken, Kids Kingdom, GEM Stores, Key Express Supermarket, and around sixty other markets, bodegas, restaurants, barber shops, liquor stores, and clothing stores. I offered myself as stock boy, hair sweeper, security guard, or anything else that was needed, but there was not a job to be had anywhere.

(But battling unemployment isn't the only fight to be waged. By the time I returned to my room, I resumed the fight that every other Harlem resident faces: the ongoing menace of roaches. They are everywhere you go—a permanent fixture in stores, on sidewalks, on walls, next to refrigerators, everywhere. As I sat at the edge of my bed resting from my job hunt, paying more attention to the *New York Times* crossword puzzle than to my cup of Dannon blueberry yogurt—which I had stirred only five seconds earlier—I take in a second spoonful and realize that one of those crunchy brown critters has already found its way from the ceiling into my breakfast snack.)

And those classifieds don't tell you how to dress once you arrive in Harlem. They don't tell you that to live in a rooming house, you better dress like a hood, but if you want to get into the more respectable Harlem establishments, you better *not* dress like a hood.

One afternoon, after visiting and viewing an exhibit on the history of blacks in film at the Schomburg Center for Research in Black Culture on 135th Street, I strolled down to 125th Street to drop in at the Studio Museum. But when I opened the door, I was met by a security guard. "What can we do for you today?"

The black guard glanced at my clothes with a wary eye. Even though I was now dressed similarly to most other black men my age on this block, he grimaced. "We're about to close."

"I've still got fifteen minutes."

Looking down at my beeper and gold chain, he smiled politely but refused to move. "Negative. We're having a private party. Why don't you call on the phone tomorrow and take a guided tour?"

As I stepped back into the street, I watched two black women hop out of a cab and walk in without being stopped.

My clothes, while ideal for helping me fit in on my block, were a problem in this other world, the one in which blacks wore business suits and carried briefcases. Dressed in dark unlaced work boots, black sweats, a $199 heavy gold chain with an Uzi pendant, beeper, Malcolm X cap, Sony Walkman earphones, black knapsack, dark sunglasses, and a black Dr. Dre T-shirt that said I GOT TO GET FUCKED UP, I was screaming adolescent ghetto defiance—a regular walking ghetto stereotype. It was probably hard for the guard to believe I was interested in surrealist paintings by early-twentieth-century Cuban-African artists.

Back in my room that evening, I figured out a solution to the clothing problem. I developed a quick-change strategy that allowed me to strip and redress myself while walking along the sidewalk day or night between appointments.

Walking out of my building in full ghetto gear and heading to a 7:45 dinner appointment at Sylvia's, I removed my dark sunglasses and Malcolm X cap. My oversized black Dr. Dre T-shirt came off to reveal a light blue button-down oxford shirt. My gold chain with Uzi machine gun pendant goes underneath the oxford.

Beeper and Sony earphones go into the knapsack and out comes my horn-rimmed reading glasses and a fresh copy of the yuppie business magazine *Black Enterprise* to hold underneath my arm. A few blocks later, my shoes are tied, college signet ring is back on my finger, and I am led by Melba, Sylvia's niece, over to a table near a photo of talk-show host Kathie Lee Gifford. I sit down at my place in the green dining room, just underneath one of the small crystal chandeliers. I am ready to be served.

Back outside, across the street, a basketball bounces repeatedly. A group of kids are cutting a larger hole in a store's damaged awning. Eight feet off the ground, it makes a great basketball hoop. When there is no playground, these kids make do.

But Ann and Gerald Watson admit that the two worlds of Harlem do occasionally collide. One example is the two-foot squiggle spraypainted on their front walk. "It must have happened last night or early this morning. Can you believe this?" Gerald asks his wife while staring at the mark, which would have gone unnoticed on any other street in Harlem.

Ann shakes her head like a suburban matron who senses that the neighborhood is under siege.

"That's going to cost us two hundred dollars to get chemically removed," says Gerald. "They come over here and forget where they are."

"When the girls were younger," explains Ann, "we gave them some pretty specific and very tight boundaries of where they could play or ride their bicycles." She goes on to say that they could not cross to the other side of 139th Street, and they could move five houses to the right or ten houses to the left. And that was it.

"But then you had a few of the kids from 140th Street—who can be pretty rough," says Harold. "I remember the time some of them were over here, right in front of our house, pulling on our daughter's hair because she had a nice bicycle. Yeah, they're a pretty rough group."

"If we ever discover crime on this block, it's minimal," explains Ken Peters.

Estelle agrees. "It's what I call quality-of-life crime—an occasional mark of graffiti, a little littering, or a broken car window. When people from the community walk down this street or in the courtyards of the Riverton over on 135th Street, they act differently," adds Estelle Peters, who is also on the board of the New York Urban League. "If a child from another part of Harlem is walking with a loud radio or making noise, his or her parent will immediately tell him, 'You don't do that kind of thing over here.' People know we're here and there is mutual respect because we have become a role model for the community."

But there are those who still resent being situated so close to the poverty and crime associated with Harlem.

"I've never liked the idea that we are right across the street from those Lincoln projects," says Madeline Waters. The wife of a surgeon, Waters, forty-five, says she is reminded of the contrasts—particularly whenever she returns each week from Joseph's, the upscale black hair salon at Sixtieth and Park. "I talk to my friends about it and they tell me to hush up." Tucking the corner of her Hermès scarf into her blouse, she steps out onto her balcony and points over to the fourteen buildings that make up the low-income housing project. The courtyards in between the buildings have worn paths. Graffiti is sprayed on the trees. Kids and adults walk around with handheld stereos and bottles of soda. Some without shirts.

"Now, I'm sure there are some very nice people over there," Waters adds, "but where else but Harlem would you find projects built right in between middle- and upper-income developments? I don't see that kind of thing near Park Avenue or Fifth Avenue, where the white people live. But I'd be accused of being an Oreo or a wanna-be if I publicly complained about this because black people are not supposed to care about class differences or the quality of a neighborhood. But many of us *do* care."

Living so close to less privileged children had an impact on the Peterses' son, Rob, while growing up. More than learning to appreciate what he had, he was oftentimes embarrassed by his large home and his street's image within the greater Harlem area.

"Even though Rob's best childhood friend was a white classmate who lived on East End Avenue, and although he knew many white classmates who had more than us," says Estelle, "he would sometimes play with kids from around the corner who hung out in Mt. Morris Park. They teased him terribly and asked him if he had a maid and chauffeur to go along with his rich family. We're certainly not rich, but to these kids who live in a public project, there is a stark contrast."

"You people aren't Africans! Half of you are walking around putting braids in your hair, trying to make it curly and wavy. The other half of you fools are burning your brains out by puttin' chemicals on it to make it straight!"

Groups gather around the lectern and listen to a very focused and eloquent man in dreadlocks and a colorful African dashiki. He stands with his back to 125th Street—just off the plaza of Harlem's State Office Building.

"Excuse me, miss," he calls to a young black woman walking by in a business suit and an attaché case. "Do you think you're an African?"

He goes on speaking through the microphone and amplified speakers, explaining how black history has been misinterpreted and rewritten.

"Imagine," he says, "Yul Brynner—a white man—being allowed to play a pharaoh in the movies. Egyptian pharaohs were black. Elizabeth Taylor—a white woman—playing our black Cleopatra . . ."

Further down the street, I got on line to go into the Apollo Theater. It was 7:15 P.M. Wednesday—amateur night. Busloads of people—black, Asian, and white—are waiting to go in.

"Ticket holders go in on the left," said a theater employee.

I realized I had bought one of the cheapest tickets (nine dollars) and crossed the red carpet and climbed two astronomically high staircases to where I squeezed into the front row of the second balcony.

The ornate theater was jammed with a young audience that was about 80 percent black and 20 percent white. Even with all the screaming and waving, it felt completely safe.

The show was not supposed to start until 7:30, but it was 7:20 and just about everybody was already waiting in their seats.

The front row, down in the orchestra, included an organized and synchronized line of teenagers—mostly young women—who seem to have a routine of shouts, arm movements, and loud laughter.

The ornate crystal chandelier dimmed and then the room got pitch-black.

And then, bam! The Amateur Night Band hit its chords. The seats shook, the chandelier appeared to tremble.

The hippest, nastiest, loudest version of Bobby Brown's "My Prerogative" rocked the building. People in my row were already hanging over the shiny brass rails.

The young host, Eric Harley, welcomed us and explained how we should applaud or boo when we select or eliminate performers.

The first group—three young black men in fades, white jackets, and T-shirts—sang a song, "Baby, It's You." Instead of relying on their great voices, they emphasized their gyrating pelvises and dropped their sex right at the foot of the stage. The front row women ate it up, and that was clearly the secret to winning the rest of the theater.

The next group, four guys calling themselves "Main Course," were slapped down within eight seconds of harmonizing for their rendition of "In the Still of the Night."

"Get the hell off!"

"That's bullshit!"

The comments were loud and ruthless. And to humiliate these guys even more, a wildly dressed hobolike clown—a familiar Apollo character—ran onstage to literally push and kick them to the outer wings. He returned with a mop and dustpan and danced to circus music.

The night was just getting started.

On this Thursday morning—or any other weekday morning—you can see groups of schoolchildren—some of them in street clothes and others in gray Catholic school pants or skirts with white shirts and maroon sweaters—walking out of the Lincoln housing project and across the sunken asphalt basketball court on their way to school. Some are escorted by their parents and some are not. Some have knapsacks. Some carry their books in plastic bags that say C-Town Supermarkets. Some are headed to parochial school. Many more are headed to public schools named Mary McLeod Bethune, Sojourner Truth, or Mahalia Jackson.

It is 7:45 A.M., and the grammar-school children almost tiptoe past the unkempt, swollen-eyed men and women already waiting by the dingy windows of the liquor store at 127th and Lenox. The kids run toward four-story rectangular school buildings behind fifteen-foot fences.

Running past me in her blue jeans and white sneakers was a public-school girl who was late for the morning bell that was already ringing on 134th Street.

"Hey, Cherisse! Cherisse! Wait up, Cherisse," she cried, running past a group of older teenagers lingering in front of a check-cashing store on Lenox Avenue. Her cornrows flapped in the wind as she chased after a girl in full Catholic-school uniform.

"Tonya, you're making me late" was Cherisse's only response as she ran into the school building with a pair of baggy black jeans and white sneakers in her hand.

When Tonya, the girl with the cornrows, got to the front door of the school, she dropped her knapsack full of books on the sidewalk, kicked off her sneakers, and unbuttoned her loose-fitting blue jeans. Underneath this bland disguise she revealed a gray plaid skirt, maroon sweater, and high kneesocks. Far enough away from the scrutiny of the gawkers and shirtless basketball players who hang out in her housing project, she slid into a pair of brown loafers, stuffed her jeans into a knapsack, then entered the beige building behind her classmates.

"I stay in Harlem because I'm around the people I understand. When I'm here, I am around the people I feel comfortable with as well as the people I can help," says Vivian Chapin. "Several years ago, a group of girlfriends and I met a bright young foster girl here in Harlem whom we mentored. She went to the old Harlem Prep, which was a moderately priced private school. Then we sent her to the University of Pittsburgh, where she majored in sociology. Now she's a computer company executive in New Jersey. If I was someplace else, I never would have met that girl. If I hadn't been in Harlem, I never would have known that she needed help."

Estelle Peters agrees that she has an important role in the Harlem community. "The people that live on Strivers Row—whether we're the old guard or the nouveau riche—we are seen as role models by a much larger black community that needs role models," she explains. "We could have moved to the suburbs of New Jersey or Westchester, but this is a black community that desperately needs an anchor. We can be that anchor. We know Harlem and its people are making a comeback. We want to be here when that happens, and we want to play a role in its rebirth."

"And it's because I see the contrast that I continue to stay involved in this community and its activities," explains Chapin. A member of the exclusive black woman's group the Drifters, a national organization of accomplished and affluent black women who raise money for minority children and youth organizations, Chapin stands in her Lenox Terrace apartment and talks about the Harlem Philharmonic Orchestra that she helped found in the 1970s. "It brought so much joy for me to see *all* of Harlem—not just the privileged families—attend a formal orchestra and concert. Kids who never heard an orchestra had the chance to see black people play Mozart, Beethoven. This is why I stay here."

"If we don't give back," says Beatrice Martin, "who will? We made this place, and we know its history." The woman turns and looks at the six-foot-tall oil paintings that line her wall. She then looks at the framed letter that Dr. Martin Luther King had sent to her in the early 1960s when she was mobilizing Harlem voters. "For the people who have been here through Harlem's heyday," adds Martin, "we know how great its residents are. Yes, the music gets loud, and yes there are guns and dope, but I know the people. I know that there are just as many of us that are doing well. And we can give back to the rest who aren't doing well."

It is Palm Sunday at Abyssinian Baptist Church on 138th Street. I squeeze past the double-parked cars with MD and DDS license plates from New York, New Jersey, and Connecticut. Glamorous black people have flooded the street and sidewalk. But there is another contingent there—people I've seen over the last three weeks sitting on the steps of walk-ups along Lenox Avenue.

As I enter one of the church's double fire-engine red doors, it occurs to me that other than at the Apollo, I had not been in any other Harlem location where I could see such a range of socioeconomic groups. I see people who are rich and people far from it.

I immediately feel the history of this eighty-five-year-old Harlem institution all around me. Looking at the eight-page program, I'm reminded that this is the most politically active black church in the country. With the exception of Reverend Wyatt Tee Walker's Canaan Baptist Church a few blocks away, it's one of the largest developers of housing for the elderly and lower-income people in Harlem. It provided the pulpit for Adam Clayton Powell, Jr., before he became a powerful congressman. It is now the home of Rev. Calvin Butts. It attracts rich, poor, and in-between from all over Harlem and other parts of the tristate area. They are here right now.

Because today is the beginning of Holy Week, the sanctuary is unusually crowded. The 9:00 A.M. worshipers are leaving and the 11:00 A.M. crowd is waiting impatiently.

"Give them room," says one of the church hostesses in white gloves, "give them room."

"Step lively, folks—get your palms and special gift, but step lively," says a tall, dark-skinned man in a blue suit who is urging slow-moving churchgoers to keep with the flow.

I stare up at the brass railings, the salmon-colored walls, and the graceful chandeliers that set off the stained-glass windows. People come from all directions. Each person is handed a special Palm Sunday gift: a fistful of palms and a silver-and-blue spray can of Raid Max Roach & Ant Killer, courtesy of S.C. Johnson & Sons. No one flinches. Not even the women in diamonds.

The only one who is offended is the minister. Reverend Butts is enraged by what he sees in the community as the selfishness of the affluent and the self-pity of the impoverished.

He looks out at the congregation, which is at least 80 percent black. Some are middle or upper income—wearing expensive conservative suits, hats, and diamond jewelry, with an occasional mink coat thrown on the back of a pew—but there are also working-class people dressed tastefully, in ties and hats, but with a little less flair. The average white congregant is far more casual—sporting accessories that the black churchgoer would never attempt—windbreakers, jeans, sneakers, and pullover shirts.

"Mommy, how come *I* can't wear my sneakers?" a young black child asks his mother as they squeeze beside me into a pew that has space for only one other person.

A woman looks over at a young white child dressed in a Barney T-shirt and Nike high-top sneakers. She then turns back, readjusting her black silk hat, and says, "Sam, it's just not appropriate in God's house." She pulls her son back in the pew seat, and he begins to swing his feet just above the floor.

"Now just imagine," the woman whispers to me while nodding toward the boy two pews behind us, "if we showed up dressed like that in one of *their* churches."

"I know, but what can you do?"

"Well, I know these poor black folks around here manage to

dress themselves up. Why can't these . . . these . . . these *visitors?*"

Reverend Butts can fully comprehend the dichotomy of the community. He sees the two worlds that exist side by side in his community, and he has a message for both of them, a suggestion of how they can better work together:

"All these broken lives amidst such affluence. If Jesus came to New York today, I believe he would break down crying. We need to be more gracious. Don't look at the poor and pity them. Find a way to reach out a hand and bring them up. If you treat a man like an animal, he'll act like an animal."

The people who heard this knew whom he was speaking to.

And Butts spoke to the less affluent as well: "The poor are mesmerized by consumerism. Stop complaining and wallowing in misery. Poor people complain, but then they buy cigarettes and crack. Poor people are without food, but they have a bottle of Colt 45."

Butts, the CEO of the Abyssinian Development Corporation and Abyssinian Church Federal Credit Union and outspoken opponent of alcohol ads and violent misogynistic rap music that consumes his neighborhood, knows his community. He knows the two groups that have stood side by side all these years.

As Willie Edwards stands at the top of the stairs on this Palm Sunday overlooking a crowded and littered Lenox Avenue, he watches the people who pass his building going up the avenue. Many carry palms. Some carry yellow or orange lilies. Some are going up to Strivers Row or to 135th Street, where they will turn right, headed for Lenox Terrace or The Riverton. Many more are going up there, but will instead turn left to return to Sunday dinner in their smaller, more modest efficiency apartments or walk-ups. As Willie stands at the steps of the four-story walk-up looking out, it's all one Harlem. The people he knows and the people he doesn't. The people who will lend him a few bucks and the people who won't.

When I get to the top of the crumbling stairs, Willie is holding the gently purring Sadie in his arms, and the early-afternoon sun beats down on us as we stare at each other. I brace myself for the inevitable financial request.

"How ya doin', Larry?"

"Fine," I answer, loosening my tie.

"Palm Sunday, huh, Larry?"

"That's right, Willie."

"Do you think—"

I look up at him menacingly as I put my key into the outer lock of the building's front door, expecting the daily request. This time I'm determined not to give in.

Willie drops his head sheepishly while cradling the purring cat in his arms.

"Do you think you could spare . . . a palm?"

I look up at him, and see how gently he cradles and strokes the sleeping Sadie. I see, for the first time, how his face is lined with compassion.

Steadying her in his arms, Willie reaches out for half my palms and then smiles at them.

After gently rubbing Sadie under her furry chin, I turn to enter the dark vestibule and climb the stairs to my room.

Names and identifying details about certain individuals have been changed.

INDEX

it harder to erase stereotypes of impoverished black community, 49–50

it's a statement that black spouses are inferior, 40–45

leaders of black community will be less loyal, 36–40

reminder of past sexual exploitation, 54–58

undermining of ability to introduce role models, 45–49

physical attraction to white women, black male's, 43–45

statistics, 33–34, 58

Supreme Court decision affecting, 33

Marshall, Thurgood, 49, 264

Martin, Beatrice Riggs, 263–65, 269, 289

Massachusetts Committee Against Discrimination, 250

Mathabane, Mark, 39

May, Lawrence T., 193

Media:

interracial marriages, treatment of, 47–49

single black leader, attempts to pinpoint a, 161–67

Men and Women of the Corporation (Kanter), 70

Meredith, James, 164

Mfume, Kweisi, 162

Michigan State University, 212

Middle class, black, 149

leadership of, issues to be addressed by, 151, 152

Miller Brewing Company, 249, 250–51

Minority-issue advisory group, 73

Minority-owned businesses, 77, 78

Miscegenation:

statutes prohibiting, 27, 32–33, 35, 65

see also Marriage, interracial

Miss America pageant, 61

Mixed marriages, *see* Marriage, interracial

Mobil Oil, 139

Monster (Scott), 164

Morrison, Toni, 219

Mortimer's, 93–95

Moseley-Braun, Sen. Carol, 157, 159, 160, 162

Motley, Constance Baker, 60

"Moving from 'Black Rage' to 'Bias Neutralizing,'" 232–53

Muhammad, Khalid, 178

Myers, Edward, Jr., 263

"My Negro Problem—and Ours" (Podhoretz), 35

Myrdal, Gunnar, 240

NAACP, 35, 38, 53, 156, 169, 219

budget of, 142

corporate contributors to, 139, 140

membership of, 139, 141

mismanagement of, 139–48

program management, 142

scope of, 142–43

weaknesses as source of black leadership, 138–48

NAACP Legal Defense and Education Fund, 140, 141

National Association for the Advancement of Colored People (NAACP), *see* NAACP

National Association of Black Social Workers, 53

National Law Journal, 237

National Urban League, 138, 145, 149, 156

weaknesses as source of black leadership, 138–39, 145, 146–48

Nation of Islam, 144, 178, 218

Native Americans, intermarriage by, 49

Navy, U.S., 192, 193

Networking, 2, 151

Newsweek, 43

New York City, New York, 78, 157–59, 162

restaurants, *see* Restaurants, black man's undercover guide to dining at ten top New York

New Yorker, The, 219

New York magazine, 1*n.*, 41–42, 76, 162, 254*n.*

New York Newsday, 222*n.*

New York State Republican organization, 164

New York Times, 56, 76, 88, 140–41, 143, 144, 158, 181*n.*, 265

New York University School of Business, 77

New York Yankees, 251

Operation Breadbasket, 150

Owens, Major, 28

Painter, Nell, 219

Park Avenue Café, 119–22

Patterson, Basil, 264

Patterson, Orlando, 39

Payson, L. G., 192

ABOUT THE AUTHOR

LAWRENCE OTIS GRAHAM is a graduate of Princeton University and Harvard Law School. The author of ten books, including *The Best Companies for Minorities,* his work has appeared in *The Best American Essays,* as well as in the *New York Times, Essence,* and *New York* magazine. His first-person undercover story, "Invisible Man," exposed discrimination in country clubs and is the subject of a Warner Brothers film. A corporate attorney and an adjunct professor at Fordham University, Graham has worked at the White House and The Ford Foundation.

A popular lecturer and commentator on minority, business, and legal issues, he was recently named "Outstanding Young Lawyer of the Year" by the National Bar Association, and the American Bar Association's *Barrister* magazine named him one of "20 Lawyers Who Make a Difference." Graham is president of the diversity consulting firm Progressive Management Associates in White Plains, New York.